ISLAMIC STUDIES

ISLAMIC STUDIES

A HISTORY OF RELIGIONS APPROACH

Second Edition

Richard C. Martin

Iowa State University

 Prentice Hall, Upper Saddle River, New Jersey 07458

Library of Congress Cataloging-in-Publication Data

Martin, Richard C.
  Islamic studies: a history of religions approach/Richard C. Martin
    p.   cm.
  Enl. ed of: Islam, a cultural perspective. c 1982.
  Includes bibliographical references (p. 256) and index.
  ISBN 0-13-205543-0
  1. Islam.   I. Martin, Richard C.   Islam, a cultural perspective.
  II. Title.
  BP162.M343   1996
  297— dc20   94-41956
                                                      CIP

Acquisitions Editor: Ted Bolen
Assistant Editor: Jennie Katsaros
Editorial Assistant: Meg McGuane
Buyer: Lynn Pearlman
Cover Art: *Stonework, Geometric Dado Panel,* Islamic Collection,
             Metropolitan Museum of Art

© 1996, 1982 by Prentice-Hall, Inc.
Simon & Schuster/A Viacom Company
Upper Saddle River, New Jersey 07458

Printed in the United States of America

10 9 8 7 6 5 4 3 2 1

0-13-205543-0

Prentice-Hall International (UK) Limited, *London*
Prentice-Hall of Australia Pty. Limited, *Sydney*
Prentice-Hall Canada Inc., *Toronto*
Prentice-Hall Hispanoamericana, S.S., *Mexico*
Prentice-Hall of India Private Limited, *New Delhi*
Prentice-Hall of Japan, Inc., *Tokyo*
Simon & Schuster Asia Pte. Ltd., *Singapore*
Editora Prentice-Hall do Brasil, Ltda., *Rio de Janeiro*

For Nia and Holly

CONTENTS

PREFACE

$\mathcal{T}$his work existed in an earlier, much shorter, version titled *Islam: A Cultural Perspective*. When that text was published in 1982, not many introductory texts for religious studies courses on Islam were available. The two best books were by well-known Orientalist scholars of great erudition, one non-Muslim, the other Muslim: H. A. R. Gibb, *Mohammedanism: An Historical Survey* (1949), and Fazlur Rahman, *Islam* (1966). Both books have been revised and reprinted posthumously and continue to enjoy an excellent reputation.

After *Islam: A Cultural Perspective* appeared in 1982, publication of books on Islam expanded greatly, relative to the past. Again, two introductory texts are worth mentioning because they are empathetic to the subject matter, informative, and have each gained wide readership: Frederick Mathewson Denny, *An Introduction to Islam* (1985) and John L. Esposito, *Islam: The Straight Path* (1988). By now, both books have appeared in second editions. Denny's book is useful for the amount of information it provides on Islamic religious practice, and Esposito's text answers the growing demand for an unbiased discussion of Islam in the modern period. I have learned much from reading and teaching with these four books, despite certain small criticisms I have of them.

The decision to rewrite and expand the earlier text and call it *Islamic Studies: A History of Religions Approach* is implicit in the title. Even though there are roughly a thousand departments of religion of one sort or another in North America, until recently very few historians of religion have been trained in the languages, texts, and history of Muslim societies. Islam specialists were often borrowed from other departments, such as history or anthropology or Near Eastern studies. Although this has begun to change, it is still the case that very few textbooks and courses on Islam in religious studies departments are about the study of religion. *Islamic Studies: A History of Religions Approach* seeks to make the academic study of religion a more prominent consideration in the study of Islam. Each of the following chapters presents not just information about various aspects of Islamic religion, but much more discussion on how religions are studied.

The point is worth belaboring, if briefly. The father of New Criticism, Northrup Fry, once remarked that students in the physical and life sciences don't describe what they are doing as studying nature; they study scientific method and particular sciences, such as "physics," "biology," or "zoology." That is, they study how to classify and explain natural phenomena according to a discipline of study they share with other scientists. In the humanities, students of literature study how to analyze a text, look for plot, evaluate style, and interpret textual meaning. Students of literature learn to talk to each other about how to explain and interpret poems and novels. In religious studies, too, it is misleading simply to say that we study religion(s). Like scientists, what we actually do is study the study of, in this case, religion(s). Which is to say, one can't just walk up to something as complex as a religion and expect to learn about it by taking it in factually. The disciplined study and reasoned interpretation of religious texts, rituals, and social practices is what characterizes the comparative study of Islam and other religions in the academy.

Another reason for rewriting and expanding the earlier text is that in the meantime the media have "discovered" Islam. Western non-Muslims generally have more images and perhaps more information about Islam than they did in 1982. Islam is now traveling on the "Great Information Super Highway," to which students and the public have increasing access. More is needed in a text on Islam than predigested information, served up in the simplest of terms. In *Islam: A Cultural Perspective*, I used a minimum of Islamic technical terms in the text, presenting instead their English equivalents for easier comprehension and retention. The matter is reversed in *Islamic Studies: A History of Religions Approach*. It is time now to end the unfortunate trend of minimizing the vocabularies of Islam and other religions in undergraduate texts. Anyone who reads computer bulletin boards or listens to contemporary music knows that today's youth are capable of learning complex computer and cultural argots. No one should approach the study of another religious system, any more than a new software, without learning the terms by which the system operates.

The reader should also note that Arabic and other Islamic terms are generally italicized only on first appearance in a chapter; thereafter loanwords into English usually appear in roman type. I have taken as an indication of American English usage of Islamic terms their appearance in the unabridged *Webster's Third New International Dictionary*. The only diacritical marks used in this text are the *'ayn* ('), for example, in the word "Shari'a," and the *hamza* ('), as in the term "Qur'an." These two diacritical marks are used in *Webster's*. Only in the Glossary have I given full transliteration of Arabic terms.

Another change since 1982 is that Islam is now recognized as a North American religion, soon to become the second largest after Christianity, and already larger than some Christian denominations, such as the Episcopal Church. Europe also has a growing population of Muslims. Of course, France, Britain, and Germany have for many years had large Arab, Pakistani, and Turkish minorities in their societies. Now, however, it is as much the Islamic and not just the ethnic identity of children in state schools, of men congregating outside a neighborhood mosque on Fridays, and of women wearing *hijab* on the streets that provide some of the new images we have of Muslims. These are media images. Often they are religious images. Religion vies with ethnicity as the greatest cause of the culture wars that are waged and the violence that erupts so frequently in the world today. The relationship between religion and conflict is an important and neglected topic in religious studies, especially in Islamic studies.

Muslim societies have also been subjected to tragic and bloody conflicts. Of those that have occurred just since 1990, we need but mention Bosnia in the Balkans, Somalia in Africa, and Ayodia in India. Perhaps the most important event with respect to the West, however, was the Gulf War in 1991. Many Muslims in the Middle East and elsewhere saw this war as a Western alliance led by Americans against Islam and Muslims. Why were Muslims around the world so nervous about Western troops with their "Patriot" missiles and "smart" bombs in the land of the sacred places of pilgrimage, Mecca and Medina? Many were asking: Have the Crusaders returned, not only to shed Muslim blood, but this time to destroy the shrine built by Ibrahim and the mosque that holds the last remains of the Prophet Muhammad? Muslims have also asked why the West, so quick to punish the Iraqis when they invaded Kuwait, has all but sanctioned the murder and rape of thousands of Bosnian Muslims, denying them even the right to arm themselves. The "New World Order" that was being proclaimed as the Soviet Empire collapsed and the Gulf War commenced has led many Muslims to believe that they have become the new "Evil Empire," the new villain in Western political mythology.

On a more personal level, I have learned more about the study of religion and about Islam since 1982. In 1984 I had the great fortune to be able to visit Pakistan, Malaysia, and Indonesia, where I visited Muslim universities and organizations and learned much about Islam beyond the Arab world. I lived in Egypt with my family from the summer of 1989 to the beginning of 1991 and watched my daughter, Nia, one of the persons to whom this book is dedicated, negotiate her way as a four- and five-year-old in a truly "multicultural" environment. I listened with fascination to her debates with Muslim, Christian, and nonreligious schoolmates about God, Santa Claus, and other important beings in the cosmologies of small children (in which Satan, interestingly, was absent). Their playful but earnest verbal combat made me realize that conflict and its resolution is an important problematic in the history of religions.

I have also had the benefit of getting to know, in recent years, the Muslim academic community in South Africa. Their struggle as a religious, and for the most part ethnic (Asian), minority in the Apartheid and post-Apartheid South Africa raises important questions about being Muslim in a non-Muslim state, and hence about the problem of religious minorities in relation to dominant traditions. Muslims find themselves on both sides of this issue of power and identity in various parts of the world today.

Closer to America than Asia, the Middle East and Africa are home to other friends and colleagues who have contributed to this work. Many colleagues, both at home and abroad, are named in footnotes; in the pages that follow, they and others will recognize how much I have learned from their books and my conversations with them. In particular, in regard to this book, I would like to mention Charles J. Adams, Juan Campo, Richard M. Eaton, Josef van Ess, Adel S. Gamal, Sidney Griffith, Hassan Hanafi, Bruce Lawrence, Gordon D. Newby, Jonathan Z. Smith, Tamara Sonn, Abdel-Kader Tayob, John Vall, Marilyn R. Waldman, and Mark Woodward. I should also like to thank Jennie Katsaros, assistant editor at Prentice Hall, for working closely and patiently with me to produce the best possible text.

The preparation of general texts should have the benefit of response from readers, and that has been the case. Several students at Arizona State University who read *Islam: A Cultural Perspective* over the years offered constructive criticism, which has led to changes made in the text of *Islamic Studies: A History of Religions Approach*. Two graduate students in particular have contributed to this volume. Katherine (Kate) Kolstad prepared a brilliant M.A. thesis on ritual purity in Islam; her findings and interpretations induced me to add Chapter 10, "Ritual Contamination and Cleansing." With Dwi Surya Atmaja I read *hadith* and *kalam* (theological) texts in Arabic, and he prepared an important M.A. thesis on the latter. I rediscovered in the process how lively and essential primary texts are, even in translation. In the following pages I have added many passages from Qur'an, hadith, and other Islamic texts, some of which I read with Dwi. I am also indebted to Ayesha Qureshi, a graduate student in Religious Studies at Arizona State in 1994–95, for assistance with research on footnotes and quotations used in the text.

I shall end by mentioning my wife, Holly. She helped me write the earlier text, *Islam: A Cultural Perspective*, and her imprint is still to be found in this book, especially in Chapter 9, on esthetics. Equally important, she joined me during sabbatical leaves in Egypt in 1982, just after *Islam: A Cultural Perspective* appeared, and again in 1989–90. Herself a Chinese literature specialist who has lived for a while in both Taiwan and China, and more recently, an English-as-a-Second-Language teacher in inner-city high schools, she has always been equal to the challenges of living and communicating in Cairo. Along with our daughter, Nia, she created an interesting life and acquired a wide variety of friends in Egypt, often learning important things about the society in which we lived that I had overlooked in my more narrow scholarly pursuits. As always, I am grateful for her supportive companionship. To Holly, too, I dedicate this book.

Richard C. Martin

1

Unity and Diversity
in Allah's
Commonwealth

GOD IS THE GREATEST

Being in Cairo for the first time should have carried no surprises, but it did. I had taken several courses in Arabic and on Islamic topics, and I had enjoyed numerous friendships with Muslim students as well as many happy moments sharing food and customs. But all of this had happened in university communities in America and Europe. Living in Egypt brought a whole new experience of Islamic culture.

The Western visitor to Cairo is impressed with the great diversity of strange sights, sounds, and smells that greet the senses. Garlic peddlers and tea confectioners call out their wares in musical tones. Bicyclists balance broad trays of flatbread on their heads as they ride through streets snarled with the traffic of man, beast, and machine. Buses are stuffed with Cairo's multitudes, jostling each other frantically for the right of passage to bureaus and bazaars. But above the clamor and din, five times each day there reverberates the central and unifying summons of Muslims to prayer. Each time it begins, *Allahu akbar*, "God is the greatest":

> *God is the greatest, God is the greatest,*
> *God is the greatest, I witness that*

1

There is no God but Allah; I witness that
There is no God but Allah. I witness that
Muhammad is His Apostle; I witness that
Muhammad is His Apostle.
Come to the prayer! Come to the prayer!
Come to the betterment! Come to the betterment!
God is the greatest. God is the greatest.
There is no God but Allah.

Allahu akbar! For more than thirteen centuries this Arabic phrase has sounded from the highest place that the muezzin, the person charged with sounding the call, could climb. From minarets of mosques, piercing upward through cluttered urban skylines, or, lacking mosques, from rooftops of houses, the call has been heard throughout the Muslim world. Five times each day this simple statement summons the faithful to prayer. It means God is infinitely greater and more majestic than His entire creation. Sung out in stylized chant, its first utterance announcing, it reaches a high note, a sensation uplifting, above the petty and mundane. In response to this declaration of divine majesty, the prayer is performed on artfully woven rugs or simple towels spread out in mosques, homes, and sidewalks—anywhere. It is an act that achieves its highest significance in the touching of the forehead to the ground as an expression of total submission to God.

Declaring boldly the greatness of Allah and submitting ritually to His will are central to Islam. The Arabic word *islam* means "submission" and "peace." A Muslim is one who submits to Allah and finds therein peace. Tradition teaches that Bilal, a black slave freed by companions of the Prophet Muhammad, was the first Muslim to chant the summons to prayer. The year was 622 A.D., year one of the Islamic calendar. In the Arabian city of Medina, from the roof of the newly built house that served as the Prophet's home and first mosque, the call sounded in tones loud and clear. *Allahu akbar.* Each day since 622 that phrase has continued to rise above the more familiar sounds of this world, declaring divine majesty and summoning the faithful to prayer.

THE WITNESS

The *shahada*, or witness, that "there is no God but Allah" and that "Muhammad is His Apostle" is the first of Five Pillars of Muslim faith and practice. All Five Pillars—the witness, the prayer, the giving of alms, fasting, and the pilgrimage to Mecca—play important roles in the intellectual and social dimensions of Islamic life. We will have more to say about the Five Pillars in this and other chapters. First, the two themes of the witness or shahada are worthy of attention.

"There Is No God But Allah . . ." Islam is one of the three great monotheistic religions to arise in the Middle East; along with the other two—Judaism

FIGURE 1.1 Muslims performing the salat, Iran. (Photo by J. Isaac. Courtesy of the United Nations.)

and Christianity—it stresses the oneness and unity of God. The word *Allah* means "the God," the same God confessed to and worshipped in the other monotheistic traditions. In the call to prayer, in the shahada, and in everyday discourse, the name Allah is constantly heard. The name also appears in Arabic writing and calligraphy in books, on mosques and public buildings, and on wall hangings in homes and offices. Allah is the central focus of Islamic religion and culture.

The affirmation of God's oneness and unity is comprehended in the important Arabic religious term *tawhid*. The early Muslim community in Arabia, where pagan polytheism had been widely practiced, regarded the *association* (in Arabic, *shirk*) of other gods with Allah as a serious threat to God's unity. Shirk was the earliest and most repugnant form of heresy. Pagan gods were familiar and pliable beings, made of stone and easily "possessed." The concept of Allah stood above such associations. As Islam spread to lands and cultures outside of Arabia, the Christian doctrine of the Trinity and the Zoroastrian dualistic conceptions of good and evil divine powers were also seen by Muslims as aberrations of God's unity, or tawhid. Muslim theologians sought arguments, both from scripture and through reason, to make persuasive the fundamental oneness and unity of Allah, excluding "lesser" gods and the plural implications of a "god-head," which threatened that unity. Muslim mystics practiced special meditations or modes of remembrance (*dhikr*) that focused the consciousness upon God,

FIGURE 1.2　"Allah" in Arabic calligraphy.

because in their view God was the only Reality. The average Muslim, even without special theological knowledge or spiritual techniques, nonetheless thinks of God in the way of tawhid.

". . .Muhammad Is His Apostle." The second phrase of the shahada declares that Muhammad is God's chosen messenger to humankind, who was sent to his own people in seventh-century Arabia. Accepting the Judeo-Christian biblical tradition in large part, Muslims believe that God had sent prophets and messengers to other nations in the past with the same revealed message Muhammad was to recite to the Arabs. Muhammad's mission brought the final positing of divine Truth, and thus Muhammad is regarded as the "Seal of the Prophets."

Muslims look to the person and example of the Prophet Muhammad as important spiritual resources. Like the other prophets recognized in the Muslim religion, including Moses, Jesus, and several other biblical and non-biblical figures, Muhammad was thought to be an ordinary mortal, a prophet raised from the midst of his own people. Far from having any notion of a divine "nature" or of divine qualities, Muslims remember Muhammad as one of the common people of his time, without formal education or literacy. The contrast between the Prophet's humble circumstances and the reverence in which he is held is truly remarkable. A visit to Muslim homes and places of business is instructive. Pictures and representations of the Prophet and his family are frowned upon and seldom seen, for reasons we will discuss in Chapter 9. Yet ask Muslims about the Prophet, and the response is always enthusiastic and respectful. Queries about Islam are often greeted with responses such as "the Prophet used to say . . ." or "Once while addressing a group of companions the Prophet did such and such."

Both the historical and the religious dimensions of Muhammad's life in seventh-century Arabia are important ingredients of any understanding of Islamic civilization. Along with the *Qur'an*, God's Word recited by the Arabian prophet, Muslims have looked for guidance in the *Sunna*, Muhammad's example as recorded by his deeds, sayings, and silent approval. His closest companions and those whom they taught during the next two generations carefully transmitted the Prophet's sayings (*hadith*) orally, until the need was felt to write them down and test them for authenticity. In matters of personal piety, public conduct, and legal transactions, Muslims often cite both the Qur'an and the Sunna of the Prophet as authorities.

The proper context for understanding both the Qur'an and the Sunna is the life of the Prophet, a story that we shall consider in more detail when we look later at the overall history of Islam. We may anticipate the main features of that story by noting the following. Muhammad was born of humble circumstances, as already noted, to a clan belonging to the powerful tribe of Quraysh in Mecca. As an orphan raised by his uncle, Muhammad had no wealth or education until he was about twenty-five. His marriage to a widowed older woman gained him an important personal relationship as well as some means and experience with the caravan trade that dominated the Meccan economy. His call to be a prophet came when he was about forty, although the message he delivered directly challenged the religious and social values of the time. Thus, he was not immediately well received, and very few people chose to follow him at first. Eventually, he and his followers emigrated from Mecca to Yathrib (later called Medina), an Arabian city that proved to be more hospitable to his leadership. The date of the emigration (*Hijra*) was 622. During the final ten years of his life, Muhammad completed delivering God's message, and, with the help of his growing number of followers, he got much of Arabia, including Mecca, to accept the religion he preached. The story of his life is dramatic and arresting. It is filled with tensions and conflict—with communities of Jews and Christians, but primarily with the tribal paganism that isolated Arabia from the world it was soon to conquer. During Muhammad's lifetime a new civilization was born that radically changed the history of the world.

QUR'AN: THE WORD OF GOD

Our initial encounter with Islam must include a grasp of the importance of the Qur'an to Muslims. The Qur'an is the book that records in beautiful Arabic style, thought to be inimitable by ordinary mortals, the divine message of Allah as it was recited by the Prophet on various occasions during his mission in Mecca and Medina. In literary form the Qur'an comprises 114 *suras* (chapters), which vary in length from a few to over two hundred *ayas* (verses). Whereas terms such as "Bible" and "scripture" are derived from words meaning "writing," the Arabic term "Qur'an" comes from a verb which means "to recite." Like other scriptures, the Qur'an is a book. It contains a message that is comprehensible and meaningful. More than that, however, the Qur'an is an oral phenomenon. Its distinctive and proper recitation is essential to the total impact it has upon Islamic culture.

A visit to a Muslim town or village quickly confirms these remarks about Muslim scripture. In both its literary and oral forms, the Qur'an is a constant in Muslim life. Everyday speech is often punctuated by verses from the Qur'an. Muslim children begin their earliest education by learning to recite it properly, with correct enunciation and intonation. An important milestone in life is reached when a Muslim is able to recite the Qur'an entirely from memory. Quranic calligraphy graces many public buildings and shrines. The Qur'an dominates Muslim culture as an ever-present symbol and reminder to Muslims of the communication of God to humankind through His Messenger, Muhammad.

For Muslims the Qur'an is a divine miracle, recited to the Arabs by specially trained reciters, using speech that even the greatest of poets are said to be incapable of imitating. Understood within the Muslim world view, the Qu'ran is the record of God's, not Muhammad's, communication to humankind. Muslims believe the Qur'an was written on a Heavenly Tablet that was the same source of revelation as that received by earlier prophets. It was delivered to Muhammad by God's angel, Gabriel. The divine nature of the Qur'an is often compared to the divine nature of Christ as conceived by most Christians. The Qur'an, not the Prophet, is the word of God.

The message of the various ayas and suras is for the most part *plain* and direct, although some passages are recognized to be *obscure* and difficult to understand. Muslims strive constantly to internalize the Qur'an through memorization and thoughtful reflection on its meanings, yet it is generally acknowledged that the complete meaning is known only to God. Nonetheless, both the plain and the obscure passages are constant subjects of intense study and interpretation. Classical commentaries on the Qur'an continue to be published and studied even as contemporary scholars offer new interpretations appropriate to changing times.

The oral form of the Qur'an, the original mode of its deliverance by the Prophet, is still maintained by schools of reciters, who take many years of training to perfect their art. Their performance is in constant demand, especially during Muslim festivals and holidays, when the beautiful and distinctive tones of quranic chanting may be heard throughout Muslim neighborhoods and villages. Even on more personal occasions, such as marriages and deaths, Muslim families often employ the services of a Qur'an reciter to enunciate God's Word properly for the joy and comfort of those present. Muslims also personally recite brief passages of the Qur'an on other occasions, particularly during daily prayers. The more devout may undertake to recite the entire Qur'an at regular intervals.

The Qur'an is authentic only in its original Arabic form, even for those Muslims who speak little or no Arabic. Thus, attempts to know and understand its meaning through translations have never been encouraged. For many persons, of course, both non-Muslims and those Muslims who do not

FIGURE 1.3 Muslim reciting the Qur'an.

speak and understand much Arabic, translations may provide the only access to the Qu'ran's meanings. A word of caution is necessary in this regard. Grasping the approximate meaning of quranic sentences, even when they are carefully translated, is not enough. From what we have just learned, it should be clear that the total effect of the Qur'an in Muslim life cannot be grasped without experiencing the esthetics of its Arabic oral and written forms. The non-Muslim student is urged to listen to authentic recordings of quranic recitation and to gaze upon the pages of graceful calligraphy in which Muslim scripture is recorded, in order to begin to appreciate its total cultural effect in Islamic societies.

THE ABODE OF ISLAM

Who are the Muslims? This question is commonly answered, "The Arabs." This is a mistaken impression which is true only insofar as Islam arose among the Arabs, its Prophet and many of its adherents were and are Arabs, and its scripture, the Qur'an, when used in worship, must be recited in its original Arabic form. The majority of the world's Arab population, living primarily in the Middle East and North Africa, is Muslim. However, Arabs comprise only about 25 percent of the present population of Islam.

In the Middle Ages the Islamic Empire stretched from Spain in the West to India in the East, from Turkey in the North to Yemen in the South—the largest empire of adjoining lands the world has ever known. Many ethnic groups became Muslim along with the Arabs.

Beyond those distant borders of the *Abode of Islam*—the part of the world under Islamic rule—Muslims penetrated at different times into Russia, China, Southeast Asia, Sub-Saharan Africa, and Europe. More recently Islam has taken firm root in North America. Muslims are found in almost every country of the world. They form a majority of the population in thirty-six countries, and nearly half of the population of four others. In 1992, the *Encyclopaedia Britannica Book of the Year* estimated the strength of Islam at 951 million people, almost one-fifth of the world's population. Islam is the world's third largest religion, behind Christianity and Buddhism, and its present rate of growth and vitality rivals both traditions.

In an important sense, the Abode of Islam knows no geographical boundaries. In the Middle Ages, boundaries between Muslim and non-Muslim peoples were occasional lines of conflict. Caliphs, the rulers of the Islamic Empire, were responsible for maintaining the peace and defending the faith and the faithful from enemy attack. Beyond the Abode of Islam was the *Abode of War*—a geographical concept often more in a religious than in a military sense. Today Islam no longer forms a single political entity. Vast in size and appeal to all races of humankind, the Islamic world is situated mainly in a broad belt of nonindustrial nations stretching across Africa, the Middle East, South Asia, and Southeast Asia. Some Islamic countries, rich in natural resources, especially petroleum, have acquired considerable economic and political power. One consequence has been a much greater visibility of Islamic religion and culture in the Western world.

Islam is often treated as an urban religion by academia, and as a religion of camel-driving nomads by Hollywood. There is much truth in the former image, but the popular image of Muslims as desert-dwelling nomads is grossly exaggerated. Great cities such as Cairo, Damascus, Baghdad, and Isfahan have been important centers of Islamic culture for centuries. Achievements in art and architecture are associated with mosques and royal buildings, which are urban phenomena. It is also important to realize, however, that Islam has been the faith of peasants as well as princes and Bedouin *shaykhs* (Arabian nomadic chiefs). Today approximately 68 percent of Muslims are sedentary rural dwellers, living primarily in agricultural communities in which family units usually extend to include large numbers of kin. A decreasing number of Muslims in modern times, about 4 percent, live in nomadic tribal structures. Both village and nomadic life, on the other hand, sustain cultural systems that have remained relatively isolated from the impact of the modern world. The less modern areas have retained elements of traditional local folk customs, although the main tenets and practices of Islam are firmly held by tribesmen and peasants.

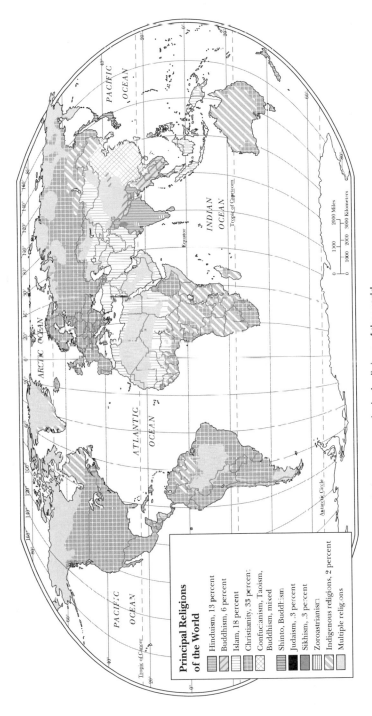

Principal Religions of the World

Hinduism, 13 percent
Buddhism, 6 percent
Islam, 18 percent
Christianity, 33 percent
Confucianism, Taoism,
Buddhism, mixed
Shinto, Buddhism
Judaism, .3 percent
Sikhism, .3 percent
Zoroastrianism
Indigenous religions, 2 percent
Multiple religions

FIGURE 1.4   Distribution of Muslim populations among principal religions of the world.

By contrast, less than 30 percent of the world's Muslim population lives in cities, although that percentage increased rapidly in the latter part of the twentieth century, as nomads and peasants alike migrated to cities to find employment.[1] In urban areas, kinship ties are qualified by much greater opportunities for education, social and economic mobility, and alternate lifestyles. Between nomadic and rural Islam on the one hand, and urban Islam on the other, there are many important cultural differences. For Islam, the challenge of the twentieth century to religion is occurring chiefly in urban areas.

SUNNI ISLAM

One's first acquaintance with another religious tradition often brings the impression that it forms an undifferentiated whole. This is never the case in Islam or in other religious traditions. Not only do Muslims belong to many ethnic groups and socioeconomic settings, but from a very early time there were significant divisions of opinion within the commonwealth, or *umma*, of Islam on *how* to be Muslim. The unity of Islam cannot be appreciated fully without a consideration of its diversity and its ability to incorporate divergent interpretations of basic beliefs.

The main body of Muslims is known by the term *Sunni*. Originally, they were known by the phrase *ahl al-sunna wa l-jama'a*, "The People of the Path and the Congregation," indicating the role of the community as a whole in following the teachings of the Qur'an and the Prophet. The recorded practice and teachings of the Prophet Muhammad were early regarded as his *Sunna*, an Arabic term meaning "path" or "way." These traditions, as we have seen, became powerful symbols for the Islamic religion, models of right belief and practice. Like all religious symbols, the collections of the Prophet's *hadith*, or "sayings," comprising his Sunna, or "authoritative example," required interpretation and application to a variety of situations in everyday life.

Majority or "Sunni" Islam ultimately settled on four schools of interpretation, whose functions were to decide upon the proper application of the Qur'an and the Sunna to virtually all aspects of the life of the community. Each of the four schools takes its name from a famous early jurist to whom later followers trace many of the school's distinctive opinions: *Hanifites* (after Abu Hanifa, d. 767), *Malikites* (after Malik ibn Anas, d. 795), *Shafi'ites* (after Muhammad al-Shafi'i, d. 820), and *Hanbalites* (after Ahmad ibn Hanbal, d. 855). Acceptable differences of interpretation exist among the four schools, and a Sunni Muslim may seek to conform his or her practice of Islam to any one of them. Beyond theoretical differences, geographic differences account for the preponderance of one or more schools over the others in given regions of the world of Islam.

What sorts of questions are decided by the jurists of these schools? The answers to many kinds of questions are sought in the Qur'an and the Sunna, and some of the most important are those pertaining to religious duties. For example, every Muslim must perform the daily prayers in a state of ritual purity. Conditions of purity are usually met by prescribed acts of cleansing (which may vary in their particulars from school to school). But what if bathing facilities are absent when the call to prayers sounds? Or what would constitute defilement of ritual purity between the moment of washing and the moment of prayer? Answers to such questions are not arbitrary but must be sought from the traditional bodies of opinion of the Hanifi, Maliki, Shafi'i, and Hanbali schools. Nor is the extent of religion in Islam determined by ritual alone. Matters pertaining to marriage, divorce, inheritance, and even proper government also come under the jurisdiction of Islamic law.

The learned doctors of law belong to a class of leaders in Islamic society known as the *ulama*. They are highly respected for their learning in the religious sciences. Islam has no clergy or priesthood as such. Members of the ulama in every village and city attain such status through social recognition of their achievement in the study of the roots of right belief and practice. With respect to Islamic law *(shari'a)*, by common agreement these roots are: (1) the Qur'an; (2) the Prophet's living example (Sunna); (3) the learned consensus *(ijma')* of the ulama; and (4) reasoning by analogy *(qiyas)* from accepted interpretations of the first two roots to new problems not directly addressed therein.

These four roots had been established as fundamental principles of Islamic law by the ninth century. Late in the seventh century, after the deaths of the four "rightly guided" caliphs (see Chapter 2 and especially Chapter 4, "Rashidun") who had been living companions of the Prophet, differences of opinion about the meaning of the Qur'an and the Sunna began to increase, as we might expect. Some jurists preferred to rely upon the Qur'an and the Sunna entirely. Others felt that even with such awesome bodies of authority as scripture and tradition at hand, an individual's exercise of reason (related to number 4 above) was necessary, especially in those cases where the Qur'an and the Sunna seemed to be silent. By the tenth century (some argue as late as the twelfth or even the thirteenth century), most jurists maintained the theory that independent reasoning was ended, other than restricted uses of analogy to the Qur'an and the Sunna. This, however, was a legal fiction; Muslim jurists have continued to reinterpret the Shari'a throughout history.

Arriving at legal opinions through the consensus of learned scholars (number 3 above) was another important principle under considerable discussion. It was based on a hadith attributed to the Prophet: "My umma (community) will never agree upon an error." In the strict sense, this has been taken to mean legal judgments. In practice, however, as we shall later see more clearly, consensus is an important social ingredient of Islamic culture. Perhaps this is another way of saying that traditional modes of thought and behavior, though these may differ from place to place, retain a sense of constancy. Even changes in custom require broad consensus based upon interpretations of the Qur'an and the Sunna.

All four roots form a concept of the revelation of God's will to the historic community of Islam. The term for this concept is *Shari'a*. Like the notion of Torah in Judaism, Shari'a is more than scripture. It implies a composite source of teaching and practice that presumes the interrelation of divine and human activity. It involves the Qur'an and the Sunna of the Prophet, and it requires authoritative human interpretation and application. Sunni Islam, comprising the majority of Muslims, has tended to place little social or religious distance between the ulama and the common people. Understanding and living by the Shari'a with the help of the ulama have played and continue to play important roles in the social and religious affairs of Sunni Muslims.

SHI'I ISLAM

A significant minority of Muslims, known as *Shi'i* (Shi'ite) Muslims or the *Shi'a*, have differed from the Sunni majority on certain religious and political matters almost since the beginning of Islam. Today about 10 percent of the Islamic population of the world is Shi'i, living mostly in Iran and Iraq. Shi'i communities also exist in many other Muslim countries, including such Sunni strongholds as Saudi Arabia. The differences between these two branches of Islam will be discussed by topic throughout this book. Such historical and religious differences as do occur should not obscure the broad lines of agreement between the two branches. It is no longer desirable, as scholars in the past have tended to do, to tell the story of Islam solely or primarily from a Sunni point of view, as if Shi'i Islam were a heterodox sect or an aberration of the "true" Islam.

Shi'i Muslims differ little from Sunnis in belief and practice. Their few points of difference, mainly in modes of leadership and piety, are nonetheless significant. During the first centuries of Islam, the majority of Muslims accepted the caliphs, or successors of Muhammad, as the legitimate political leaders of Islam. Many, however, sought guidance in both political and religious matters from spiritual leaders descended from 'Ali son of Abu Talib, Muhammad's cousin and son-in-law. 'Ali, who was recognized by most Muslims as the fourth caliph of Islam, was assassinated in 661. The civil strife that resulted in his assassination left an indelible mark upon the Islamic umma. The partisans (singular, *shi'a*) of 'Ali accepted his sons and their descendants as their spiritual leaders, or *imams*. For the Shi'a, allegiance to 'Alid imams tended to replace loyalty to the figure of the reigning caliph, and at times even to the Sunni ulama. The Shi'a believe that Muhammad passed on a significant part of his teaching directly to 'Ali, and hence to subsequent imams. Although the twelfth and last imam disappeared late in the ninth century (expected someday to return), the Shi'i ulama carry on the distinctive teachings and interpretations they trace back through the imam lineage to the Prophet. The teachings of the sixth imam especially, Ja'far al Sadiq (d. 765), became the basis of the *Ja'fari* school of law, which serves the same function in Shi'i Islam as do the four schools in Sunni Islam. Like their Sunni counterparts, the Shi'i ulama of the Ja'fari school are concerned to keep Islam on the track of the Shari'a (divine legislation) according to the four roots mentioned previously. In addition to their pious learning in these roots and in the teachings of their imams, however, the Shi'i ulama have often assumed a stronger role of leadership; with their charisma, they have been able from time to time to rally great masses of Shi'i followers under their persuasion.

The emotional intensity that characterizes Shi'i Islam culminates on the 10th day of Muharram (the first month of the Islamic calendar). On this date in 680, in Karbala, Iraq, Husayn, the son of 'Ali and grandson of Muhammad, was brutally murdered by troops of the Umayyad Caliph, Yazid. On each anniversary of this event, the Shi'a reenact the events of Karbala during the first ten days of the month. The scene is one of emotional bereavement. Black tents are set up, and the attire and gestures of mourning are assumed. For nine days, representing the days of siege by Yazid against Husayn and his family, those who have gathered hear the story of Husayn's demise dramatically retold.

On the 10th of Muharram, emotions reach a crescendo in the staging of the Karbala tragedy. Actors representing both sides in this sacred drama—the forces of Yazid and the 'Alid family of Husayn—recreate the religious Passion of Islamic (particularly Shi'i) History. Other protagonists onstage include the Angel Gabriel, the slain Husayn, and the deceased Prophet Muhammad. Toward the end of the Passion, the central theme has become clear: Suffering and martyrdom are exalted virtues, the way to salvation. Through the ultimate vicarious suffering and martyrdom of Husayn, sinners are released from the flames of Hell. Muslims who witness the drama are also participants, for the plot of the story is ingrained in their shared consciousness of this event. It is a moment of catharsis, indicated by the final line of one version of the Passion, uttered by a chorus: "God be praised! By [Husayn's] grace we are made happy, and by his favor we are delivered from destruction. . . . We were thorns and thistles, but now are made cedars owing to his merciful intercession."[2]

Remembering the tragedy of Husayn on the 10th of Muharram is a recommended religious act for Sunnis as well as for the Shi'a. The dramatic reenactment of these events and the emotional identification with their meanings, however, is a special characteristic of Shi'i Islam. In Chapter 12 is a description and brief analysis of the *ta'ziya*, the Passion of 'Ali's family. The history of Shi'ism has included periods of political protest and uprisings, and consequent repressions. During such periods, the imams and the ulama who have since represented them have often served as leaders of spiritual and political resistance. In this context, the Passion of Husayn has served as a symbol of the ultimate promise of salvation. Participation in the Passion is participation in a salvation history that has distinct tones in Shi'i Islam. In the pages ahead it will be important to distinguish the differences of tone without losing sight of the essential agreement of faith and practice between the two branches, Sunni and Shi'i Islam.

THE COMMON DENOMINATOR

Let us return to consider in brief the Five Pillars of Islam. They are: (1) the witness; (2) the prayer; (3) the alms; (4) the fasting; and (5) the pilgrimage. We have already seen how the witness, or shahada, contains two essential themes in Islam, when a Muslim declares: "I witness that there is no God but Allah; I witness that Muhammad is His Messenger." The other four Pillars are known as the religious duties ('ibadat). The rules governing these acts of worship in particular have been carefully argued and expounded by each of the Sunni and Shi'i schools of law, with slight variations among them. This is because the Pillars are considered "obligatory" for all Muslims, whereas other Acts of Worship are "recommended." Without going into the complexity of Muslim worship at this point, let us nonetheless consider the main features of worship.

The Religious Duties

Prayer (**Salat**). Performing the daily prayers is the second Pillar of Islam. As in other religions, prayer is an act of communication between human beings and God, and Muslims may choose to pray at many times and for a variety of reasons. Five daily prayers, known in the Arabic singular as *salat*, are considered a duty for all Muslims, and on these occasions preparations in ritual purity are required. Salat must be said and performed while facing in the direction of Mecca. It may be performed virtually anywhere except on Fridays, when at the midday call to prayer Muslims should gather at a nearby mosque. There a sermon is heard, and then the prayer is performed in uniform rows of worshippers.

Alms (**Zakat**). The mission of the Prophet Muhammad was directed in part against the injustices that the tribal Meccan economy imposed upon widows, orphans, and others without means. The *zakat* is a form of giving to those who are less fortunate, and, as the Third Pillar, it is obligatory upon all Muslims with the means to do so. In general, the schools of law have interpreted this Pillar to mean that one should give a certain amount from that part of one's wealth and assets each year in excess of what is required for a respectable standard of living. Normally this should be done before the beginning of the month of Muharram, the first of the new year. Each Muslim may choose the form and recipient of his zakat. Giving the zakat is considered an Act of Worship because it is a form of offering thanks to God for the means of material well-being one has acquired.

Fasting (**Sawm or Siyam**). Another expression of thanksgiving is the Fourth Pillar, fasting. Like the zakat, *sawm* is considered meritorious whenever it is performed (without detriment to one's health), but it falls as a duty to all Muslims to fast in particular during the ninth month, the month of Ramadan. During Ramadan, refraining from food, drink, and sexual activity during daylight is enjoined upon all Muslims except those who are in ill health. This restriction also applies to pregnant and menstruating women and to persons engaged in strenuous work or demanding travel. One's duty then is to make up lost days of fasting at a later time. Each day of Ramadan, the time of fasting is from just before sunrise to just after sunset. Breaking the fast is otherwise permitted, and often evenings during Ramadan are joyous and sumptuous occasions in Muslim homes. It is reported that the Prophet often fasted, particularly when he was directing his attention toward God in meditation. Sawm during Ramadan or any time is recognized as physically demanding but spiritually rewarding.

Pilgrimage (**Hajj**). The pilgrimage season begins in the tenth month, the month following Ramadan, and lasts through the middle of the twelfth month, Dhu al-Hijja. The Fifth Pillar requires all Muslims who are physically and financially capable of it to make the *hajj* to Mecca once during their lives. The actual rites and prayers take place at the sacred Ka'ba in Mecca and at other locations nearby. The rite of pilgrimage is very old, having existed in pagan forms long before Muhammad. Muslims associate the origin of the hajj and the founding of the Ka'ba with the prophet Abraham (Ibrahim). Today the hajj is a spectacular gathering of Muslims at Mecca from all over the world, numbering about two million people each year.

Striving (**Jihad**). Although it is not universally recognized as a Pillar of Islam, *jihad* is a duty in one form or another. The general meaning of the term is "striving for moral and religious perfection." Jihad is the form that patriotism and citizenship take within the Islamic umma. Because Islam regards itself as a universal religion, jihad can be in the service of the spread or defense of Islam. This sense of jihad is often translated as "holy war." In the event of attack from outside forces, jihad calls for fighting and, if necessary, dying for the sake of Islam. In this case it is a duty that falls to all able-bodied male Muslims. It is true that the cry of "jihad!" has been raised from time to time in Islamic history, but it is the broader meaning of striving within the context of one's life and community for moral and religious perfection that is the main sense of this duty in Islam. One who so strives is known as a *mujahid*. Every Muslim can and should be a mujahid.[3]

Being a mujahid, a striver for moral and religious perfection, involves numerous forms of public and private devotion that characterize the "practice" of Islam generally. We will encounter some of these in greater detail in Chapters 11 and 12. Among the most important dietary laws are the quranic injunctions against eating pork and drinking alcohol. Muslims are also enjoined to respect their parents and elders, to help provide for close relatives and kin, and to give to the poor and disadvantaged when at all possible. On the other hand, murder, theft, fornication, adultery, lying, cheating, and wrongly accusing or testifying against someone are all strictly forbidden by the Shari'a.

Iman: Islamic Beliefs

The term *islam* in a technical sense means "the practice of the religious and social duties" outlined above. There is another term, *iman*, which means "faith," and like the Five Pillars, iman can be divided into parts or categories. In Chapter 6 we will consider the content of Muslim faith and thought in more depth. As we proceed to learn about Islamic history and culture generally in the next few chapters, it will be useful to bear in mind the six parts of iman or "faith," which answer the question: faith in what?

1. *God and His Attributes.* Belief in Allah and His unity *(tawhid)* entails belief in His attributes such as knowledge and speech. God's attributes are inherent in His being and not apart from Him. In popular piety, it is believed that God has ninety-nine beautiful names or attributes, and rosaries of thirty-three beads are used to conduct private devotions that consist in remembering God by naming his attributes.
2. *Prophets.* The Muslim belief that Muhammad is the Messenger of Allah is grounded in the belief that many prophets preceded Muhammad. Selected from among ordinary mortals to bring the divine message to humankind for their guidance, prophets and messengers were necessary for salvation. From Adam (the first), to Muhammad (the final "Seal"), prophets have taught humankind about matters of faith and practice necessary to salvation.
3. *Angels.* In addition to the earthly messengers of God's will, Muslims believe there are numerous invisible beings who execute the commands of God in the invisible, supramundane sphere. The most important of these are: Gabriel, the messenger of God's will to His prophets; Michael, in charge of the natural world; Israfil, who trumpets in the Last Judgment; and Azrael, the angel of death.
4. *Sacred Books.* Belief in sacred books or scriptures sent to confessional communities, particularly to the Jews and Christians, is the fourth category of iman. It follows from the aspects of faith just mentioned, for God's communication to His prophets through His angels has resulted in other sacred books. In addition to the Qur'an, Muslims acknowledge the Torah of Moses, the Psalms of David, and the Gospel of Jesus as previously sent scriptures.
5. *The Last Day.* Muslims believe that the world as we know it will end in divine destruction followed by a Day of Resurrection at which all of humankind, past and present, will be brought to strict account for the degree to which they kept the faith

and the practice enjoined upon them by their prophets. Those who obeyed God and His messengers will henceforth enjoy Paradise; those who did not will suffer in Hell. Those who had iman, "faith," but who nonetheless sinned in significant ways will suffer temporarily before attaining Paradise.

6. *Predestination.* The sixth part of faith is the omnipotence of God, that is, belief in His total power (*qadar*) as Creator to shape and determine the course of His creation. The paradox of divine power and agency in all events versus human responsibility for moral and immoral acts indicates that the frequent charge of fatalism against Islam is no more true than in any religious tradition that believes in divine predestination. Belief in predestination, or qadar, is a positive affirmation of God's power and majesty for most Muslims, and not an excuse to become resigned to the way things are in the world.

These general descriptions of the terms iman and islam—that is, of faith and practice—apply throughout the tradition. Like believers in other religious traditions, Muslims vary in the intensity of their faith and the diligence of their practice. Some are very pious, however, and one important form of pious devotion throughout the centuries has been Islamic mysticism, known in Islam as *tasawwuf*, or "Sufism."

MYSTICAL ISLAM

From the interior of a compound in North Africa, the name of Allah may also be heard—as it frequently is throughout the Muslim world—but not from a muezzin, nor at intervals prescribed by the Shari'a. Those who utter it call themselves Sufis. They are Islamic mystics, gathered in a community around a spiritual master, or Shaykh. Such communities have existed for a long time in Islam, and those who have chosen the path of mysticism have been Sunnis in some cases, Shi'ites in others.

In Sufi gatherings, the two syllables *Al-lah* dominate the atmosphere. In quiet moments in his or her own cell, each devotee softly murmurs the divine name repeatedly. "Allah." One so occupied is conscious of nothing else. At other times the divine name is more audible, more disturbing. A French physician attending to the health of a Sufi Shaykh reported the following experience:

> Fairly often . . . while I was talking directly with the Shaikh, the Name "Allah" had come to us from some remote corner of the zawiyah [Sufi convent], uttered on one long drawn out, vibrant note:
> "A. . .l. . .la. . .h!"
> It was like a cry of despair, a distraught supplication, and it came from some solitary cell-bound disciple, bent on meditation. The cry was usually repeated several times, and then all was silence once more.

"Out of the depths I have cried unto thee, O Lord."

"From the end of the earth will I cry unto Thee, when my heart is overwhelmed: lead me to the rock that is higher than I."

These verses from the Psalms came to my mind. The supplication was really just the same, the supreme cry to God of a soul in distress.

I was not wrong, for later, when I asked the Shaikh what was the meaning of the cry which we had just heard, he answered:

"It is a disciple asking God to help him in his meditation."

"May I ask what is the purpose of his meditation?"

"To achieve self-realization in God."

"Do all disciples succeed in doing this?"

"No, it is seldom that anyone does. It is only possible for a very few."

"Then what happens to those who do not? Are they not desperate?"

"No: they always rise high enough to have at least inward Peace." Inward Peace. That was the point he came back to most often, and there lay, no doubt, the reason for his great influence. For what man does not aspire, in some way or other, to inward Peace?[4]

Peace. Submission. Two sets of notions—one a state of mind and a social ideal, the other a conscious attitude and a physical posture—all comprehended in the notion, *islam*. But beyond the religious denotations of peace and submission, the word "Islam" and its adjective "Islamic" connote many things: the Arabesque style of art; the exquisite Persian miniature paintings; the architecture of magnificent mosques; the literature of the *Thousand and One Nights*; the poetry of Omar Khayyam; the philosophy of Averroës, and much more. These more familiar hallmarks of Islamic civilization are but the tip of the iceberg. Islam means religion. It also means a great civilization that has subsumed many cultures, achieving a remarkable unity.

Contrary to this picture of a culturally diverse yet religiously unified civilization, many non-Muslims in the West, particularly in more recent times, conjure images of conflict, violence, and social upheaval when the topic of "Islam" comes up. Therefore, we close this overview of the Islamic tradition by considering another manifestation of Islam—one that the media have dubbed "fundamentalism," borrowing a label from a movement with the same name in early twentieth-century Protestantism in Britain and North America. In this last example, we leave aside traditional Islamic names for groups and movements, such as "Sunni," "Shi'i ," and "Sufi," and turn to a more recent nomenclature that has crept into (some would say, dominates) public discourse about Islamic religion.

As we turn to this topic, we are reminded of a principle of scientific inquiry, that the investigator in the act of research, the scholar or student, inevitably influences the object of his or her study, in this case Islam. That is to say, studying a religion is an active, not a passive, pursuit. Therefore, what Americans and Europeans have come to regard as Islamic fundamentalism can be seen in large part as a product of the creative imagination of social scientists and reporters.[5]

Islamic Revivalism

In 1949, a reticent and reflective middle-aged Egyptian toured the United States. Sayyid Qutb had been born into humble, rural circumstances in Egypt in 1906. Like many Egyptians educated between the two world wars, Qutb received both a traditional early education (based on memorizing the Qur'an) and higher training in Western literature and thought. After schooling, he joined the Egyptian Ministry of Education as an inspector of schools. It was in this capacity that he participated in a mission to examine several local public educational systems in the United States, a country and culture much admired by many Egyptians and others in the Muslim world for its modernity and technology. However, what Sayyid Qutb experienced in American society ran counterintuitive to his own growing self-identity as a pious Muslim intellectual. For one thing, Qutb was dark-complected, and America at mid-century was experiencing socially accepted public expressions of racism. Qutb's visit to the United States also occurred during the immediate aftermath of the Arab-Israeli war, with the defeat of the Palestinians and the founding of the State of Israel. America was, on the whole, strongly pro-Israel and anti-Arab. For Qutb and others, the link between racism and anti-Arab sentiments on the one side with America on the other—a society dominated by capitalist economic values, materialism, and Christianity—seemed obvious enough. Qutb's experience was symptomatic of a much larger movement going on in the so-called "Third World," and particularly in the Muslim world.

Sayyid Qutb, however, became what he did following his trip to America not simply because of what he experienced there, but because of what he experienced when he tried to bring about change in Egypt through Islamic revival. The American experience simply reinforced for Qutb a sense of distrust and a feeling of alienation from Islamic constructions of "the West."[6] He joined an organization called the Muslim Brotherhood. He wrote many pamphlets and books, sounding a call for Muslims to return to the fundamentals (*usul*) of their religion. His writing soon became strident as he argued that existing governments in Muslim countries were not truly Islamic and would have to be replaced by Muslim leaders who ruled according to the social and moral precepts established in the Qur'an and by the Sunna of the Prophet.

In 1966, Sayyid Qutb was executed, having spent much of his life since returning from America in Egyptian prisons, where he had done much of his writing. As one biographer has said, summing up Sayyid Qutb's legacy, "[s]ince his execution in Cairo in 1966, his writings have inspired numerous revivalist movements throughout the Muslim world. They have captured the imagination and the commitment of young Muslims and transformed them into working for the cause of Islam in the world."[7]

The use of the term "Muslim" as title for the Brotherhood signaled the growing belief among many Muslims in the twentieth century that Islam was the most valid and just way of life, commanded by God, revealed in the Qur'an, and exemplified in the practice of the Prophet Muhammad. There was nothing new in that conviction on the part of men like Sayyid Qutb; nor was the belief that Dar al-Islam, the world of Islam, stood in periodic need for renewal of faith and practice focused on God. A widely held belief among Muslims throughout the centuries has been that great religious leaders were "Renewers" (singular, *mujaddid*) of religion in their time, and that a Renewer would appear at the beginning of each century of the Islamic Era. What has been distinctive about twentieth-century Islamic movements for religious renewal and revival is the direct challenge these movements have mounted against all governments and ideologies considered to be non-Muslim. Men and women like Sayyid Qutb argued that capitalism, communism, and secularism, represented by the governments of the former Soviet Union, Europe, the United States—all the modern -isms and -ologies—have failed. In their view, crass materialism, sexual license, and social injustice are rampant in those very Western countries that are trying to impose their values and influence on Muslim societies. Moreover, in the Muslim critique, Christianity, Judaism, and the other world religions have not provided solutions to modern political, economic, and social problems.

The most telling and frequently heard slogan among the "Islamists" (*Islamiyyun*), as those who have striven for the revival of Islam are called, is: Islam is the Solution! Many also call themselves Mujahidun, "Strivers [in the Path of God]," a term we have already encountered among the religious duties. They are also known by the Arabic term for "fundamentalists," *usuliyyun*. However, this latter term was not simply borrowed from the West. Usuliyyun is a term that throughout Islamic history has denoted those who have based their interpretation of religious law on a strict reading of the usul "roots" rather than on rational argument. In the ninth century in Baghdad, one such movement was led by Ahmad ibn Hanbal (d. 855), who was introduced above and to whom we shall return in Chapter 7. "Hanbalism" has been associated with several historic Islamic revival movements. In modern times (as similarly in the past), the efforts of Islamic revivalists have run counter to the interests of the Westernized regimes in the Muslim world, leading to conflict and violence.

In this introductory chapter we have surveyed the main expressions of Islam—Sunni, Shi'i , and Sufi. We have also addressed the periodic tendency in history for reform movements to arise, seeking to rid Islamic society of what Islamists see as un-Islamic influences and to restore an Islamic basis to society. These aspects of Islamic societies—orthodoxy, suffering and martyrdom, mysticism and asceticism, and efforts toward renewal—are well known in the history of religions more generally. Chapter 2 presents an overview of the major periods, themes, and counterthemes of Islam in history. Ideas and theories in the comparative study of religions will be introduced from time to time, to help interpret Islamic religion in light of the broader experience of human history. It is hoped that students of religion generally, as well as specialists in other traditions, will find much in Islam that is common and universal among the world religions, as well as much that is distinctive, interesting, and valuable in the Islamic contribution to world history.

NOTES

1. On the demography and ethnography of Islam today, see Richard V. Weekes, ed., *Muslim Peoples: A World Ethnographic Survey*, 2d ed. rev. in 2 vols. (Westport Conn.: Greenwood Press, 1984).
2. G.E. von Grunebaum, *Muhammadean Festivals* (Atlantic Highlands, N.J.: Humanities Press, Inc., 1976), p. 94. Used by permission of Humanities Press, Inc., New Jersey 07716.
3. The Arabic term *mujahid*, meaning "the one who performs jihad," has a plural form, "*mujahidun*" (or "*mujahidin*" [pronounced mujahideen]), which is often assumed by Muslim political groups struggling against governments and forces perceived to be against Islam. This political sense of the term mujahid is only one aspect of the more general meaning of mujahid.
4. Martin Lings, *A Sufi Saint of the Twentieth Century: Shaikh Ahmad al-'Alawi; His Spiritual Heritage and Legacy*, 2nd ed., rev. and enl. (Berkeley, Calif.: University of California Press, 1971), p. 22. Used by permission of University of California Press and George Allen & Unwin Ltd.
5. The role of the scholar in constructing the object of his or her investigation, religion, has been essayed by Jonathan Z. Smith. See especially Jonathan Z. Smith, *Imagining Religion from Babylon to Jonestown* (Chicago and London: University of Chicago Press, 1982), pp. xi–xii.
6. An informative historical survey of Islamic attitudes toward the West is given by John O. Voll, "Islamic Renewal and the 'Failure of the West'," in *Religious Resurgence: Contemporary Cases in Islam, Christianity, and Judaism*, eds. Richard T. Antoun and Mary Elaine Hegland (Syracuse, N.Y.: Syracuse University Press, 1987), pp. 127–44).
7. Yvonne, Y. Haddad, "Sayyid Qutb: Ideologue of Islamic Revival," in *Voices of Resurgent Islam*, ed. by John L. Esposito (New York and Oxford: Oxford University Press, 1983), p. 67. The passage on Qutb is based on Haddad's brief but excellent study.

2

Islam in History: Overview and Themes

"TRADITION" IN ISLAMIC HISTORY

Celebration of the fourteenth centennial of the Prophet's Hijra from Mecca to Medina began in November 1979.[1] In this chapter we will survey the main events of those 1,400 years, looking at the major periods of Islamic history as well as certain themes that characterize the study of Islam. In subsequent chapters of this section on history we will concentrate on select personalities and moments within that span.

The historian's task of reconstructing what "happened" during the many centuries since the Hijra has been facilitated by the preserved writings of Muslim scholars and travelers throughout the centuries. Islamic documents and records are plentiful and diversified. Regarding the earliest centuries, however, the task is somewhat difficult. Few records or statements exist from non-Islamic sources about Islam during the first two centuries after the Hijra. Furthermore, to a large extent Islamic traditions about those first two centuries have survived mainly in texts dating from the third century after the Hijra onward. This gap is not unique to Islamic history. Historical analysis of the founding periods of all the major religious traditions presents similar difficulties. Our main sources of information about the founding years of

Christianity, Judaism, Buddhism, and several other traditions are characterized by scriptures and pious recollections appearing in later texts. Thus historians are faced with a dilemma. It would be a mistake to throw out all "religious" literature as unreliable versions of what actually happened and why, as many historians have advocated. It would also serve no useful purpose to accept religious texts uncritically in the search for verifiable historical information, for determination of historical fact must hold up to critical examination. In religious as in other literature, ambiguities, contradictions, and anachronisms that beg to be explained appear regularly. In their investigations of the formative years of a given religion, and in the absence of independently reliable historical documents, scholars of religions have used such terms as "tradition" and "sacred history" to designate a religions's view of its own unique history.

It is usually held that history began when humankind learned to write and keep records. In the Middle East, writing dates from circa 3,000 B.C. Yet until much more recently, only an elite few could read and write. Information was gained and passed on orally—a method of learning and shaping one's world view that has flourished in human civilization, sometimes independently of literary traditions. It is partly in this sense that we will speak about the Islamic religious *tradition*. Notwithstanding the absence of full and unambiguous documentary evidence dating from the time of the events themselves, the written texts from later centuries are obviously the result of a tradition in the making since the earliest times.

In the next few pages, a brief overview of Islamic *history* will be sketched. In Chapters 3 and 4, we will consider in more depth some aspects of the *tradition*, or sacred view, which gave Islamic history its shape as viewed within world history.

FOURTEEN CENTURIES OF ISLAM

Arabia dramatically entered the stage of world history in the seventh century, although it had been playing a regional role for several thousand years. South Arabia had once been known as the Kingdom of Sheba, and it became a source of frankincense, myrrh, and other spices and exotica from the East, destined for Mediterranean markets. Less important on the larger world scene was the nomadic population of Central Arabia.[2] Its main city, Mecca, was barely known to the rest of the world until just before the time of the Prophet. Yet it was from Central and not South Arabia that the Islamic Empire was launched across North Africa and the Middle East.

The occasion for the early seventh-century outpouring of Arabs into Syria, Iraq, and Persia, as well as later journeys into Egypt and North Africa, was a new vision of monotheistic religion inspired by the Prophet Muhammad. Born of humble circumstances in the city of Mecca late in the sixth century, Muhammad began in about the year 610 to preach a message that challenged the Arabs. His message attacked the tribal provincialism, social injustice, and polytheistic paganism that differentiated the Arabs from their more urbanized and cosmopolitan neighbors in Byzantium and Persia, and the settled peoples of Syria and Iraq. Although Muhammad died before the Arab armies came to expand their control significantly to lands outside of Arabia, the message he recited in the form of Revelation accompanied his most trusted companions and generals. Thus the Prophet's message took root where Arabs established political control throughout the Middle East. The history of Islam, then, begins properly with the Prophet Muhammad and the Revelation recited by him to the peoples of Mecca and Medina, about which we shall have more to say in Chapter 3.

It may be useful to think of the outpouring of Arabs from the Arabian Peninsula in the seventh century as a *Völkerwanderung*, a mass migration of people not unlike earlier migrations in the Middle East. For example, late in the third millennium B.C., Semitic peoples had migrated into Mesopotamia and established the ancient Babylonian Empire. The quranic and biblical stories of Abraham's migration from Ur of the Chaldees (Babylonia) to Haran and then to Palestine corresponds to what we know of such a Völkerwanderung from Mesopotamia to Palestine circa 2,000 B.C. The conquest of Canaan (Palestine) by the Hebrew people several centuries later was part of a large pattern of migration which included the Philistines and other newcomers to that area. Migrations such as these inevitably involved wars and conquests. They also brought new ideas, as Semites, Persians, and other peoples encountered one another and established new civilizations on top of older ones. The older civilizations were not always destroyed in the process; each new conquering people took command but absorbed much of the culture of the previous landlords, adding new ideas and developing distinctive forms. Thus, power in the Middle East had already changed hands many times prior to the Arab conquests in the seventh century. A successful economy of agriculture and trade had existed for nearly four millennia, and in this context, cultural achievements in writing, literature, monumental architecture, and legal institutions had left a rich heritage on which the Arabs and the people they conquered could now build an Islamic Empire.

Two great empires gave way to the Arab conquests. First, the troops of Byzantium—the Eastern Christian Empire with its capital in Constantinople—were pushed out of Syria and Iraq by Muslim armies. Christians and Jews living in these lands were not greatly affected by the changing of the guard. Many became Muslim, but the existing culture was left more or less intact. Byzantium retained its strength in Anatolia (modern Turkey) until the thirteenth century, when the first Ottoman Turkish Muslims challenged Byzantine control of Anatolia and the Balkans. During the eight centuries of

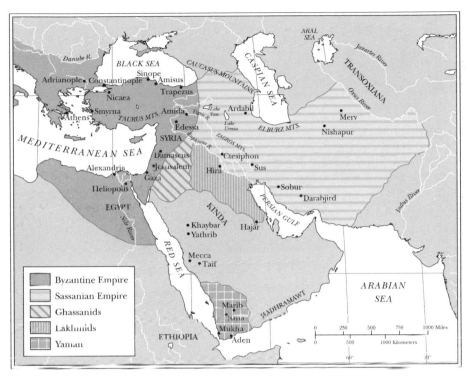

FIGURE 2.1 The Byzantine and Sassanian Empires and their client states in the sixth and seventh centuries at the rise of Islam.

coexistence between Islam and Byzantium, the occasional military clashes did not prevent important cultural exchanges.

The Sassanian Persian Empire fared less well when the Arab armies marched across the Middle East. The Persians had already played out their resources after centuries of conflict with the Byzantine Empire. By the middle of the seventh century, the last Persian king was assassinated, and the once great Persian Empire fell to the Arabs. The political and cultural implications of this change of balance in the Middle Eastern powers was considerable. Henceforth the ethnic and cultural composition of the Abode of Islam was a mixture of Arab, Persian, Turkish, Armenian, and other Middle Eastern peoples.

The Classical Age

From the seventh to the thirteenth centuries, Islam formed an empire dominated by the office of the caliphate. We will pay closer attention to some of these caliphs or rulers of Islam later in this chapter.

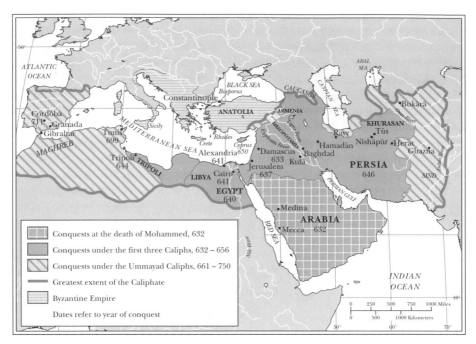

FIGURE 2.2 The Caliphate at its greatest extent.

The First Four Caliphs (632–661). Following Muhammad's demise, the first caliphs ruled from Medina in Arabia. They were known among Sunni Muslims as the Rashidun, or "rightly guided" caliphs, because they had been companions of the Prophet and learned directly from him how to live according to his Sunna "example." By the end of this period, Medina proved to be an impractical command post for the growing empire. Arab militias led by able commanders had conquered and begun to settle in Iran, Iraq, and Egypt. The question of leadership over the expanded Muslim community precipitated civil strife (*fitna*), a topic to which we will return later in Chapter 4.

The Umayyad Caliphs (661–750). The next period of the caliphate was under an Arab dynasty that ruled in Damascus, Syria, known as the Umayyad caliphate. This was the period of the consolidation of Arab rule and gradual growth of Arabic and Arab influence over the still existing languages and institutions of previous civilizations. The religion of the Muslim conquerors was adopted by many of the conquered peoples, and a mode of coexistence was worked out with those in religious communities who did not convert to Islam.

In culture the Arabic language expanded beyond local Arabian *oral* traditions of poetry and Islamic worship to become an important *literary* language. The Arabic Qu'ran played a key role in this development. Also important was the contribution of the caliph 'Abd al-Malik (reg. 685–705), who made Arabic the official language of government records and discourse (replacing Greek, old Persian, Syriac, and other established literary languages). Soon literature about the Prophet and various aspects of Islamic religion appeared. Muslim scholars sought to broaden the base of the language by consulting pure Bedouin usage and by writing grammars and dictionaries. The works of earlier Greek philologists appear to have been fundamental to this enterprise. In art, the field of architecture dominated as the Muslim conquerors continued the ancient Middle Eastern mode of cultural expression through monumental architecture. One of the signal achievements of the Umayyad Age was the Dome of the Rock Mosque in Jerusalem, built by Caliph 'Abd al-Malik in 691.

Spain (711–1492). In the year 711, Umayyad forces crossed the Straits of Gibraltar and established a branch of the Umayyad caliphate in Spain. The crossing over into Europe of Muslim forces in that year was the result of a long march across North Africa. In France, at Poitiers and Tours, the Muslims were defeated in 732 by Christian troops under the command of Charles

FIGURE 2.3 Dome of the Rock shrine, Jerusalem. (Courtesy Israeli Government Tourist Office.)

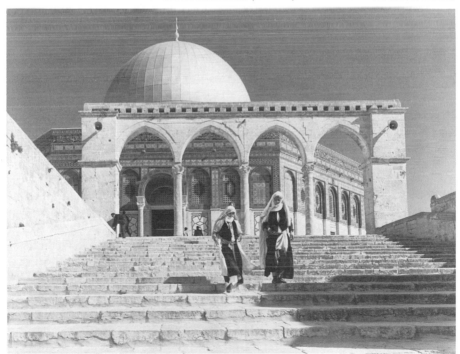

FIGURE 2.4 Court of the Lions, Alhambra, Granada. Moorish (Nasrid), 1354–1359.

Martel. Thereafter, the border between Christendom and Islam in Western Europe, which was frequently crossed from both sides, was drawn in a moveable political line across northern Spain. The *reconquista* (reconquest of Spain by Christian forces) began in the eleventh century, about the same time as the Crusades. Southern al-Andalus, as the Arabs called the Iberian peninsula (Andalusia in English), remained in Muslim hands until the reconquista was total and complete in 1492. During five centuries of Islamic rule, Arab culture flourished under the Spanish Muslims (Moors), and al-Andalus served as an important point of contact between Christendom and the Islamic world. In literature, philosophy, and architecture, the Spanish Muslims made several notable achievements that have survived to this day. An example is the richly decorative design of the Alhambra. The writings of the Moorish philosopher Averröes inspired considerable philosophical discussion in later Medieval Europe. The Spanish language itself bears witness to the Islamic heritage, for it has served as a conduit of many Arabic words into other Western languages.

The Abbasid Caliphs (750–1258). In 750 the Umayyad caliphate in Damascus fell to another Arab family, the Abbasids. The Abbasid caliphate established its own capital, Baghdad, along the banks of the Tigris River in

Mesopotamia. Under Abbasid rule, Arab hegemony gave way to increasing influence from other elements within the Islamic population. At first the Abbasid caliphs were able to coordinate successfully and productively the tensions between Sunni and Shi'i Muslims, Arabs, Persians, Turks, and other ethnic groups, and the various social and professional classes of the older civilizations still living in the Middle East. But such diversity within the vast Islamic Empire had a centrifugal effect, and the caliphate in Baghdad started losing control over people and lands that were distant from the capital.

Eventually the centrifugal effect also became centripetal. Turkish and Persian Muslim dynasties grew independent and powerful enough to make demands upon Baghdad. A radical Shi'i dynasty known as the Fatimids ruled first in North Africa, then in Syria and Egypt from 909 to 1171. Under the Fatimids, Cairo became an important political capital; its institutions of learning and culture rivaled those of Baghdad. Today in Cairo, Muslim students from all over the world attend al-Azhar University, built by the Fatimids more than a thousand years ago, two centuries before universities were established in Medieval Europe. Originally Shi'i, al-Azhar is now a Sunni university.

Although the Abbasid caliphate remained the central symbol of political authority throughout these upheavals, first the Persian Shi'i dynasty known as the Buyid (945–1055) and then the Turkish Sunni dynasty known as the Seljuqs (1055–1258) brought the Abbasid caliphate under their respective controls. Throughout the Abbasid Age, regardless of these political shifts, the level of cultural achievement remained high. It was during this period that ancient Persian reemerged as a Middle Eastern vernacular language, using Arabic script and absorbing many Arabic words. Persian became a potent medium, not only of Islamic religious literature along with Arabic, but also of several distinctively Persian genres of *belles-lettres* and poetry. Chiefly in Baghdad, classic governmental, educational, and religious institutions, such as hospitals and academies of science, as well as highly developed commercial markets were established and thrived.

The Abbasid Age was also the period in which the classic schools of Islamic law and theology flourished. Disciplines that studied the four roots of the Shari'a (see Chapter 1) branched out into the four orthodox schools that are accepted in Sunni Islam. The Shi'a formed schools or traditional interpretations of their own. The important oral tradition of sayings attributed to the Prophet Muhammad, known as *hadith*, was written down and codified. Since the Abbasid Age there have been six orthodox collections, the best known of which is the *Authentic* by al-Bukhari (d. 870). Traditional religious disciplines, such as law, quranic studies, and studies of the prophetic traditions, went on mainly in mosque schools. Late in the Abbasid Age, enlightened patrons separately endowed academies known as *madrasas*. Well-known professors were appointed to the faculties of these institutions and were paid salaries, replacing the more informal arrangements of the earlier mosque schools.

The First Six Hundred Years in Retrospect

The first six centuries of Islam were characterized by the gradual evolution and stabilization of Islamic religious, political, and cultural systems. Even with the dramatic success of Muslim Arab armies in the first thirty years after Muhammad's death in 632, the "Islamization" of older Near Eastern societies nonetheless took several centuries. During this period of time the Muslims destroyed relatively little of what they conquered, but they changed some of it significantly. Arab commanders and warriors, despite some looting and confiscation, left much of the land under the administration of the previous tenants, until the caliph 'Abd al-Malik accelerated the process of Arabization. Muslim tribal groups from Arabia established garrisons adjacent to the major population centers of Iran, Iraq, and North Africa. Baghdad, begun in 750 more than a century after the death of Muhammad, was the first major "Islamic" city to be established apart from the garrison towns. Abbasid rule accelerated the urbanization of Islamic civilization.

Scholars estimate that not until about the year 1000 did the Muslim population exceed that of non-Muslims living under Islamic rule. Many such non-Muslims were scriptuaries, known to Muslims as "People of the Book," primarily Christians and Jews. Under Islamic law, people with scripture were known as *dhimmis*. Dhimmis formed tolerated religious communities that were protected under Islamic law and rule. Indeed, Islamic society during these first several centuries comprised a great many Islamic sects as well as non-Muslim peoples. Therefore, when we refer to "Islamic society" in the past, as well as in the present, we are speaking of a society in which not everyone is Muslim. Indeed, in medieval Islam, as we shall see when we discuss Baghdad, different groups of Muslims and non-Muslims lived in clearly divided neighborhoods or sectors of the city.

By the time Shi'i Buyid warlords forced their military will on the Abbasid caliphs after the mid-tenth century, the office of the caliphate had passed its peak and was in decline until it was effectively destroyed three centuries later. With the Sunni Seljuq Turkish warlords came a new style of control over the caliphate, one that generated many of the classical Islamic religious and cultural institutions we know today. As one historian summarized this period of Islamic history through the mid-thirteenth century,

> The process of forming a Middle Eastern Islamic civilization occupied six hundred years from the beginning of the seventh to the beginning of the thirteenth century. However innovative, Islamic civilization was constructed upon a framework of institutions and cultures inherited from the ancient Middle East. . . . The characteristic changes of the Islamic era were the formation of new political

and social entities, the organization of new religious communities, and the generation, out of the elements of the past, of a new cultural style.[3]

Islamic Commonwealth After the Caliphate[4]

With the invasion of the central Islamic lands by Mongol warriors, the Classic Age of the empire under the institution of the caliphate came to an end. Indeed, we can only imagine what those decades of invasion and destruction must have been like for the Persians, Turks, Arabs, and other Muslims who lived and died in the path of the Mongol hordes. Originating in Siberia, the Mongols swept out of the East through Russia, China, and Central Asia, much as Arab tribal warriors had swept out of the West from Arabia several centuries earlier. Was Islam, with its traditions of urban civilization and high culture, ultimately to be destroyed ironically as it had first appeared, at the hands of tribesmen on horses?

The Mongols invaded the Middle East under the brilliant command of Chingiz Khan. His son, Hulagu, captured Baghdad in 1258; the Abbasid caliphate and its Seljuq lords were destroyed. But the true irony was that in just a few decades, many of the Mongol lords who occupied the Abode of Islam would themselves became Muslims, and the general shape of Islamic civilization remained remarkably stable without the caliphate as its central political symbol.

The Mamluks (1250–1517). Not all of the Abode of Islam fell to the Mongols. In Egypt and Syria, an independent Islamic government had been set up that was able to resist Mongol pressures. The leaders of this regime were called the Mamluks. Originally Turkish slaves (*mamluk* means "owned"), they were strict Sunni Muslims. In art and literary scholarship, the Mamluk period was productive. Culture was supported by royal patronage. The religious notables, or ulama, were allowed complete authority over Islamic faith and practice. To this end the Mamluks maintained the fiction of a caliphate by permitting figurehead caliphs to sit in Cairo for a while. Their most impressive literary achievements were in historical writing. One scholar of the period, Jalal al-Din al-Suyuti (1445–1505), wrote histories of Islam and scholarly studies of the Qu'ran that soon gained great prestige throughout the Islamic world. In less scholarly circles, some of the popular romances and tales of *The Thousand and One Nights* were generated in the Mamluk period.

The Ottoman Turks (1412–1918). The Muslims known to most Europeans after the sixteenth century were called Saracens. In fact, they were the Ottoman Turks, a Sunni Islamic empire that lasted until the beginning of the present century. At the height of their power, the Ottomans took possession of much of the western portions of the Abode of Islam and marched as far as Austria in Europe before they were repulsed. Alarm over the Saracen threat appears in the writings of such figures as Martin Luther, signaling the serious military and psychological threat posed by the Ottomans. Basing themselves mainly in Anatolia (modern Turkey), they took possession of Syria, Egypt, and North Africa. Through the use of a highly trained paramilitary force known as the Janissaries, and a supply of hand guns and artillery, the Ottoman sultans were able to capture and control large territories with relatively small forces. Their greatest prize was Constantinople, captured from the ailing Byzantine Empire in 1453. Renaming it Istanbul, the Ottomans made it their capital, adding splendid monuments of their own to its many architectural treasures. During the latter period of Ottoman rule, the Islamic lands paying tribute to the sultans in Istanbul were rewarded with serious neglect, causing cultural stagnation in the eastern and southern Mediterranean regions. The present century has seen a remarkable reversal of this trend.

The Safavids of Persia (1500–1779). At the same time that the Ottomans were establishing hegemony in western Islam, a Shi'i dynasty gained control of Persia. Known as the Safavids, they established their capital in Isfahan, making it one of the most beautiful cities in the Islamic world. They retained power until the mid-eighteenth century, when they were overthrown by Muslim warlords from Afghanistan. Mistrustful of Ottoman intentions, with good reason, the Safavid kings, or *shahs*, established diplomatic and economic ties with European powers. In art and architecture, a distinctively Persian expression of Islamic culture developed. An outstanding example may be seen in the magnificent buildings erected by Shah Abbas (1587–1628).

The Mughals of India (1526–1730). While the Ottomans and Safavids were carving out their empires, Turkish and Afghani warlords moved into India to establish the Islamic empire of the Mughals (a form of the word Mongol). Sunni in religious persuasion, the Mughal rulers made Delhi their capital. There and elsewhere they built impressive royal palaces and mosques. The best known of these is the Taj Mahal (see Figure 2.5).

The Mughal emperors ruled an Indian population of which the vast majority was Hindu, not Muslim. The remarkable growth of Islam within this context was due not so much to the Sunni religious commitments of the rulers but rather to the Sufis, or mystics, whose modes of piety were particularly at home in the Indian environment. Later in this chapter we will take a closer look at one Mughal emperor in particular, the famous Akbar.

From India, Muslim missionaries went to Malaysia and Indonesia, where Islam has grown with amazing vitality. Today Islam is quite strong throughout Southeast Asia, a fact that Westerners often overlook, so strong is the association of Islam with the Middle East. Another area of vital growth for Islam is the continent of Africa. South of the Sahara, where Islam had not penetrated in the initial push across North Africa to Spain, Islam is now growing rapidly, as black tribal groups confront the twentieth century.

FIGURE 2.5 The Taj Mahal, India. (Courtesy of the United Nations.)

Islamic World Since the Nineteenth Century

This brief historical sketch of the history of Islam concludes with a look at the past two centuries. Because of the impact the West had on the Islamic world during the nineteenth and twentieth centuries, and more recently, with the counterimpact of Islamic nations on the West, distortions are difficult to avoid. After the decline of Ottoman, Safavid, and Mughal power in the eighteenth century, European powers began to encroach upon Islamic lands, often in the form of economic and political meddling, buying influence by supporting the extravagant tastes of corrupt sultans and rulers. Fixing blame for the decline of Islamic governments during this period is dangerous and not essential to our purpose here. More broadly, Europe was gaining a position of superiority in the important spheres of the military, economics, and technology. Islam seemed on the decline.

One important exception was Egypt. In 1805, a Turkish subject, Muhammad 'Ali, with nominal connections to the Ottomans in Istanbul, set himself up in Cairo as ruler of a state that included Egypt and Syria, and for a while Arabia. Not unaware of the European advantage, Muhammad 'Ali sought to

Westernize the Egyptian economy and many traditional Islamic institutions. His successors were less capable rulers, and from the mid-nineteenth century until 1956, Western powers, notably the British, were able to maintain a strong presence in Egypt.

With the collapse of the Ottoman Empire after World War I, the modern state of Turkey emerged under the brilliant leadership of Ataturk. Even more than Muhammad 'Ali, Ataturk believed that the road to recovery would have to be paved by Western forms of modernization. He had the capital moved out of traditional Istanbul to Ankara. The Arabic script in which the Turkish language had been written since the time of the Ottomans was replaced by the Latin alphabet of European languages, and the Turkish language itself was modernized. Those religious practices regarded as excessively emotional, such as certain Sufi dances, were severely constrained by governmental decree.

In many ways, Ataturk's reforms were successful. He and the "Young Turks" who aided his efforts rapidly formed a modern state—one in which the role of Islamic traditions was much less in evidence than elsewhere in the Islamic world. More recently there have been signs of a resurgence of popular Islamic religious sentiments in the general population of Turkey, of the type mentioned at the end of Chapter 1. The Islamic world's most radical attempt to de-Islamize traditional culture in favor of Western modes has proved to be a pendulum that has started to swing back.

In Iran, the Safavids were replaced by the Qajar dynasty. Internally, except for some sectarian uprisings, the nineteenth century was relatively peaceful under the Qajars. Externally, the British and the Russians were mounting pressure on the borders of Qajar Iran. In 1925 the Qajars were overthrown by the Pahlavi shahs, who labored to turn Iran into a modern state under their tight control. The Pahlavi government was opposed by Muslim religious and nationalist groups that wanted reforms but not at the expense of their religious and national heritage. The second and most recent Pahlavi shah was overthrown in 1979. The popular religious uprising that helped to make this revolution possible is but another sign of the widespread longing for a return to more traditional forms of Islamic government and ways of life in the Muslim world.

ISLAM AND CHRISTENDOM

An enduring theme in the history of Islamic studies has been the relationship between the World of Islam and Christendom. That history has been marked by both constructive as well as destructive events and moments. Rich cultural exchanges have taken place, such the translation of the works of Aristotle into Arabic by the Muslims, then into Latin by medieval Schoolmen. On the darker side were the Crusades, holy wars mounted in Europe to wrest the Holy Land from "Saracen infidels"—that is, Muslims. Do these historic points of contact between Muslims and Christians around the Mediterranean have any bearing on the relationship between Islam and the West today? The answer has to be yes.

A well-known U.S. political commentator remarked in the spring of 1992 that we may be coming to the point where we (he meant the Christian West) will have to recognize that the birth of Muhammad was as important in world history as the birth of Jesus. The context of this remark was a Sunday morning television news discussion of the decision of the Algerian government to rescind the recent elections in which the Islamist Party, known by the French acronym "F.I.S." (Islamic Salvation Front), had won enough seats in a recent election to control the parliament. Widespread fear was expressed by Western world leaders and media pundits that "Islamic fundamentalism" might be able, through democratic means, to bring down the Westernized governments of Algeria and other states in the Muslim world. In this case, the conflict is not between Islam and Christendom, but rather its more modern, political manifestation, Islam and the West.

This concern in public discourse about Islam indicates a longstanding conflict between Islam and Christianity, the Middle East and the West. Any study of Islam by non-Muslim Western students and scholars must be conscious of this conflict, which is often lurking beneath the surface of Western remarks made about Islam, like the one cited above about the importance of the birth of Muhammad in history. Similarly, Muslim reactions to the Western studies of Islam are also often influenced by this historical conflict. Therefore, in addition to the relationship between Muslims and the Christian communities living under Islamic rule in Dar al-Islam, we need to understand something about the historical relationship between Dar al-Islam on the one side, and Western Christendom and the modern West on the other. Another boundary between Islam and Christendom was established in the fourteenth century, when Turkish forces in Anatolia and the Balkans positioned themselves between Europe and Latin Christianity to the West, and the Baltic region, Russia and Orthodox Christianity to the East. A few words about these historical relationships between Muslim and Christian civilizations are in order.

Early in the Christian encounter with Islam, Muslims were interpreted by Christians in light of Genesis 16:1–16 and 21:12–14 as descendants of Abraham through Ishmael, his son through his concubine Hagar. Prior to the eighth century, Christians had identified the Jews as descendants of the Ishmaelites, a marginal people. The Venerable Bede (d. 735) made the identification of Muslims as descendants of Ishmael, and Christians as the descendants of Isaac. Theological polemics between Muslims and Christians, from Baghdad to Granada, were driven by such passages from the Bible and the Qur'an. Until the eleventh century, however, more religious disputation occurred between Muslims and Christians within Dar al-Islam, rather than on the borders, such as in Spain and Sicily.

In the period between 1100 and 1500, Latin Christianity became more aware of the world of Islam than previously. The most positive contribution to this awareness was that made by Peter the Venerable (ca. 1094–1156), Abbot of Cluny, France. Peter commissioned the translation of the Qur'an and other Muslim religious texts in a body of literature that has come to be known as the "Cluniac Corpus." The Cluniac Corpus of translations of Islamic texts into Latin in the eleventh century marked the beginning of serious study of Islamic religion. Until this time, most writing about Islam by Europeans had focused on the figure of the Prophet Muhammad. These included salacious accounts of Muhammad as an imposter, a licentious womanizer, an apostate Christian, a magician, and so on.

More widely known and referred to in modern times are the Crusades, which began in the eleventh century and continued for the next two centuries. The Islamic world remained largely untouched by the Christian/ Muslim skirmishes and wars going on in Palestine and Syria, and it wasn't until the twelfth century that successful Muslim counteroffensives were mounted. The famous contest between Saladin (Salah al-Din al-Ayyubi) and Richard the Lion-Hearted, as well as the conflicting theological commitments to Jerusalem by both sides, is captured in the following account of an exchange of letters between the two commanders. The first is from a letter sent in 1191 by Richard, King of the Franks, to Saladin, Sultan of the Muslim Ayyubid dynasty:

> I am to salute you, and tell you that the Muslims and Franks are bleeding to death, the country is utterly ruined and goods and lives have been sacrificed on both sides. The time has come to stop this. The points at issue are Jerusalem, the Cross, and the land. Jerusalem is for us an object of worship that we could not give up even if there were only one of us left. The land from here to beyond the Jordan must be consigned to us. The Cross, which is for you simply a piece of wood with no value, is for us of enormous importance. If the Sultan will deign to return it to us, we shall be able to make peace and to rest from this endless labour.

After reading this "offer" from Richard, Saladin consulted with his advisors then sent back this reply:

> Jerusalem is ours as much as yours; indeed it is even more sacred to us than it is to you, for it is the place from which our Prophet accomplished his nocturnal journey and the place where our community will gather [on the day of Judgment]. Do not imagine that we can renounce it or vacillate on this point. The land was also originally ours, whereas you have only just arrived and have taken it over only because of the weakness of the Muslims living there at the time. God will not allow you to rebuild a single stone as long as the war lasts. As for the Cross, its possession is a good card in our hand and it cannot be surrendered except for something of outstanding benefit to all Islam.[5]

Such irreconcilable theological differences between leaders who respected each other and who could otherwise cut deals with each other are characteristic of a relationship between Islam and the West that on occasion could be quite productive

In the late fourteenth century, the Christian states of northern and eastern Europe mounted another crusade, this time not to take the Holy Land (for which all earlier attempts had been ultimately unsuccessful), but rather to check the advance of the Ottoman Turks on the medieval Kingdom of Serbia. At the famous Battle of Kosovo in 1389, the Turkish Muslims defeated the Serbs and took control of the western Balkans (former Yugoslavia), on the "doorsteps of Europe." In 1529 and again in 1683, the Turks laid siege, unsuccessfully, to Vienna (Austria). The long contest for the Mediterranean between the Muslim Ottoman Empire and the Christian Habsburg Empire ended eventually in stalemate.

The Ottomans, however, had succeeded in driving a wedge between Western and Eastern Christendom, Rome and Byzantium. Their most lasting heritage in Eastern Europe was in the Balkan states. With the conquest of Constantinople of 1453, the Orthodox heritage of Byzantium moved east to the steppes of Central Asia and Russia. One result of this Islamic expansion into Eastern Europe was to suppress the ancient conflict between Roman and Orthodox Christianity.

Another result, far less positive, was to open another front of Muslim/Christian political and religious conflict, which has lasted down to the present, this time with Eastern Orthodox Christianity. Kazakh, Tatar, Uzbek, and other Muslim peoples settled the steppes of Eastern Europe and Central Asia, in the wake of the Mongol invasion into that territory in the thirteenth century. For the next few centuries, Orthodox Christian Muscovy and Islamic Istanbul struggled to control the region. In 1773, Catherine the Great ended religious persecution and gave greater freedom to Muslims under Russian rule. However, the Russian nobles soon began to seize Tatar estates, forcing the Muslims to flee to the Ottoman Empire. With the fall of the Ottoman Empire and the rise of the Communist, secularist Soviet Union at the end of World War I, great numbers of Muslims (as well as Orthodox Christians) again lost their religious freedom. Seven decades later, the collapse of the Soviet empire in 1990 freed Muslims and Eastern Orthodox Christians to resume public practice of their traditional religious rites. The challenge to both traditions, Muslim and Christian, as they rediscover and reconstruct their religious heritages, will be to defuse the ancient conflicts that are so deeply rooted in their shared history.

We close this chapter, then, with an observation. Throughout the Islamic world during the past two centuries, Muslims have been struggling to reform and redefine their faith over and against the challenges of modernization, foreign intervention, and internal corruptions. The average person in the West has been largely unaware of these developments until quite recently. Often described as a "militant revival" of "fundamentalist" Islam, the reforms that are going on now in several parts of the Islamic world are part of a much longer and less ominous process when seen in perspective. It is hoped that this study of Islamic religion and culture will provide some insight into why hundreds of millions of Muslims struggle to preserve and live within their Islamic heritage.

Our next task is to look more closely at Islamic religious history and religious interpretation of history.

NOTES

1. Islamic years are reckoned on a lunar calendar of about 354 days. Each century of our Western solar calendar is equivalent to about 103 lunar years. Writers on Islamic topics usually list together the A.H. and A.D. dates of events. For example, "al-Ghazzali (d. 505/1111)" means that the Muslim theologian al-Ghazzali died in the year 505 after the Hijra, which corresponds to A.D. 1111. To make things simpler, only the A.D. dates will be cited in these pages.
2. For critical reassessment of how important Mecca was at the time of the rise of Islam, see Patricia Crone, *Meccan Trade and the Rise of Islam* (Princeton, N.J.: Princeton University Press, 1987).
3. Ira M. Lapidus, *A History of Islamic Societies* (New York and elsewhere: Cambridge University Press, 1988), p. 225.
4. For the distinction between "empire" and "commonwealth" as it is meant in this context, students of history may wish to consult Garth Fowden, *Empire to Commonwealth: Consequences of Monotheism in Late Antiquity* (Princeton, N.J.: Princeton University Press, 1993).
5. Francesco Gabrieli, trans., *Arab Historians of the Crusades*, trans. from Italian by E. J. Costello (Berkeley and Los Angeles: University of California Press, 1984 [1957]), pp. 225–26.

3

Quranic Cosmology
and the Time
of the Prophet

SACRED BLUEPRINTS

Why do the religious practices of the Sioux Nation seem so different from those of Zen Buddhists in Japan? We can account for physiological differences among people in terms of biology and genetics. Cultural differences, including religious beliefs and practices, are seldom determined by biology, however. Cultural characteristics are transmitted socially—in the home, on the playground, in schools, and in religious institutions and ritual practices. Historians of religion and anthropologists have developed a set of concepts for the analysis and comparative study of religion and culture. We begin this chapter with a brief consideration of the concepts of cosmology, world view, ethos, and pathos. Then we will see how they apply to the study and understanding of Islam.

In a well-known comparative study of Islamic culture between Indonesia and North Africa, the anthropologist Clifford Geertz discussed the significance of sacred symbols for the study of religion: "What sacred symbols do for those for whom they are sacred is to formulate an image of the world's construction and a program for human conduct that are mere reflexes of one another." Geertz went on to define this process in terms of the notions of world view and ethos. The passage is worth quoting.

In anthropology, it has become customary to refer to the collective notions a people has of how reality is put together as their world view. Their general style of life, the way they do things and like to see things done, we usually call their ethos. It is the office of religious symbols, then, to link these in such a way that they mutually confirm one another. Such symbols render the world view believable and the ethos justifiable, and they do it by invoking each in support of the other. The world view is believable because the ethos, which grows out of it, is felt to be authoritative; the ethos is justifiable because the world view, upon which it rests, is held to be true. Seen from outside the religious perspective, this sort of hanging a picture from a nail driven into its frame appears as a kind of sleight of hand. Seen from inside, it appears as a simple fact.[1]

To these two notions of world view and ethos, the historian of religion can add two others—cosmology and pathos—in order to understand better the textual and social record of Islam in history. Sacred symbols of Islam, such as the Ka'ba in Mecca, which we shall discuss below, play a complex role in historical consciousness and ritual activities of Muslims. We need a few conceptual categories, such as those suggested by Geertz, in order to analyze the rich data of Islamic religion.

The four interrelated categories—cosmology, world view, ethos, and pathos—can be characterized as follows. *Cosmology* is the cosmic structure and dynamics of total reality that is represented by a foundational text such as the Qur'an, and which may operate as a template for a ritual system. We will consider the quranic cosmology below, with its notions of creation, the sharp distinction between the Creator and Creation, and the symbolic mechanisms for communication between these two realms. *World view* reflects historically and locally rooted perceptions of the physical and social environment. One scholar describes world view as follows: "Inside our heads, in our thoughts, and in our language, we carry a more or less coherent model of the world—a world view—a way of making sense of our environment, social and physical."[2] The anthropologist Dale Eickelman has stressed that world views are socially constructed and socially transmitted, and thus may vary from one historical and geographical context to another. World views integrate notions of family, ethnicity, and sexuality, for example, with values and beliefs from the Qur'an and the Sunna of the Prophet, or the teachings of the Shi'i imams.[3] Although socially communicated and shared, Islamic world views are ultimately individual, and thus Muslims, like all religious people, have different attitudes among themselves about things that matter to them.

The third category is *ethos*. As the passage from Geertz indicates, ethos is the local system of cultural values and norms of behavior that the community self-consciously attempts to set in practice and to keep in place from one generation to the next. The Islamic ethos is derived in large part from the Sunna or practice of the Prophet Muhammad, which is recorded in the hadith. Local legends and cultural heroes often account for other characteristics of social ethos, as for example the Bedouin in classical Arabic poetry.

FIGURE 3.1   Muslim children singing the national anthem on the playground of a religious school in Egypt. (Photo by the author.)

Variations in ethos occur between rural and urban environments, and between Arabs, Bengalis, Iranians, and other ethnic groups. Seyyed Hossein Nasr has characterized the transcultural perception of the Islamic ethos, although he did not use the term, as follows:

> For nearly fourteen hundred years Muslims have tried to awaken in the morning as the Prophet awakened, to eat as he ate, to wash as he washed himself, even to cut their nails as he did. There has been no greater force for the unification of Muslim peoples than the presence of this common model for the minutest acts of daily life. . . . It is this essential unifying, a common *Sunnah* or way of living as a model, that makes a bazaar in Morocco have a 'feeling' or *ambiance* of a bazaar in Persia, although the people in the two places speak a different language and dress differently. There is something in the air which an intelligent foreign observer will immediately detect as belonging to the same religious and spiritual climate. And this sameness is brought about firstly by the presence of the Quran and secondly, and in a more immediate and tangible way, through the 'presence' of the Prophet in his community by virtue of his *Hadith* and *Sunnah*.[4]

The final category is *pathos*. It was Geertz who offered the best characterization of religious pathos, although he, too, did not use the term. "There are at least three points," Geertz reasoned, "where chaos—a tumult of events which lack not just interpretations but *interpretability*—threatens to break in upon man: at the limits of his analytic capacities, at the limits of his powers of endurance, and at the limits of his moral insight."[5] To this notion of the occasional uninterpretability of some things in life in accord with one's religious and moral convictions, unresolvable conflicts of interpretation leading to communal violence are also an indication of the pathos of a religious tradition.

Although the history of Islam can be told without reference to God, angels, Satan, and so on, history as it is understood within the Muslim umma is based on the quranic symbol system. We turn now to consider the quranic cosmology.

QURANIC COSMOLOGY

The second sura of the Qur'an, the Sura of the Cow, begins with a long account of generic distinctions between those who believe in God and His revelation and fear him (in Arabic, the *mu'minun*), those who reject God (the kafirs), and those who attempt to deceive both believers and God by professing faith falsely (the *munafiqun*, Qur'an 2:1–29). The munafiqun, usually translated as "hypocrites" or "backsliders," are described with reference to striking metaphors: deafness, lightning that blinds, covenant breakers, followers of Satan. The struggle between Truth (*sidq*) and Lie (*kadhb*), and between acceptance/belief (*iman*) and rejection/unbelief (*kufr*), is a powerful thematic characterization in the opening verses that speak of conflict in the human condition.

The opening passage of the second sura is followed by verses on the creation of Adam and the refusal of Iblis among the angels to "bow down" to Adam. Then there is the story of the primal man Adam and his wife in the Garden, God's instruction of Adam in the names of things and in obedience to Him, and Satan's successful deception of the First Parents, which caused them to be expelled from the Garden (2:30–39). Thus, the struggle between Truth and Lie, doing good and sowing disorder, is a cosmological problem and a fundamental one in Islamic symbolism. The story continues in the second sura with an account of Israel's covenant with God, with brief mention also made of the Christians and Sabaeans—other people with scriptures, or "People of the Book." Then there is the Israelites' breaking of the covenant and rejection of God's signs, and their consequent punishment, of which it is said that God made an example of them (2:40–86). The following passage from the Sura of the Cow dwells on the role of prophets sent by God to various communities to warn them to fear God and obey His prophets:

> We gave Moses the Book and after him followed up with Messengers, and gave Jesus son of Mary clear [signs] and confirmed him with the Holy Spirit. So whenever a Messenger comes to you with that which you desire not, do your souls become inflated with arrogance? (2:87)

Then follows the judgment on those confessional communities that reject their messengers:

> The Jews say "the Christians have nothing [true to stand on]" and the Christians say "the Jews have nothing [true to stand on]," although they recite a similar

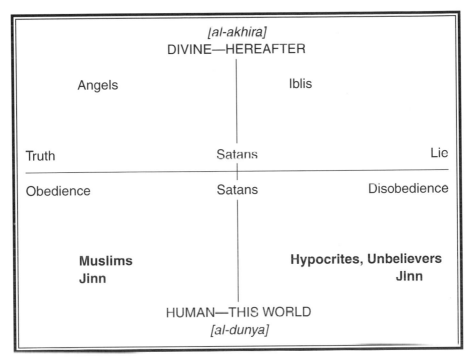

FIGURE 3.2   Diagram of the quranic cosmology.

book. In likewise, those without knowledge say the likes of what [Christians and Jews] say. On the Day of Resurrection God will judge among them regarding that in which they differ. (2:113)

With verse 122 begins a section on Abraham, the founder of the Ka'ba in Mecca, who prays: "O Lord, make Muslims [literally, 'those who submit to You'] and [make] our progeny your *umma muslima* ['community that submits to you.']" (2:128)

The sacred narrative of this cosmology shifts to the umma in Arabia and to the Messenger to the Arabs (Muhammad is meant but not named), beginning with verse 142 of the Sura of the Cow. Here the themes of going in the Straight Path (*sirat al-mustaqim*) versus going astray or being led astray come to denote the Arabs and their Prophet in particular. To stay on the Straight Path requires an effort, that is, jihad, in the path of God, a fundamental notion of the Qur'an which we discussed in Chapter 1. This dimension of the quranic cosmology can be represented with the diagram in Figure 3.2.

The two axes of Figure 3.2 indicate the divine versus the human, and the here and now (*al-dunya*) as opposed to the hereafter (*al-akhira*). The sacred is distinguished from the profane both with respect to space (heaven and earth) and time (now and the hereafter). The quranic cosmology is dynamic. Satans and angels can impose themselves into the human plane, al-dunya.

God sends His word down to messengers and through them to humankind, and the latter through prayer and ritual express themselves to God.

Elsewhere in the Qur'an, in a well-known passage, the unity of humankind that is contained in primordial time in the seed of Adam is presented as follows:

> And when your Lord drew forth from the descendants of Adam, from their loins, their seed, and caused them to testify concerning themselves [saying]: Am I not your Lord? They said: Truly, we so testify; Lest you say on the Day of Resurrection: Verily, of this we were unmindful. (7–172)

Among the implications of this passage is that the seed of Adam, containing the whole of humankind throughout all the ages, is primordially Muslim and thus in a state of primal peace. To be non-Muslim or to fall from Islam, then, is an accident of history, al-dunya, not an essential attribute of humanity as defined in quranic cosmology, al-akhira.

The Qur'an stresses that humans who walk in the Straight Path must be morally aware of their actions. Moral awareness is framed in the quranic concept of *taqwa* (piety, fear of God), which Fazlur Rahman translated with the phrase "to protect oneself against the harmful or evil consequences of one's conduct."[6] Again, the consequences are unavoidable on the Day of Judgment, al-akhira. Only a life of service (*'ibada*) to God, ritually encompassed by the religious duties (the *'ibadat*, including the Five Pillars discussed in Chapter 1), is appropriate to those who are believers (mu'minun), as opposed to unbelievers, that is, kafirs. The quranic cosmology, therefore, admonishes humanity to live by the Qur'an, which refers to itself as a Book of Guidance, to follow prophets and messengers sent to humankind, and to build a community, an umma, that will ensure the ability of humans to accomplish these ultimate ends.

A final note on quranic cosmology is that it is not historical in the strict sense. It is primordial and prehistorical. Cosmology is a system of symbols that act as lenses through which to see and interpret events in history. Thus, historical time, the world today, is seen and understood in terms of the struggle between those who believe and those who don't, the temptations by satans, etc. With this in mind, we turn from cosmology to consider historical time, from the Qur'an to Islam in history, without losing the perspective of quranic symbolism. Throughout the rest of the book we will use terms like world view, ethos, and pathos in the senses discussed above.

FROM COSMOLOGY TO HISTORY

Islam stands in the light of history as the last of the three monotheistic religions to arise in the Middle East. Affinities among Judaism, Christianity, and Islam have been noted. The political and cultural symbiosis of these three religious communities in the Middle East during the past fourteen centuries, despite heavy polemics and occasional conflict, has been possible largely because of their compatible religious world views. In Western scholarship, Islam is often seen as having originated as an Arabian expression of monotheism, the last in a long and dynamic succession of Middle Eastern empires and states in antiquity. Islamic sacred history takes account of this overall development of the three faiths that trace their origins to Abraham and Adam.

The early Islamic community was conscious of having roots in earlier civilizations, for it believed that monotheistic religion was older than either Christianity or Judaism. But, as has been noted, Muslim historians wrote about the ancient past with a much different sense of history than that of Western historians. As we have seen, the Jewish and Christian communities that fell under Muslim rule were able to enjoy special status as "People of the Book." This term occurs in the Qur'an; it refers to those confessional religious communities to whom Muslims believed Allah had already sent prophets and scriptures. Many of the early Islamic historians began their works with the general Judeo-Christian-Islamic notion of God's creation of the world. This was usually followed by stories of prophets, from Adam to Jesus, who were sent to various peoples prior to Islam. These stories formed a prologue to the sending of the Prophet Muhammad to the Arabs. As one scholar of Islam has said:

> The Qur'an's own presentation of the pre-Islamic history of God's revelatory activity demonstrates how thoroughly the sending of Muhammad and the revelations to him are felt as rooted in an earlier *Heilsgeschichte* [sacred history], the knowledge of which is essential to the Muslim. Nevertheless, the scholarly concern with the precise "origins" and "authenticity" of materials with a pre-Islamic background such as those found in the Hadith is only one type of concern. Of potentially greater significance for the historian who is trying to understand early Islam is the more subtle question of the meaning and function of such materials in the individual and collective life of the early Muslims.[7]

Although some of the prophets of the Islamic tradition are foreign to the Bible, the classic concept of sacred history in Islam was much closer to the concepts of early Judaism and Christianity than any of these ideas are to modern ideas of history.

The Middle Eastern monotheistic traditions share a common lore about the past that includes creation myths, legendary patriarchs and prophets, divine acts of reward and punishment directed at nations, and manifestations of God in word (scripture) and deed (history). Sacred history located the religious community within an overall divine plan. The very structure of the divinely created *cosmos* also provides proper orientations that place one in harmony with the divine will. For example, highly significant in the Islamic cosmology is the sacred Ka'ba in Mecca. A rectangular house that enshrines a black stone in the eastern corner, the Ka'ba is the focal point of all

Muslims in the rituals of prayer and of pilgrimage. Muslims believe that the Ka'ba achieved fundamental significance long before the sending of Muhammad, Jesus, and Moses as prophets. Tradition teaches that the sacred Ka'ba was founded by Abraham (Ibrahim in Arabic). The Prophet Muhammad, then, appeared in a moment of sacred history that had begun with Adam and the creation of the world, and the Ka'ba was seen as the center of a number of sacred sites and ritual orientations; indeed, the Ka'ba is the center of a cosmos religiously conceived by Muslims. The proper understanding of Islam as religion begins with a knowledge of sacred history and of the cosmological views of the Islamic community.

MUHAMMAD IN THE PROPHETIC TRADITION

In Islamic sacred history, Muhammad ibn 'Abdallah, an orphan raised under the protection of the powerful Quraysh tribe of Mecca, was called by God at the age of forty to recite a message that was eternally inscribed in Heaven. That message directly challenged the tribal society into which he was born and whose protection he enjoyed less the more he spoke Allah's truth. That message was, in its essentials, similar to the divinely sent word borne by others, including Moses (Torah), David (Psalms), and Jesus (Gospel)—a message that Muslims believe the Jews and Christians had not only not heeded, but also altered to suit their own ends. The *sending* of the Prophet Muhammad is seen by Muslims as the final historical positing of the timeless scripture. *Qur'an* is the Arabic word for the recitation of the message from God that Muhammad delivered during his lifetime. As *Seal* or last of all the prophets since Adam, the unlettered Muhammad had uttered the word of God in miraculously eloquent Arabic to a people whose cultural pride lay in their oratory and poetic skills. Herein lay the chief sign of his prophetic calling.

The quranic cosmology clearly identifies Muhammad's prophetic mission to the Arabs in the context of previous divinely sent messengers to various peoples of the Earth. Both Muslim and non-Muslim scholars have frequently observed that the present collection of the Qur'an probably does not reflect the original order in which the verses were recited by the Prophet. The result is a text that often seems to be disjointed and difficult to comprehend in translation to non-Muslim readers. Nonetheless, many of the 114 suras of the Qur'an can be seen to form narrative wholes or structures with specific messages boldly stated. One such sura, the twenty-sixth, is called the Sura of the Poets, and it carries the specific message of Muhammad's prophetic mission against the background of other prophets sent by Allah.

The Sura of the Poets begins (Qur'an 26:1–9) with a general consolation from Allah to the Prophet concerning the Arabs' failure to heed the message of Allah through his Messenger, Muhammad. In the opening verses we hear Allah saying (verses 2–9):

These are signs of the Scripture that makes clear.
Perhaps you torment yourself [O Muhammad] because they believe not.
If We willed, we could send a sign down upon them that would force them to bow
    their necks [in acceptance]
No new remembrance is brought to them from the Merciful that they do not
    renounce.
They charge lies! So tiding of what they used to scoff at will be brought to them.
Don't they see the Earth, how we have produced in it every fruitful pair?
Truly in this is a sign, though most of them believe not.
Truly your Lord is Mighty, the Beneficent!

In the next large section of the sura (10–91), we learn of seven other messengers who preceded Muhammad: Moses, Abraham, Noah, Hud, Salih, Lot, and Shu'ayb. Notice that three of them—Hud, Salih, and Shu'ayb—are not biblical figures. There is some trace of these three in the folklore and records of Middle East sources outside of the Bible and the Qur'an. What captures our attention, however, is that all seven forerunners of Muhammad are similarly presented in the narrative of the sura. God sent each to his own people with the message: "Won't you fear God? Truly I am a faithful messenger unto you. So fear God and obey me." (In the longer passages on Moses and Abraham, this common formula is stated in different words.) Thereafter we find mention of the specific ways in which each people have transgressed God's will. For example, Moses charged Pharaoh with obstructing God's command to let the Israelites go free; Abraham condemned the idol worship of his clan; and Shu'ayb accused his people of dishonest business practices. In each case the people rejected the messengers raised from their midst, in some instances after first asking for a sign that would prove the messengers were sent from God. The subsequent refusal to accept these signs proved disbelief and rejection of Allah and His messenger. The seven passages on earlier messengers end with the announcement of divine retribution against the seven nations.

Note that each of the seven passages ends with the phrase: "Truly herein is indeed a sign; yet most of them believe not. And truly your Lord! He is indeed the Mighty, the Merciful." By combining the names of both biblical and local Arab figures of legendary times in similar prophetic roles, the Qur'an declares that the sacred history of Islam is comprehensive of not just the Arabs but all other Middle Eastern peoples. In this view, the Arabs had always been a part of the divine scheme of salvation about which both Jews and Christians had already had much to say.

The final passage of the sura (verses 192–227) ties the examples of the seven prophets and nations to Muhammad as messenger to his own people (192–196):

Truly [the Qur'an] is sent down by the Lord of the Worlds,
Brought down by the Faithful Spirit.

*Upon your heart [O Muhammad], that you may be one of the warners in clear
  Arabic speech.*
Truly it is in the Scriptures of the Ancients.

The divine commands and prohibitions—the *Guidance*, as these are often
called—reflect the pure monotheistic religion of Abraham more than they do
that of any other prophet. Like Muhammad, Abraham had discerned the impiety and wickedness of idol worship among his kin. But the banishment of
Abraham's wife, Hagar, and their son, Ishmael (Isma'il in Arabic), had an
important consequence not mentioned in Judeo-Christian scripture. According
to Islamic tradition (sacred history), when Hagar and Ishmael were banished,
Abraham escorted them to Mecca, where he helped Ishmael construct the
house for the sacred black stone, the Ka'ba. Hence the Ka'ba is regarded by
Muslims as the first house of worship. According to tradition, from that archaic
moment the Ka'ba remained a place of worship for Arabs, but by Muhammad's
time it had degenerated into a shrine of pagan idols of the sort Abraham had
renounced. That period of "ignorance" and social "crudeness," in which
humanity had lost touch with God and His messengers, is known as the
Jahiliyya. The notion of Jahiliyya, which denotes pre-Islamic times but has come
to connote any condition in which Islam is not adequately observed, is an
important aspect of temporal and behavioral symbolism in quranic cosmology.

One of Muhammad's last acts was to perform the pilgrimage to Mecca,
where he asserted the Abrahamic meaning of that rite, of the Ka'ba, and of
several other sacred sites in and near Mecca. Thereby the Prophet established, indeed reestablished, the annual pilgrimage of Muslims to the first
house of worship. What had been a local pagan rite among the Arabs
became a sacred duty for all Muslims throughout the Abode of Islam.

Islamic sacred history begins, then, with Allah and the creation of the
world. Messengers/warners had already been sent to various communities
of humankind by the time of Muhammad. In many ways, Abraham, as presented in the Qur'an and Islamic tradition, became the most significant
example for Muslims because of his pure monotheistic belief and his dis-
avowal of the idol worship that corrupted his clan. Islamic tradition identifies a remnant community of these pure monotheists, known as Hanifs, in
Arabia during the pre-Islamic (Jahiliyya) period. Although the Qur'an was
specifically an Arabic scripture, received in the time of the Prophet, it carefully wove into the fabric of Muhammad's biography an overall history of
humankind. A consideration of that biography is next.

MUHAMMAD IN HISTORY

Information about Muhammad's life prior to his fortieth year is sparse. It is
commonly agreed that he was born around 570 in Mecca. His father, 'Abdallah, died a few months before he was born, and his mother Amina died

when he was six. Since he was an orphan, his economic fortunes and social standing were not promising. Formal education as we think of it in modern times did not exist in traditional pastoral societies like those of Arabia, and, like so many people of the Bedouin tribal environment, Muhammad was functionally illiterate. What he learned of the cosmopolitan culture streaming in and out of Mecca may have been enhanced by traveling with caravans to Syria. There the older manifestations of Judaism and Christianity would have appeared in noticeable contrast to the pagan culture of Arabia.

At age twenty-five Muhammad married Khadija, then a widow of forty, who entrusted to him the management of her family's caravan business. With this marriage Muhammad moved from the immediate protection of his uncle Abu Talib to a position of some limited social recognition in the Quraysh tribe of Mecca.

It was fifteen years after marriage to Kadija, when he was forty, that Muhammad first experienced in a traumatic way the voicing of the message for which he has been remembered. Muslim historians themselves have differed on whether or not the many stories about Muhammad's special gifts and powers—some of them quite fantastic—were actually true. Truth in Islam *is* the Qur'an. It is revered as the document of Allah's revelation conveyed through His Messenger, Muhammad. Both as revelation and as foundation for the Prophet's sacred biography, the Qur'an is the apogee of Islamic salvation history.

The moment that marks the irruption of sacred time into the life of the Prophet is known in Islam as *laylat al-qadar*, the Night of Power, the night between the twenty-sixth and twenty-seventh days of the ninth month on the Muslim calendar, Ramadan. On this occasion Muhammad is said to have first experienced his call to prophethood. Tradition has elaborated the circumstances of this occasion. Muhammad often retreated to hills near Mecca to brood and meditate on the spiritual malaise of the Meccans. On one such occasion, at the age of forty, he was moved by a strange experience. A bright, blinding light appeared on the horizon; it was a manifestation of the Angel Gabriel. Here the Qur'an speaks for itself (in Arabic, the style is simple and direct): "Recite, in the name of the Lord who created, created man from a clot. Recite, and thy Lord is the most Bounteous, who teaches man what he does not know." (Sura of the Clot 1–5 [Qur'an 96])

The Qur'an relates that when Allah required Moses to appear before the great Pharaoh and demand freedom for the Israelites, Moses was sore afraid. Allah assured him that divine signs would enable him to convince Pharaoh and his chiefs. So, too, later sacred biographies and commentaries explained that on the Night of Power, Muhammad was filled with fear and awe, reluctant to go out and face the powerful Quraysh tribe of Mecca with Allah's message of judgment. But Muhammad was reassured that he would not be left to his own resources. As Muhammad had feared, the Quraysh did scoff, saying he was mad or infused with poetic enthusiasm. Like Pharaoh and the

FIGURE 3.3　Arabia at the time of Muhammad, seventh century.

folk of earlier prophets, the Quraysh asked Muhammad for a sign of his prophethood. The Qur'an relates that Muhammad challenged them to "bring a *sura*" as eloquent and beautiful as those of the Qur'an, which, in the irony of typical sacred biographies, was Allah's word recited on the lips of a common illiterate man. Later Muslim theologians explained that the failure of the Quraysh to match Muhammad on these occasions was the sign of his prophethood, a sign the Quraysh significantly refused to acknowledge.

　　The Quraysh, Muhammad's tribe, had established supremacy in Mecca by virtue of its monopoly over the caravan trade; given the nature of the terrain of Arabia, it was convenient for such commerce to pass through Mecca, which maintained caravanserais (inns with large courtyards) for the traders and their camels. The Quraysh also controlled the pagan shrines around Mecca, including the Ka'ba. Throngs of pilgrims streamed into Mecca during the sacred months each year. Huge fairs provided additional attractions, and revenue for the Quraysh. Although Muhammad had been orphaned in infancy, his uncle, Abu Talib, had raised the young lad in this environment and saw to his protection now; family connections were essential to tribal society. But effective protection wore increasingly thin when, after the Night of Power, Muhammad assumed the role of Prophet/Warner. At first he had recited short piercing messages attacking the social injustices and pagan worship that had come to thrive in Meccan society. Then his uncle and guardian, Abu Talib, died in 619, as did Muhammad's beloved wife, Khadija. With two of his most important sources of human support gone, the next three years were extremely trying for the Prophet. Thus in 622, upon the invitation of the town fathers there, Muhammad and his followers made the fateful Hijra (emigration) to Yathrib (henceforth called the City of the Prophet, *madinat al-nabi*, or simply Medina). This moment is reckoned as the beginning of the year 1 (A.H. 1) in the calendar used in the Islamic world.[8] It was a pivotal moment between failure and success for Islam, a poignant midway in sacred time.

Tradition tells us that at the time of the Hijra small groups of men, women, and children were quietly slipping out of the city of Mecca. Followers of the Prophet Muhammad, they were headed for the city of Yathrib and a new life of religious freedom without persecution. Earlier Muslim expeditions to the nearby Arabian city of Ta'if and faraway Ethiopia had not produced an acceptable place for Islam to flourish. Two years before the Hijra, at age fifty, Muhammad had initialed an agreement with the town fathers of Yathrib, pledging to help them overcome the tribal factionalism that sorely divided their city. This may seem odd, since tribal sanctions and oppression were the very forces that drove Muhammad and his followers out of Mecca. Implicit in the warnings Muhammad had voiced to the Meccans, however, was a message of peace. In spite of the abuse this had earned him, Muhammad's honorific title, "al-Amin" (the trustworthy), was a recognized trait of his dealings, even with those who rejected him.

In Mecca, from the Night of Power until the Hijra, Muhammad had served in the role of Messenger/Warner to the few who would listen and respond. In Medina, Muhammad was in a position to assume a role of leadership which enabled him to create an Islamic umma, or "commonwealth." The revelations continued to come to him, but now they had less to do with warnings about the Day of Judgment. The continued Guidance of Allah through His Messenger laid down the fundamentals of law for the Islamic umma as well as other practical directives.

Three problems confronted the Prophet during the remaining ten years of his life, which were spent in Medina. First, he needed to pull the Islamic community together and complete his role as a prophetic conduit of divine revelation as well as provide for the viability of an ongoing umma through his own words and example. Second, he had to deal with opponents from other religions, primarily the Jews, but also continued resistance from Arab pagans. Third, his departure from Mecca did not end that city's general dislike of him or his goal of including it within the Islamic umma. From the Hijra in 622 until his death in 632, the Prophet Muhammad succeeded in overcoming all three obstacles.

As leader in Medina, Muhammad served first as an arbiter to that city under a mandate to help end the quarreling among its chief clans. At first only the *Emigrants* from Mecca, known as the Muhajirun (those who emigrated by making the Hijra from Mecca to Medina), looked upon him as their Prophet. But slowly many Medinans also became Muslims; these were called "helpers," known in the Islamic tradition by the Arabic term *ansar*.

Tribal factionalism also accounted in part for the Prophet's trouble with the Jews, for some of the tribes in Medina were composed of Jews who had been living there for generations. At first Muhammad sought friendly terms with them, seeing much in common between Islam and their faith. During the earliest period in Medina, for example, Muslims joined the Jews in praying in the direction of Jerusalem. But the Jews mistrusted him and gave assistance to his enemies, the Meccans, against him. The matter became serious enough for Muhammad to have to deal harshly with the Jewish tribes in order not to have conspirators within his own ranks. In the end they were forcefully expelled from Medina.

The most serious skirmishes, however, were with the Meccans. Two major battles were waged between the Meccans and the Prophet's troops of Medina, one at Badr and the other at Uhud. The first limited successes of the Muslims evolved into a definite victory at Badr in 624, but a major setback occurred and the Muslim forces were nearly destroyed by the Meccans a year later at Uhud. By 630 the Meccans had been compromised enough to negotiate for terms of a peace treaty with the Prophet, at a place called Hudaybiya. The Muslims asked primarily for the right to make the pilgrimage to Mecca. At first the Meccans consented but arranged to be absent from the city when the Muslims arrived. But by 632, when Muhammad himself made the pilgrimage, the Meccans and many Arabs outside the two cities had been absorbed into Islam. Muhammad, the Messenger/Warner from God, had also become a statesman for the people of Central Arabia.

Muhammad's death in 632 marked the closing of sacred time. He was a Messenger who ultimately had been received by his own people. The foundations of the Shari'a were henceforth laid down for the historic community of Muslims. Earlier that year Muhammad had made the pilgrimage to Mecca, the first since the Hijra. It was a ritual that already had deep significance for the Arabs. In a farewell sermon delivered from a small rocky promontory called the Mount of Mercy, at one end of the Plain of Arafat, a sacred station of the pilgrimage just outside of Mecca, Muhammad is reported to have said the following: "I have left with you something which if you will hold fast to it you will never fall into error—a plain indication, the book of God and the

FIGURE 3.4   Vaulted arches of the Prophet's Mosque, Medina. (Courtesy of the Ministry of Information, Kingdom of Saudi Arabia.)

practice of His prophet, so give good heed to what I say. Know that every Muslim is a Muslim's brother, and that the Muslims are brethren."[9]

Muhammad fell ill on his return to Medina, and he died at his home shortly thereafter. Sacred time had come to an end. Historic time resumed, but under a new dispensation. The historic community of Islam now held a world view that was to shape its response to the challenges that lay ahead. The sacred biographies that tell the story of Muhammad's life reverently express in historical terms the remembrance of what had taken place in sacred time. The most tangible results are the Qur'an, the Book of God, and the Sunna of the Prophet. We have seen that the Qur'an tells of how prophets of old had said to their people: Keep your duty to Allah and obey me! Now Islam as it faced the vicissitudes of historic time had a vision of its mission to do just that.

SACRED TIME AND SACRED BIOGRAPHY

At this point, a word about interpretation should be entered. The foregoing biography of Muhammad's life is a composite drawn from several sources.

Historians have long labored to sort out the underlying facts. But asking whether or not the founder or Prophet of a religion lived and did all that is ascribed to him is a question with limited value to our present concern. Even if it were answerable, we would not be much closer to understanding Islam. It is true that Muhammad is less ancient than such figures as Jesus, Moses, and the Buddha. Nonetheless, our information about his life comes from later generations of pious followers who received information about him by word of mouth. They proclaimed the story of Muhammad's prophetic role as a religious truth. Strictly historical assessments of this sacred expression of biography are difficult, if not impossible, to make.

The sacred time par excellence of Islamic history covers the twenty-two-year period (610–632) during which Muhammad served as the vehicle for Allah's revelation. Information about those years forms a sacred biography, for which the main source is the Qur'an. More information is contained in the transmitted traditions or hadiths about the Prophet's Sunna. Pious biographies about the Prophet appeared during the eighth and ninth centuries. These provided the next generations with fuller accounts of the life of one who continued to affect human affairs in times and places far removed from the revelation.[10]

Muslims are very clear that the events of the Prophet's life form articles of faith that transcend history as it is usually judged. Most Muslims also assert the factual historicity of the biographical picture of Muhammad as presented in sacred literature. But another kind of question about Islamic conceptions of the Prophet is more pressing in the comparative study of religions. How have Islamic views of the Prophet served as paradigms for social and personal modes of behavior in cultures where Islam was and is a way of life? What important human concerns are being expressed in the ways the Prophet has been understood by those in different generations and cultural settings in Islam? When Muslims of the seventh and eighth centuries wrote the biographies we now possess, they communicated within a culture with which they shared a common world of symbols and meanings. These will seem strange to us if taken as bare facts without interpretation. The process of interpretation belongs to this entire study. It is appropriate, then, to view the biographical picture of the religious figure Muhammad with respect to the sacred time that his biography epitomizes.

In discussing the time of revelation in Islam, the term "sacred time" has been used. The meaning of sacred time as it applies to a wide variety of religions, past and present, has been described by the historian of religions, Mircea Eliade. Eliade holds that for many of humankind's religions, the most sacred time is a "primordial mythical time made present."[11] In the religions of antiquity and among many nonliterate peoples, myths relate a course of events such as the creation of the cosmos out of chaos and the establishment of a world order. This mythical time is made present by the periodic retelling of the myth of Creation and by the performance of sacred rituals. At the beginning of each year the ancient Sumerians and Babylonians, for example, recited myths of Creation in dramatic ritualized reenactment of sacred time. The original creation of an orderly cosmos out of chaos could be appropriated in ritual to revitalize historic time. The forces of dissipation and disorder in human life were thereby brought under control.

The matter is somewhat different in Judaism and Christianity, and especially in Islam. It has been noted that Creation and the divine sending of Messengers form an essential part of Islamic sacred history. But the most sacred time was an historic moment sanctified by the revelation to Muhammad, the Seal of the Prophets. As such, the time of revelation to the Arabs through Muhammad was discontinuous with ordinary time. The second caliph, Umar, is reported to have said: "In the time of the Apostle of God, people were judged by revelation. Then revelation was cut off, and now we judge you by those works of yours that are apparent to us. . . ."[12] One historian of Islamic religion has noted:

> While Muhammad still lived and prophecy and revelation in Islam continued, an order of existence prevailed that was unattainable in subsequent times. Human affairs stood under the special "judgment" of the prophetic-revelatory event. . . . For most Muslims, the "cutting off" of revelation at the Prophet's death marks not only the end of one historical order and the beginning of another, but also the transition from one order of being to another. Once past, "the time of the Apostle of God" became—most vividly for those who had participated in it and the early Muslims after them, but in a real sense for all Muslims—a wholly different mode of time: a time made holy by divine activity, "a time out of time," what Mircea Eliade has called "sacred time."[13]

The religions of antiquity vivified the powerful paradigm of mythic time in their own lives through the retelling of myth and its ritual reenactment. Christians participate in the sacred time of Christ's incarnation in the ritual of the Eucharist or Last Supper. For Muslims the sacred time of revelation is most dramatically experienced in the proper recitation of the Arabic Qur'an. We will return to this theme later in the book. Let us now consider a few important "moments" in Islamic history.

NOTES

1. Clifford Geertz, *Islam Observed: Religious Development in Morocco and Indonesia* (Chicago and London: University of Chicago Press, 1971 [1968]), p. 97.
2. Michael Thompson, *Rubbish Theory: The Creation and Destruction of Value* (Oxford: Oxford University Press, 1979), p. 57.
3. Dale F. Eickelman, *The Middle East: An Anthropological Perspective*, 2d ed. (Englewood Clifs, N.J.: Prentice Hall, 1989), pp. 228–31.
4. Seyyed Hossein Nasr, *Ideals and Realities of Islam* (Boston: Beacon Press, 1972), pp. 82–83.

5. Clifford Geertz, "Religion As a Cultural System," in *Anthropological Approaches to the Study of Religion*, ed. Michael Banton, A.S.A. Monographs 3 (London: Tavistock Publications, 1966), p. 14.

6. Fazlur Rahman, *Major Themes of the Qur'an* (Chicago and Minneapolis: Bibliotheca Islamica, 1980), pp. 28–29.

7. William A. Graham, *Divine Word and Prophetic Word in Early Islam* (The Hague: Mouton Publishers, 1977), p. 2.

8. On the variance between the A.D. and A.H. dating systems, see Note 1 to Chapter 2.

9. Ibn Ishaq, *The Life of Muhammad: A Translation of Ishaq's Sirat Rasul Allah*, trans. Alfred Guillaume (Lahore: Pakistan Branch, Oxford University Press, 1955), p. 651.

10. A useful translation of the classical biography of Muhammad is Ibn Ishaq's biography, available in English translation (see previous note). The history of this important text and its formation in early Islam is the subject of an important study by Gordon Darnell Newby, *The Making of the Last Prophet: A Reconstruction of the Earliest Biography of Muhammad* (Columbia, S.C.: University of South Carolina Press, 1989).

11. Mircea Eliade, *The Sacred and the Profane: The Nature of Religion*, trans. Willard R. Trask (New York: Harper and Row, Publishers, Inc., 1961), especially Chapter 2.

12. Graham, *Divine Word*, p. 9.

13. Graham, *Divine Word*, p. 9.

4

Select Persons, Places, and Events

STORIES AND THE MONOTHEISTIC TRADITIONS

In the history of the world's great religions, the stories of key individuals are widely known among ordinary people. For Christians, the list may vary, but it probably includes stories about Jesus, the Apostle Paul, the conversion of the Emperor Constantine, the rule of Charlemagne, and the struggle between Martin Luther and the Roman Catholic Church. Stories about the lives of those who shaped the past are a popular form of historical knowledge. Stories about kings, saints, heroes, and fabulous places permit popular lessons to be drawn by the great majority, who treat such stories with more interpretive license than do academic historians. In the monotheistic traditions of Judaism, Christianity, and Islam, such stories function within a framework of sacred history that connects a sacred time in the past with the present moment in a learnable anthology of key persons, places, and events.

The annals of Islamic history record many such stories. Certain caliphs, saints, and other noteworthy figures appear as models to be emulated or avoided. To tell about them all here is neither possible nor necessary. Certain places—lands, cities, shrines—also became objects of stories, legends, and historical writing. A select few examples will suffice. We will focus on the "rightly guided" caliphs of the Sunni tradition, on the city of Baghdad, and on Akbar, the Mughal emperor of India. The good and the bad that are attributed to them contain lessons that have served as meaningful illustrations within the Islamic tradition.

An attitude of critical skepticism toward all but the soundest evidence in reconstructing the past is not essential to our purpose here. Although the assumptions implicit in popular ideas about the past are often challenged in critical historical investigations, our present aim is to discover the narratives held to be true within the Islamic tradition. What Muslims believe about the past is more appropriate to our present concern than the ascertainable facts of history.

THE RASHIDUN

Although Islam has been remarkably uniform in the expression of its main beliefs and practices for the more than thirteen centuries of its history, important divergences did occur after Muhammad's demise in 632. Muslims locate the source of these problems in the first major period following the death of the Prophet. This is known among Sunni Muslims as the Age of the Rashidun, or "rightly guided ones" (632–661). Much like Emperor Constantine in Christianity and Emperor Asoka in Buddhism, the four Islamic rulers known as caliphs in the Age of the Rashidun occupy an important place in the historical consciousness of Sunni Muslims. (Shi'i Muslims recognize only one of the four, 'Ali, as a rightful successor to Muhammad.) Theirs was the transitional age from a simple community established by the Prophet to a major religious tradition that constituted an empire. Such figures as Jesus, the Buddha, and Muhammad did not speak directly to the question of how and by whom their followers should be led in the years and centuries to come. There has been much debate within Islam about the legitimacy of the Rashidun caliphs and about their faithfulness to the mandate of the Shari'a upon them as heads of the Islamic community. This discussion has had far-reaching consequences.

Abu Bakr

Islamic tradition relates that when Muhammad died in 632, survivors at his bedside were thrown into confusion. The Messenger of Allah's Word was mortal, as he himself had claimed. But the voicing of the Guidance of Allah's Word, the Qur'an, was complete at the time of his death. Who would lead the umma which had formed around that Word and Guidance? How could those who had braved considerable abuse from their own clansmen continue without the Messenger of Allah?

Immediate steps were taken to choose a caliph to stand at the head of the Islamic umma. Such a person would be a spiritual leader, or imam. He would also be a political figure. All agreed that Muhammad's function as Prophet and Messenger of God could not be served by anyone present. The sacred time of revelation had ended. Among the reactions reported of those present on this solemn occasion was that of 'Umar ibn al-Khattab, one of the Prophet's closest companions. Originally a fierce Meccan opponent of Islam, 'Umar converted four years before the Hijra to Medina, and he became one of Islam's most ardent adherents. 'Umar was just as intense in his reaction to Muhammad's demise. According to the early tenth-century historian al-Tabari, 'Umar reportedly cried out:

> Some of the hypocrites allege that the Messenger of God is dead. By God, he is not dead, but has gone to his Lord as Moses b. 'Imran went and remained hidden from his people for forty days. Moses returned after it was said that he had died. By God, the Messenger of God will [also] return and will cut off the hands and feet of those who allege that he is dead.[1]

By contrast, when Abu Bakr learned of Muhammad's death, he went to the mosque where 'Umar was ranting, kissed the corpse of Muhammad, then asked 'Umar to be quiet. When he would not, Abu Bakr stepped before the people assembled to grieve for the Prophet, and said:

> "O people, those who worshipped Muhammad, [must know that] God is alive [and] immortal." He then recited the verse: "Muhammad is only a messenger, and many a messenger has gone before him. So if he dies or is killed, will you turn back on your heels? He who turns back on his heels will do no harm to God; and God will reward the grateful" [Qur'an 3:144]. . . . 'Umar said, "By God, as soon as I heard Abu Bakr recite it, my legs betrayed me so that I fell to the ground, and my legs would not bear me. I knew that the Messenger of God had indeed died."

It is further reported that Abu Bakr said on that occasion: "Whoever worships God, God is alive and immortal; whoever worships Muhammad, Muhammad is dead!"[2] Abu Bakr's realism was in keeping with the teachings of the Prophet about himself and about God.

We have already noted that Muslims believe that Muhammad had not designated a successor, nor had he stated whether or how one should be chosen. The lack of guidelines was further complicated by vested interests within different parties. The Emigrants from Mecca claimed longer and closer ties as members of Muhammad's clan, the Quraysh. They too had been the targets of rejection by Muhammad's opponents in Mecca. Among the Emigrants from Mecca were some members of the Prophet's own family, led by his cousin 'Ali. They believed that 'Ali stood closer to Muhammad than anyone else. Those who thought of 'Ali in this way came to be called the Shi'a. They believed 'Ali was the legitimate successor of the Prophet. The people of Medina, however, had made the Hijra possible by inviting Muhammad and his Meccan followers to their city. Known as the Helpers, the Medinan party preferred a caliph (who after all would rule in their city) from among their own ranks. Although each group had its special interests, the need for unity prevailed. The electors chose Abu Bakr to be imam of the nascent Islamic umma, caliph of Islam. Some say it was 'Umar himself who urged the selection of Abu Bakr.

The choice of Abu Bakr was a good one. Other candidates such as 'Ali and 'Umar were more polarized. Abu Bakr was a middle-of-the-road candidate, an elder statesman acceptable to the largest number of people, according to Sunni sources. In the two short years until his death in 634, Abu Bakr was able not only to consolidate Islamic rule in Arabia by quashing apostate rebellions in southern and eastern Arabia, but also to send forth his armies into Syria and Iraq, where they met with considerable success against the forces of the Byzantine and Sassanian Empires. Tradition pictures him as a modest man of high moral standards, with humility regarding his role as leader. The main source of wealth for the growing community of Islam was the spoils gained in war, and most Muslims believe that Abu Bakr faithfully followed the quranic teaching that all true believers had equal rights to booty thus gained.

'Umar ibn al-Khattab

Much of tradition relates that the younger, more energetic 'Umar was Abu Bakr's designated choice of a successor. There is not total agreement about this, for according to Arab custom, a man who possessed manly and fair-minded qualities that the rest were willing to recognize would be the one to rise to power. Such a man became the tribal leader when the rest swore allegiance to him. There is some indication that neither the party of partisans (Shi'a) of 'Ali, nor the Helpers (ansar) of Medina were particularly happy with the choice of 'Umar, or with the principle of designating one's successor. Nonetheless, the majority of those who had been Muhammad's companions accepted 'Umar as the second caliph of Islam. Once again the choice seems to have been fortunate, for during the ten years of 'Umar's reign (634–644), Islam became a world phenomenon. As military advisor to Abu Bakr, 'Umar already had demonstrated the expertise that enabled him to continue Muslim conquests with brilliant success. His armies took control of Egypt in North Africa, and they had pushed Byzantine and Persian troops out of Syria and Iraq. By the time of 'Umar's death in 644, Persia was near total collapse. By 651, the last Persian king or shah of the Sassanian Empire had been assassinated. As one historian put it: "The power which had been the colossal rival of Rome and Byzantium, both the dream and the nightmare of the desert nomads, was lying vanquished at the Arab's feet."[3] 'Umar's role in setting this in motion is perhaps the reason he designated himself "Commander of the Faithful," in addition to the title of caliph.

Some historians have seen the military successes of 'Umar as almost inevitable, given the changing balances of power in the Middle East at the time. Byzantium and Persia were exhausted after centuries of confrontation over the territory that lay between them, namely, Syria and Iraq. This was the Fertile Crescent of biblical times. But other, more far-reaching institutional developments are assigned to the legacy of the second caliph of Islam. He is said to have adopted fair means of treating his non-Muslim subjects, particularly Jews and Christians. Islamic law referred to them as having the status of *dhimmi*, "people of the covenant." As conquered peoples who did not convert to Islam, they were guaranteed basic rights and freedom of worship in exchange for a poll tax paid into the central treasury in Medina. 'Umar's organization of the military included the founding of garrison towns (*amsar*, not to be confused with *unsar*, "helpers") at strategic locations within the conquered territories. Many of these became important Islamic cities of a much different character than the urban centers that had been formed by older, non-Muslim civilizations in the ancient Near East. 'Umar provided for civil stability by appointing in each province a judge known as a *qadi* to settle the inevitable disputes that arose, especially in the more distant centers of Islamic population. Much of what already existed as "Guidance" in the Qur'an achieved under 'Umar the status of public ordinance. Pilgrimage to Mecca, the prayerful observance of the month of Ramadan, and punishments for drunkenness and adultery became matters regulated in the public domain under his command.

What sort of man could achieve all this? We are not well enough informed to do more than guess. As with so many patriarchal figures of the past, we are better informed about what tradition has made of 'Umar than we are about the real man. But the Islamic memory of this rightly guided caliph, as shaped and preserved by tradition, is nonetheless of value. The very fact that the Sunni majority and the Shi'i minority have perpetuated quite different pictures of each of the rightly guided caliphs is significant. Each strand of Islamic tradition could make use of 'Umar's reputation for astute political handling of generals who acquired too much power in the field, cutting them off when necessary. This could be seen as being either in the best interest of Islam or solely in 'Umar's self-interest.

Death came to 'Umar on November 3, 644, from the dagger of a Muslim governor's Christian slave. The motive was apparently bitter resentment at heavy taxes imposed on those least able to afford them. Such resentment may have been widespread. Thus, as with so many shapers of history, the portrait of 'Umar contains many lines both light and dark, and the variety of interpretations of his achievements tells as much about the later painters of these portraits as the man himself. But in an important sense, that is exactly what we are looking for—Islamic interpretations of that period of sacred history when the Rashidun established Islam as a world religion.

'Uthman ibn 'Affan

More controversial than 'Umar was his successor, 'Uthman ibn 'Affan, the third rightly guided caliph, who ruled from 644 to 656 in Medina. He was a member of the great Meccan family of Umayya, which would later rule Islam from Damascus, Syria, for nearly a century (661–750). The events surrounding 'Uthman's rule and eventual assassination provided the Umayyad family with just the right motive for a parting of the ways with 'Ali ibn Abi Talib, the fourth and final rightly guided caliph according to Sunnis.

'Uthman appears to have had much going for him. He was credited with having converted to Islam during the early Meccan period of Muhammad's prophethood. 'Uthman's family wealth was a product of the lucrative caravan trade that earned profits for Meccan merchants. These families formed the aristocracy of western Arabia. The aristocratic families had resented Muhammad's prophecy, much of which had been directed against them, and very few of them had become Muslim until they had been forced to capitulate to the forces of the Prophet near the end of his life. Even then, the extent of their piety has frequently been questioned. Thus the early conversion of 'Uthman, a Meccan aristocrat and man of the world, was all the more significant. It should also be noted in this context that even though Islam was ideally an egalitarian community that stressed the brotherhood of all believers, aristocratic families such as the Umayyads did not readily relinquish their political expectations of wielding power.

During the period of Muhammad's prophethood and the reigns of the first two caliphs, 'Uthman had a reputation for being a loyal Muslim. Some have said his reputation was undistinguished by additional qualities that either favored or disfavored his selection as third caliph. He was chosen, in fact, by a council, called a *shura*, which 'Umar had appointed on his deathbed. There is speculation that 'Uthman was the shura's compromise choice among other strong candidates. 'Uthman's policies as caliph were basically those established by 'Umar, and the difficulties 'Uthman eventually faced were bound to arise as Islam expanded rapidly from a local Arabian cult to a world religion and empire.

Tradition divides the reign of 'Uthman into six good years and six bad years. His detractors spread the story that halfway through his reign he committed the clumsy (but symbolic) act of dropping the prophetic emblem into a well. A more probable cause of the "bad years" was that far away in Iraq, economic stability lagged far behind the rapid expansion of Islamic rule. By now the field generals of the conquests had become sufficiently powerful to pose a threat to the central caliphate in Medina.

Lists of typical grievances made against 'Uthman have been preserved. One of the most serious charges was nepotism, that he favored his own family when making appointments to lucrative posts. As with other events in the patriarchal period of the Rashidun, tradition viewed these policies in different ways. Some regarded these appointments as grossly unfair. Others saw in them a clever move by 'Uthman to diminish local thrusts toward independence. Some have argued that he simply invoked loyalties within his clan to preserve political cohesion. In addition, 'Uthman is said to have required that the soldiers who took spoils of war give some of them to the governors of provinces and other officials, many of them members of his own family.

Tradition also assigns to 'Uthman the decision to produce an official recension of the Qur'an. It is not known with certainty how much if any of scripture had been written down in the Prophet's own lifetime. During the early years of the Rashidun caliphs, certain individuals learned by heart the entire body of Muhammad's recitations. These individuals were known as reciters, and they enjoyed considerable prestige within the Islamic umma. However, many of the oral reciters died in wars against apostates in eastern Arabia, and therefore preservation of the text of the Qur'an was becoming a matter of concern. Soon written copies or parts thereof appeared in various locales, and tradition preserves some account of their textual variations. 'Uthman's effort to establish by central authority an official written version was marred by the suspicion in certain quarters of political maneuvering. Other versions of the text survived for a while. The 'Uthmanic recension may also have been resented by reciters, whose ritual function of oral recitation was thereby diminished; they recited from memory, not from a text. The official Arabic text of the Qur'an that is used by Muslims today is traced to the 'Uthmanic recension. Again, we have an example of a patriarchal achievement that was not without differences of appreciation within early Islamic society.

The third caliph also died at the hands of assassins. A contingent from Egypt bearing economic grievances angrily presented their case before the caliph at his home and headquarters in Medina. An altercation developed, and the embittered Egyptian Muslims laid siege upon his house. Umayyad forces were dispatched by Muawiya, Governor of Syria and a relative of 'Uthman, but they did not arrive in time to save the caliph from an ignoble death. Nor does there appear to have been much of an effort on the part of important Muslims in Medina, including 'Ali and other members of the Prophet's family, to come to the aid of 'Uthman. This event began what Muslims call the *fitna*, the first civil war in Islam. It stands as a watershed in Islamic history, for after 656, religious and political loyalties flowed in different directions. The era of the rightly guided caliphs was not yet over, but the unity achieved by the Prophet was now a complex balance of differing loyalties.

'Ali ibn Abi Talib

When Muhammad had been orphaned as a child, his uncle, Abu Talib (the father of 'Ali), brought him into his household. In this environment began the lifelong association between the Prophet and his cousin 'Ali, born several years later. 'Ali was among the first two or three Meccans to convert to Islam, and family ties were made stronger when 'Ali married Muhammad's daughter, Fatima. In keeping with the tribal structure in Arabia, 'Ali was closely identified with the effect of Muhammad's actions upon others in Arabia. This was true of the difficulties faced by Muhammad. When Muhammad decided to leave Mecca for Medina under unpleasant pressure, it was 'Ali who provided a foil to divert attention from Muhammad's escape. After Muhammad's death, those devoted to 'Ali, if not 'Ali himself, believed 'Ali was the first and foremost successor to the Prophet. In fact, the partisans of 'Ali (Shi'a) have preferred the term "imam" (spiritual leader) to "caliph" as a designation for the position of leadership they believed 'Ali received directly from the Prophet. Among the later Shi'a, 'Ali became something of a legend, characterized both as warrior and as saint. Typically, he was credited with killing 523 enemies with his own bare hands in a single day of an early battle. Along with heroic feats are legends of miracles which are held to be special signs of his divine favor.

'Ali played only a modest role in attempting to soften the tempers of 'Uthman's enemies. When 'Uthman was murdered, 'Ali at first hesitated to assume the role of leadership that many thought should have been his in the first place. On Friday, June 5, in the year 656, many Muslims finally paid allegiance to 'Ali as caliph in the mosque of the Prophet in Medina. The fact that many others withheld or refused allegiance made 'Ali's caliphate the weakest politically of all the Rashidun. Shortly after his investiture, 'Ali left Medina, never to return.

For the next five years 'Ali engaged in a series of attempts to force others to recognize his right to hold office. He first went to the Muslim garrison town of Basra, in Iraq, to put down the rebellion of certain Meccan Muslims who had been inciting feelings against him. Leading the rebels were two Meccan aristocrats, Talha and Zubayr, along with the Prophet's wife Aisha. In 656 'Ali and his forces met them and defeated them. This was called the Battle of the Camel, because Aisha, the popular younger wife of the Prophet Muhammad, rode into battle with the rebel forces astride a camel.

Next 'Ali went to another important garrison town, Kufah, to establish allegiances there. Then he marched to the Plain of Siffin near the ancient Mesopotamian capital at Ctesiphon, where he engaged the forces of Muawiya, the governor and a relative of the slain caliph 'Uthman. 'Ali's troops fared well at first, but then Muawiya ordered a rather curious stratagem. At the advice of a lieutenant, the Syrian troops under Muawiya attached leaves of the Qur'an to their lances as they rode forth into battle. The troops of Iraq under 'Ali's command were intimidated by this sacred symbol of divine judgment. 'Ali was forced to accept Muawiya's terms—to submit to arbitration the matter of 'Uthman's as yet unavenged murder.

The issue of whether or not 'Uthman's murder had been justified was a festering sore that infected 'Ali's caliphate throughout his reign. 'Uthman's aristocratic Meccan family, now the powerful Umayyads of Syria, followed

Arab custom in demanding blood revenge for the third caliph's murder. But many other Meccans and Medinans, as well as a growing number of non-Arab Muslims outside of Arabia, especially those in Iraq, were in sympathy with the complaints against 'Uthman; they saw his murder as just. The arbitration that took place in 658 between the negotiators for 'Ali and those for Muawiya ended in Muawiya's favor: 'Uthman's murder should have been avenged. 'Ali was held in contempt by Muawiya for having failed to bring justice. Against the protests of many of those who had supported 'Ali, Muawiya soon proclaimed himself the rightful caliph of Islam.

The opposition to Muawiya did not produce much support for 'Ali. Many seceded from his party, accusing him of weakness in handling the matter. They had felt all along that 'Uthman deserved his fate. Although 'Ali was pursued by Muawiya's troops to Kufah in southern Iraq, he was actually felled by an assassin's poisoned sword in an ambush in 661. Thus ended the brief Age of the Rashidun.

The fitna that ended the caliphates of Muhammad's close companions was to remain an important issue throughout Islamic history. However political these events may seem to the outsider, the presence of conflict in the formation of religious traditions was often a key element within each tradition. Whether more abstract, as in the Persian dualism between the forces of Light and Darkness, or whether more concrete, as in the ancient Israelite conquest of Canaan, the Near Eastern religions especially placed great emphasis on unity precisely because disunity was both a cosmic and an historical threat.

For Islam, the religious dimension of the conflict raised questions that would have to be answered. What sins should exclude one from membership in the Islamic umma? Who is a believer? The tension between defining right belief and achieving political cohesion was a chief legacy of the Age of the Rashidun to subsequent history.

'Ali's legacy has been enormous. His followers (and indeed, most Muslims) have perpetuated a memory of him that is extremely pious. For some of the Shi'a, the honors have reached divine proportions. For all of Islam, a favorable memory of the fourth caliph survived the ignominy of his five-year reign. Seen both as a warrior and as a saint, he is also remembered as an extremely selfless, giving person, attentive to the needs of others. His strength of character and pious devotion to Islam rank him among the authoritative sources of traditions about the Prophet's Sunna, especially among the Shi'a.

THE GOLDEN AGE OF THE ABBASIDS

History lends itself to explanation by comparisons. What was happening in Persia when Rome fell? What was the China of Confucius like as compared with the India of the Buddha (roughly contemporary)?

A period of high cultural achievement in Islam took place during the first phase of the Abbasid Empire, which lasted in its entirety from 750 to 1258. Historian Philip Hitti chose the year 800 as a poignant moment for comparison with medieval Europe. In that year, on Christmas Day, Charlemagne was crowned Holy Roman Emperor in St. Peter's Basilica in Rome by the Christian Pope. Europe was emerging from the so-called Dark Ages to become a vast civilization for which the Christian religion would provide a unifying world view. The term "Christendom" designates Christian civilization in Europe during the Middle Ages.

In 800, Baghdad was the capital of Islamic power and culture, and al-Harun al-Rashid was its caliph. In almost every respect, the Abbasid Empire surpassed the Holy Roman Empire.[4] The Abode of Islam under Harun was first of all much greater in extent and population than European Christendom. Moreover, Harun and his successor, the caliph al-Ma'mun, established academies in the arts and sciences in which scientific, literary, and philosophical treatises from Greece, Persia, and India were translated into Arabic and studied seriously.

The Arts and Sciences in Abbasid Times

We owe a great debt of gratitude to the Abbasid scholars and their enlightened royal patrons for preserving and furthering the great literary and scientific achievements of antiquity. For example, some of Aristotle's works would have been lost forever had not the Abbasid scholars made careful translations, often comparing several old Greek manuscripts and choosing the best readings from among them, passage by passage. We have noted that Muslims held special respect for those they called "People of the Book," the people of scriptural religions. Often in these academies, Muslims, Christians, and others worked together in a common scholarly search for truth about the past.

In addition to Aristotle and the Greek philosophers, Abbasid intellectual tastes ranged from mathematics, astronomy, geometry, and optics to medicine, pharmacology, music, poetry, and the literary arts. Studies in these areas were often implemented in special academies—"think tanks," we might call them today— established by royal patrons. The House of Wisdom was built in Baghdad by the Caliph al-Ma'mun (reg. 813–833). It included a library and apartments for those appointed as "Fellows" to the academy, and a stipend was paid to the scholars who worked there.

A famous appointee was the Christian Arab scholar Hunayn ibn Ishaq (pronounced Iss-hak), whose knowledge of Greek and Syriac—the two languages in which much of Hellenistic philosophy was written at that time— proved to be invaluable in the task of translation. The genius of the Arabic translations of this period (there had been earlier literal translations into Arabic) was that the abstract conceptual ideas of Greek philosophy were rendered creatively and accurately into Arabic.

Many Muslim philosophers and theologians were to use these translations in the elaboration of Islamic thought. Perhaps the most famous figure to do so was Avicenna (a Medieval Hebrew corrupt version of the Arabic Ibn Sina), who lived two centuries after Ibn Ishaq. Avicenna wrote several commentaries on the Arabic translations of Aristotle's philosophy. These commentaries were not merely explications of the earlier texts, but also probing philosophical exercises into the meaning that Aristotle's work held for the intellectual understanding of Islamic belief. They introduced a lively controversy among philosophers and theologians in Islam. Later, Christian theologians such as St. Thomas Aquinas, and Jewish thinkers such as Moses Maimonides, would take up the arguments that Avicenna and others had advanced.

At the same time that the Abbasid scholars were championing what Muslims referred to as the sciences of antiquity, Muslim religious scholars were everywhere present in mosque schools, studying the roots of Islamic religion. Those roots were discussed in Chapter 1: Qur'an, the Sunna of the Prophet, learned consensus, and reasoning by analogy. The scholars of the Abbasid Age continued to write valuable treatises on the meaning of the Qur'an. In the new intellectual environment of Baghdad, these treatises developed sophisticated analyses of grammar and lexicography; hence scholarly grammars and dictionaries of the Arabic language were written. In the time of the early Abbasid caliphs, important collections of Hadith, or sayings of the Prophet, were written down and codified. Islamic law had become an independent discipline and served as an important stabilizing force in Islamic society. Theologians endeavored to rationalize the roots of Islamic belief, and important theological controversies raged in the various schools that centered in Baghdad and elsewhere in the Abode of Islam.

Coming to Terms

It is important to remember that the Islamic Empire, like Christendom, was a total society comprising many ethnic groups and confessional religions. We have used the term "Christendom" to refer to the society or portion of the world in which Christianity and Christian institutions prevail or once prevailed, as for example in Medieval Europe, while the term "Christianity" refers more narrowly to the Christian religion. The terms "Islam" and "Islamic," however, serve to designate both the total culture and the religion, and therein lies some confusion.

The distinguished historian Marshall G. S. Hodgson offered a solution to this problem of terminology that we will follow henceforth in this work. Hodgson restricted the term "Islam" to refer to the religion of Muslims, but not to those aspects of society and culture that have little to do with religion. For the latter, Hodgson recommended the adoption of two additional terms, "Islamdom" and "Islamicate." "Islamdom," according to Hodgson, signifies "the society in which the Muslims and their faith are recognized as prevalent and socially dominant. . .a society in which. . .non-Muslims have always formed an integral, if subordinate, element, as have Jews in Christendom."

The term "Islamdom" has an odd ring to it, and we will use it sparingly. The term "Islamicate," on the other side, is used in Hodgson's work (and in a growing number of writings about Islam) to "refer not directly to the religion, Islam, itself, but to the social and cultural complex historically associated with Islam and the Muslims, both among Muslims themselves and even when found among non-Muslims."[5] We have also used the distinctly Islamic terminology Dar al-Islam, "Abode of Islam," and Dar al-Harb, "Abode of War." The Abode of Islam meant, for Muslim jurists, that territory ruled by Islam in which the Shari'a is in force. Nowhere are such conceptual distinctions more appropriate than in the discussion of the Golden Age of the Abbasids.

Those Christians, Jews, and others who preferred to remain within their own religious traditions were allowed to do so by the Muslim authorities. The Arabic term for such persons is *dhimmi*; it denotes people belonging to a non-Muslim religion that is tolerated and protected under Islamic law—that is, a non-Muslim whose religious belief is included within the Islamic view of sacred history. Practically speaking, the dhimmis had their own religious courts and intellectual institutions within Islamicate society. Christians caught stealing were handed over to the Bishop's courts, Jews to the Rabbis'. Often under the Abbasids, Christian and even secular intellectuals would engage Muslims freely in argument over religious and philosophical matters. Caliphs such as al-Ma'mun enjoyed bringing the leading proponents of various doctrines into the royal chambers to debate such matters as the divinity of Jesus (opposed by Jews and Muslims) or the truth of Aristotle's philosophy (opposed by the orthodox scholars of all religions). In the cosmopolitan atmosphere of Baghdad, many ideas from far and wide were aired. As noted already, when it came to establishing cross-cultural institutions such as academies, hospitals, and bureaucratic institutions, intellectuals were appointed on the basis of pertinent skills, with little regard for religious persuasion. Such was the climate of Abbasid Baghdad.

Baghdad, City of Peace

It might be useful to ask what connection this unfolding of Islamic culture in the ninth century has with Islamic sacred history and the notions of sacred time described earlier. What Islamic symbols were appropriated and borne out in Baghdad, the City of Peace, which was deliberately constructed as an Islamic city? When the Arab dynasty of the Umayyads collapsed in 750, the seat of power in Damascus, Syria, was destroyed, and the new capital was erected in Iraq. This change of location symbolized the decline of predominantly Arabic expressions of political and cultural modes, and the ascendancy of other elements in Islamicate society.

The city of Baghdad itself is interesting in this respect. The Abbasid caliph al-Mansur directed his architects to build a round city more than a mile and a half in diameter, encircled by a rampart wall. Towers were situated at the four points of the compass, and beneath these were the main gates into the city. The four entrances faced the main overland routes for which Baghdad served as a crossroads. While the Meccan Ka'ba remained the sacred focal point of the Islamic religion, Baghdad became the new cultural and political axis of the Islamic Empire, replacing Damascus of the Umayyads. The road between Baghdad and Mecca remained open and heavily traveled by Muslim pilgrims and religious scholars. But what bearing did the sacred space and time associated with Mecca and Medina have upon Baghdad?

The construction of the original city of Baghdad suggests that beyond its political and economic importance, it was intended to have special symbolic significance.[6] The city was regarded by some as the "navel of the universe," a designation that had been applied already to sacred cities such as Jerusalem. Yet Baghdad was basically a secular city. As one penetrated the walls through its gates, the first circle of buildings past the ramparts consisted of dwellings and shops. The homes were organized into neighborhoods formed of ethnic and tribal groups representing the wide diversity of peoples that comprised Islam under the Abbasids. The houses themselves appeared uninviting from the outside; they opened out only cautiously onto the street, where rougher elements were often about. The main functional access was to the courtyards, where families and clans congregated in the traditional Middle Eastern fashion.

In the center of the city were the caliphal palace and the royal mosque. Here architectural facades were richly artistic and symbolic. It was to the center of the city that the great political, religious, and cultural figures of the day found their way. In the large reception hall of the imperial complex, statesmen, scholars, envoys, and travelers from around the world came to plead their cases and celebrate their causes. In the adjoining royal mosque, a directional reminder indicated another center of high importance. The *mihrab*, or prayer niche, a common feature of all mosques, faced in the direction of Mecca. This directional orientation is called the *qibla*. Five times each day in the royal mosque, as in all mosques and places where they paused to pray, Muslims oriented themselves on a point beyond the secular involvements of Islamicate society to another, more sacred center: Mecca. All Muslim leaders of the prayer would mention the name of the caliph in Baghdad, but when the caliph himself prayed, he joined all Muslims in facing the Meccan Ka'ba.

It has been suggested that the circular city of Baghdad was a "conscious attempt to relate meaningfully to the conquered world, by islamizing forms and ideas of old."[7] The history of Middle Eastern civilizations holds many examples of new sacred sites and cities built on top of old ones. Human pathos results from conflicting claims made about possession and heritage of a sacred place, such as between Jews and Muslims at Temple Mount in Jerusalem, and between Hindus and Muslims in Ayodya, India, where a mosque was built on ground where a Hindu temple once stood. In many cases, however, older ideas and forms were given new expression and recognition by Muslim craftsmen and architects, resulting in great monuments of distinctive character. As we have seen, the older civilizations of the Jews and Christians were not obliterated by Islam, but rather were incorporated within Islamicate society.

The sacred history implicit in the Qur'an gave new meaning to the symbols of a basic world view shared by the peoples of the Middle East for four millennia. The sacred time of quranic revelation was regarded by Muslims as the "Seal" of previous dispensations. With the building of Baghdad, Islam centered itself in Mesopotamia (modern Iraq), in which the Christian, Zoroastrian, Manichaean, and other religious cultures had flourished. Since the Babylonian Exile in the sixth century B.C., for example, great Jewish communities and academies of learning had lived on continuously in Mesopotamia, and before that, the great civilizations of Babylon, Akkad, and Sumer. Physically, much of the past had been buried by the winds of time. Culturally, each new civilization uncovered and gave new life to world views and cultural modes that had been long evolving.

The ideas of the day that were aired in ninth-century Baghdad reflected the diversity of peoples who streamed in and out of the Islamic capital. They reflected a long cultural history with sacred and secular dimensions. By inviting and absorbing these many influences, Islam (and here we can say "Islamdom") declared that human culture, since the dawn of time, had served a divine plan and Islam was now its culmination.

BEYOND THE CALIPHATE: AKBAR OF MUGHAL INDIA

From the beginning of the sixteenth to the end of the eighteenth century, the Islamic commonwealth—that is, the Islamic world after the demise of the great caliphal empire and the Mongol interlude—was comprised of three politically independent regimes: the Ottoman Turkish, the Safavid Persian, and the Mughal Indian empires. The caliphate established by the Rashidun, which had risen to great heights of power under the Umayyads and the Abbasids, had been destroyed by the Mongols in the thirteenth century. Muawiya's victory over 'Ali had long before signaled the drifting apart of a new political center of Islam (Damascus) from the sacred geographic symbols of Islam's center (Mecca and Medina).

With the later collapse of the caliphate, what changes in the religion and cultures of Islamic peoples actually occurred? Although Islam had run out of territories it could conquer and realistically manage within one political system, it nonetheless was able to Islamize those who invaded its borders. Thus the Mongols, who ravaged Central Asia and sacked Baghdad, ended up becoming Muslims, as Turkish and Persian warlords had done earlier. The Ottoman, Safavid, and Mughal states that arose in the sixteenth century, however, established new Islamic capitals independent of each other: Istanbul, Isfahan, and Delhi, respectively. These cities were located at or beyond the outer circle of Islamdom as it had existed at the end of the Age of the Rashidun.

The relocation of political capitals brought about a flowering of culture, as Islam acquired new patrons and confronted new ideas. Probably the most dynamic area of religious ferment was that of India. Back in the Age of the Rashidun, Muslim troops had already penetrated the Sind in Northern India, thus bringing limited Arab influence to the Indian subcontinent. Later, extremist Shi'i missionaries also gained some footing. But it was Islamic mysticism that proved to be the most fertile expression of Islam on Indian soil. In turn, Muslim travelers such as the great al-Biruni brought back to the Islamic heartland amazing accounts of Indian culture and ideas. Until the sixteenth century, however, Islamic political involvement in India was managed chiefly by Turkish warlords in Afghanistan. Then, in 1524, a Central Asian Turkish lord named Babur established the empire of the Mughals in India. The challenge of this enterprise for Babur as a Sunni Muslim was considerable. Consolidating the vast territory of India into an Islamic state, and working out a cultural symbiosis with Hinduism, was a political task without precedent.

Emperor Akbar of Mughal India

One of the most fascinating stories of Mughal rule concerns Akbar (reg. 1556–1605), grandson of Babur. Under Akbar, the Muslim royal court in Delhi became a center of radical religious eclecticism in which elements of Hinduism, Jainism, Zoroastrianism, and Christianity were combined with Islam to create what Akbar intended as a new religion, known as the Divine Religion. By most measures of orthodoxy in both Sunni and Shi'i Islam, Akbar's unrestrained policy of religious eclecticism was an affair of appalling license and apostasy. His experiments in amalgamating elements of the various religions of his subjects, a venture in which he took a personal interest, did not long survive his death. The very failure of this attempt is significant to the history of Islam. It showed that even though the caliphate could no longer serve as the central symbol of Islamic unity (the Meccan Shrine and the Arabic Qur'an remained such symbols), and even though Muslim rulers were frequently tempted to act independently of the constraints placed upon them by the Shari'a, the Islamic umma was able to resist and overcome harmful ruptures.

FIGURE 4.1 A scribe, attributed to Bichitr. India, Mughal Period, ca. 1625. (Courtesy of Arthur M. Sackler Museum, Harvard University, Cambridge, Massachusetts.)

We should not dismiss Akbar as a malevolent fool. Nor should we overlook the possible motivations he might have had in creating the Divine Religion, precisely because it did draw from the various traditions of the people who came under his rule. Under the Rashidun, the majority of non-Muslim subjects had been Christians, Jews, and Zoroastrians. As we have seen, Islamic sacred history regarded the Christians and Jews as People of the Book, and they enjoyed a special status as dhimmis. Most of the dhimmis of the Middle East adopted the Arabic language, even for writing their own religious literature. Islamic sacred history was more hostile to the Zoroastrian religion of the Persians. The Arabic label "zindiq" became a broad term for heresy, especially the various forms of dualism and skepticism that took root in Persia.

The Mughals of India were not directed by a central Islamic caliphate in Medina, Damascus, or Baghdad. India had for centuries been a pluralistic society of Zoroastrians, Hindus, Jains, Christians, and Muslims. Like other religions in India, when Islam became the religion of the rulers, it formally became the state religion, but it could not form the same kind of natural symbiosis with Hinduism and Zoroastrianism as it had with Judaism and Christianity in Mesopotamia during the days of the caliphate. Nor could Muslims realistically declare a state of siege against religions not recognized in the

Qur'an, as they had earlier with the zindiqs of Persia. In view of these changes in the situation in which Muslims found themselves in India, Akbar's experiment appears less damning. Even his Muslim subjects were drawn into religious error from the point of view of strict orthodoxy, because of their everyday contact with the other religions of India.

Perhaps more significant than the cultural patterns of Mughal India was Akbar's own spiritual odyssey. Like the Abbasid caliphs of ninth-century Baghdad, Akbar invited representatives of the various religions of his subjects to debate their beliefs with one another in his presence. Until 1578 he remained a Sunni Muslim. But from that date he entered into a personal crisis that sent his courtiers scurrying for alternative religious views that might appease his spiritual restlessness. Certain influential mentors suggested that he might become the *Mujaddid*, the "Renewer of Religion," that Muslims expected to appear at the beginning of each century, and significantly, Islam was approaching the anniversary of its first millennium. Thus Akbar came to believe he was a prophet, and some say he conferred divine status upon himself. The call to prayer and exchange of greeting with the phrase *Allahu Akbar* (God is Greatest) bore the connotation of "God is Akbar" among his disciples.[8]

So into his new Divine Religion Akbar accepted many teachings which were by no means necessarily compatible. At one point he became persuaded of the truth of Persian dualism. At another, a Hindu teacher convinced him that since the longest sura of the Qur'an was named the Sura of the Cow, the Qur'an itself was proof of Hindu sanctity for that animal. He also came to share the Jain dislike for killing, and the Catholic Christian ideal of celibacy. Vegetarianism, which is not required or recommended in Islam, was adopted. And he maintained within the confines of his palace a sacred eternal flame, the chief symbol of Zoroastrian Fire Temples.[9]

It is interesting to note that modern historians disagree about Akbar's relation to Islam. Sunni Muslims, of course, have located him outside the pale of Islam. Their reasons are easy to understand and require no comment. European historians regard him as an apostate, a denier of his own religion, while Indian historians see him as a liberal Muslim. Commenting on these two latter views, Aziz Ahmad has surmised that "the Western assessment is based on the polemical position that Islam is incapable of liberalism, and since Akbar was a liberal he must have necessarily ceased to be a Muslim. The Hindu historians who wished to evolve a modus vivendi with Islam in India regard Islam as a liberal religion and Akbar as a good Muslim with some heretical views."[10] Ahmad's view is itself polemical, but his judgment is not without merit, for the tenets of Sunni Islam, especially among the Arabs, are usually taken by Western scholars to be the norm, and all other expressions of Islam, including Shi'i Islam, are then dismissed as deviations from the norm. In the academic study of religion, a less biased approach is required.

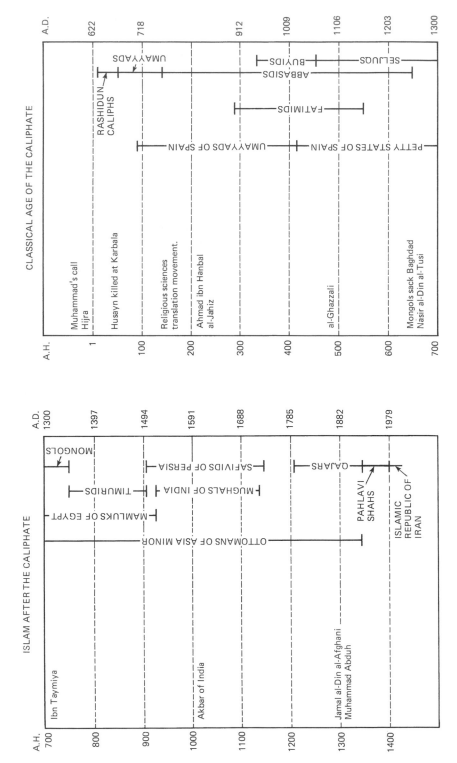

FIGURE 4.2 Chronological chart of Islam. (Adapted from B. Lewis, *Islam and the Arab World.*)

Akbar died in 1605 and was succeeded by his son, Salim, who became known as Jahanjir. Akbar's several close disciples in the Divine Religion did not long perpetuate his eclectic religion. For one thing, Islam, Hinduism, Jainism, Zoroastrianism, and Christianity were much too traditional and firmly rooted in Indian soil to be drastically altered in popular piety for very long. The pluralism that has always been characteristic of Indian culture did not require the different traditions to dissolve into one another. Yet non-Muslim religious beliefs and practices, forbidden by strict Sunni and Shi'i law, were at the popular level of religion in India to be found among common folk, especially those drawn to Islamic mysticism. Those affected did not regard themselves as non-Muslims or heretics. Perhaps Akbar simply believed that the ambiguous boundaries between the different traditions could be freely crossed to the enhancement of all. Or perhaps his failure to achieve a lasting new religion is the lesson to be learned here. In any event, his story is an indication of the kinds of problems and opportunities created by the expansion of Islam into lands and cultures that were much different from the central Islamic lands of the Middle East.

Another way to make this last point about the expansion of Islam into new and different cultural environments, with which we close this chapter, is that Islam is a universal religion that is necessarily manifested in historically distinct particular moments and places. The relation of the universal (Islam) and the particular (Muslims and Islamicate society in history) is a tension that is often felt within Islamic studies, as it is in studies of Christianity and other religions. As historians of religion, we can only approach ideas about what is thought to be universal and absolute by examining the particulars through which it can be observed.

NOTES

1. Muhammad ibn Jarir al-Tabari, *The Last Years of the Prophet*, trans. Ismail K. Poonawala, vol. IX of *The History of al-Tabari (Ta'rikh al-rusul wa'l-muluk)*, ed. Ehsan Yar-Shater (Albany, N.Y.: State University of New York Press, 1990), p.184.
2. al-Tabari, *Last Years*, p. 185.
3. Francesco Gabrielli, *Muhammad and the Conquests of Islam*, trans. Virginia Lulin and Rosamund Linell (New York: McGraw-Hill Book Company, 1968), p. 132.
4. See Philip K. Hitti, *History of the Arabs* (New York: St. Martin's Press, 1937). The comparison occurs on p. 298 of the tenth edition, published in 1970.
5. Marshall G.S. Hodgson, *The Venture of Islam*, 3 vols. (Chicago: University of Chicago Press, 1974), Vol. 1, pp. 58–59.
6. The point is made by Oleg Grabar, *The Formation of Islamic Art* (New Haven, Conn.: Yale University Press, 1973), p. 67.
7. Grabar, *Formation*, p. 72.

8. Aziz Ahmad, *Studies in Islamic Culture in the Indian Environment* (Oxford: Clarendon Press, 1964), p. 171.
9. Ahmad, *Islamic Culture*, pp. 170–71.
10. Ahmad, *Islamic Culture*, p. 175.

5

Boundaries of *Community,* *Faith,* and *Practice*

ESTABISHING BOUNDARIES

Measures of orthodoxy in religion and politics are matters of perspective. One is regarded a heretic, dissident, or subversive if he or she does not adhere to religious and political norms that prevail within a given group. Prevailing norms of right belief indicate how a community chooses to define itself. Along with some sociologists of religion, we may say that communities establish religious and political *boundaries*, beyond which those persons and movements that threaten the collective sense of identity are exiled. Concepts of personal and group identity are based on notions of the "Other." This exile and otherness can take the form of actual physical expulsion, but more often it is expressed in subtler forms of alienation, such as labels applied to those who don't conform. In our own culture, media labels such as "Militant Islam," "Pro-Choice," and "Pro-Life" signal the existence of boundary concepts. When labels such as "secular humanist," "bleeding-heart liberal," or "racist" are used, they indicate that both the accuser and the accused have different definitions of right belief and action in a given social, political, or religious community.

In the 1960s, anthropologist Fredrik Barth approached the discussion of culture in terms of ethnic boundaries. Like many anthropologists, Barth had conducted research into premodern tribal societies; he wanted to understand the cardinal importance of ethnicity and its persistence as a way of keeping one social group distinct from another. In his words, the ethnic boundary

> entails a frequently quite complex organization of behaviour and social relations. The identification of another person as a fellow member of an ethnic group implies a sharing of criteria for evaluation and judgement. It thus entails the assumption that the two are fundamentally 'playing the same game'. . . . On the other hand, a dichotomization of others as strangers, as members of another ethnic group, implies a recognition of limitations on shared understandings, differences in criteria for judgement of value and performance, and the restriction of interaction to sectors of assumed common understanding and mutual interest.[1]

Much of what Barth and others have said about ethnicity could also be said about religion, with respect to how groups define themselves and define outsiders, "others," through religious regulations and rituals. Restrictions on marriage to persons outside the umma, religious duties including purity laws, theological debates about who is a righteous member of the community who should be revered, and who is sinner who should be excluded, are all boundary concepts. Boundaries indicate the points at which societies, groups, or communities find or imagine themselves to be confronted by the "Other." Boundaries go beyond the geographical to include the cultural, mythical, and ritual lines that are disputed in court, in religious councils, sermons, coffee houses, and over the dinner table. Boundaries may also be defended on the battlefield, preserved in rituals and purity laws, crossed legally and illegally for trade, and for conversion, to name only a few functions of religious boundaries.

Barth and others have spoken of "boundary maintenance," to indicate the cultural mechanisms by which a group protects its identity and purity. Boundaries, to pursue the metaphor, can be crossed for a variety of reasons, but visas and border checks may be required, or have to be circumvented, to pursue the metaphor further. This is roughly what we mean by the saying: "When in Rome, do what the Romans do." All cultures have moral and social rules that identify, mark, and control outsiders who come into the community. The pathos of boundary maintenance—what happens when it breaks down?—is exemplified by the bitter conflict that erupted among Serbians, Croatians, and Bosnians when the former Yugoslavia fractured politically in 1991. This tragic crossing of many kinds of boundaries—by military force, systematic rape in front of husbands and children, unceasing attacks on unarmed civilians, bombing of mosques, churches, museums, and hospitals—has little to do in this case with linguistic or ethnic differences, but rather with historic religious conflicts in the region. As we saw in Chapter 2, communal commitments to Eastern Orthodox Christianity, Roman Catholicism, and Islam produced and maintained the boundaries that divided and separated these groups when Yugoslavian national unity collapsed.

In order to understand the role of religion in the formation of boundaries in Islamic history and culture, we turn now to consider the Islamic discourse on self-identity and relations to the "Other," that is, to non-Muslims and to groups of Muslims with which one does not primarily identify. It should be noted that the mostly Arabic terms that frame this discourse arose out of the historical experience of Muslims, especially in the early history of Muhammad and the Rashidun, when major fitnas (religious uprisings introduced in Chapter 4) occurred within Islamicate society, and again, in the nineteenth and twentieth centuries, in the colonial experience of Islam under European hegemony. Let us discuss briefly these terms, including some we have used already, that connote boundaries.

The term *zindiq* (heretic, dualist) signifies a conceptual boundary drawn around the Islamic tradition as a whole. "Sunni" and "Shi'i " are labels indicating divisions within Islam. Other terms exist, including ones for social and cultural distinctions. The term *shirk* (compromising God's absolute unicity by associating other beings with Him—that is, polytheism), for example, functions as a boundary maintenance term. In nascent Islam it was the quranic term for pagan Arabs who did not accept Islam; in modern times, secularized leaders and groups of lapsed Muslims are often accused of shirk. The process involved in the use of these terms is a very important one in the study of the religions of humankind. It is possible to argue that orthodox articles of faith are often the result, not the cause, of internal religious conflicts. If we take the view that countermovements against the mainstream of a tradition may express real human needs and aspirations, then we must be prepared to look beneath the surface when pejorative labels are used.

Islamic history has been a dynamic drama of different social, political, and religious movements, each searching to define its own legitimacy in terms of the central symbols of the Shari'a. Where there was stress between groups, boundary concepts and labels came into use. A few persons and movements in particular are characteristic of countercultural movements in Islam. In our discussion of these paradigm cases, lines between religious heresy and political dissidence cannot be sharply drawn. The language employed to deal with all perceived threats to the collective identity within Islam has usually been religious.

However much in contempt they may be held by a community, dissidents and counterforces often play a significant role in the formation and consolidation of the beliefs and practices within the public consensus. Heresy calls for greater clarity on such matters as "Who is a Muslim?" and "Who is a member of the Islamic umma?" Dissidence can serve to raise public consciousness of instability and inequity within the social fabric. As in other religious traditions, Islamic religious language about heresy and unorthodox ideas assumed a particular world view. Basic to that world view was the

Shari'a, with its central symbols of the Qur'an and the Sunna of the Prophet. The sacred history of which these symbols formed the central core provided a means by which to identify threats to the collective identity and to explain the import of their dangers to the common people. This interpretive activity has taken place in sermons and in lessons drawn in everyday discourse from the Qur'an, the Sunna of the Prophet, the lives of respected saints and spiritual leaders, and the like.

EARLY SECTARIAN BOUNDARIES

Sectarian Divisions During the Age of the Rashidun

The religious significance of the assassination of 'Uthman and the unsatisfactory arbitration between 'Ali and Muawiya lay in the subsequent emergence of three sects: Khawarij (Kharijites), Murji'a (Murjiites), and Shi'a. Each developed a different notion of its collective identity, and thus each saw differently the boundaries of right belief. The Khawarij (Seceders) believed that faith was demonstrated in righteous acts; without faith made explicit in public behavior, one could not claim to be a Muslim. Conversely, sinful acts committed by any Muslim, including the caliph, breached one's confession of faith and claim to be a Muslim. 'Uthman, the Khawarij argued, had acted contrary to the mandate of the Shari'a. Therefore he—and all others who committed grave sins—should be expelled from the Islamic umma. When 'Ali lost the round of arbitration with Muawiya on this matter, the Khawarij were those who withdrew from 'Ali's forces to form a separate sect. Mostly Arab at first, the Khawarij had nonetheless resented the aristocratic families of Mecca, such as the Umayyads.

The Murji'a (Postponers) held that outward acts of faith and sin could not be judged by human beings, even pious Muslims of impeccable faith and morals, except insofar as the common good was affected. They believed that the decision regarding 'Uthman's or any Muslim's status as a believer or sinner must be left to Allah, that is, postponed until the Day of Judgment. The Murji'a believed that sin did not imply that one should be excluded from the community. Those who held this more moderate attitude fell more or less in line with Muawiya and the Umayyad caliphs, though not without criticism of their alleged lack of piety.

The Shi'a (partisans of 'Ali) were not happy with either development after the arbitration at the Plain of Siffin. In their view, the office of the caliph had already been greatly abused. But they also mistrusted the Khawarij, who wished to let the umma as a whole, rather than an imam descended from the House of the Prophet, be responsible for judging whether or not human acts were contrary to God's will. Khariji communalism was a social reflex on

Arab tribal custom. The Shi'a further believed that 'Ali possessed special charisma and the proper understanding of how to apply the Shari'a to everyday life, and that this gift had been passed on to him by the Prophet himself, but not to the first three caliphs. Thus the proper source for interpreting the Shari'a was the imamate—the office of the true line of successors to the Prophet through 'Ali—not the caliphate or the ulama. Although the Shi'a soon found themselves in opposition to both the central caliphate of the Umayyads in Damascus and the sternly resisting Khawarij, many of the non-Arab peoples in Iraq who became Muslims were drawn to their cause. Both religious and social explanations have been offered for this, but it is fair to say that the various groups of Shi'a formed a cluster of forces resisting Arab hegemony in Middle Eastern politics after the rise of Islam. Whether viewed religiously or politically, many of the early Shi'i groups seem to have been underground movements that gave vent to the hopes and aspirations of both Arabs and non-Arabs who felt oppressed by the policies of the Umayyad Arab caliphate.

THE IMAMATE

Whereas the Sunni caliphate can be discussed in the political terms of dynasties, the Shi'i imamate focuses on 'Ali and the descendants of his family (known as Alids). For the next several generations after the Rashidun, the Shi'a swore allegiance to 'Alid imams, often in opposition to the caliphate and to the political and religious sensibilities of the Sunni majority. The complex history of the imamate cannot be told in detail here. The many inconsistencies between Sunni and Shi'i accounts of that history make the task extremely complicated. The general picture that emerges in these sources shows that 'Ali's two sons, Hasan and Husayn, became the second and third imams after 'Ali. They and their followers suffered persecution, resulting in the martyrdom of Husayn at Karbala in Iraq in 680 (see Chapter 1). Far from suppressing the movement, Husayn's murder by the Umayyad caliph Yazid gave impetus to the Shi'i cause.

Twelver (Imami) Shi'a

After 680, nine more imams of the Alid line became the spiritual leaders of the main body of Shi'a. The twelfth and final imam of that branch, Muhammad al-Muntazar, disappeared as an infant in the year 873. This began what is known in Twelver Shi'i symbolism as the Lesser Occultation. In 941 began a period which has lasted to the present day, known as the Greater Occultation, during which the return of the twelfth imam has been anticipated by Twelver (imami) Shi'a. For the Twelver Shi'a—the main body of the Shi'a in the Islamic world today—this disappearance or *occultation* of the twelfth imam constituted a distinctively Shi'i interpretation of sacred history. The imam, though absent from human affairs since that time, is expected to return as the *Mahdi,* the divinely "Guided One," the restorer of religion and faith to the Islamic umma. In fact, the doctrine of a future restorer is found in some Sunni works, although the term Mahdi is not always used. The idea has been popular among the Shi'a and among the masses of Muslims, particularly in times of stress and turmoil within the Abode of Islam. Actual leadership within the Twelver Shi'a community since the occultation of the twelfth imam has been conducted by living representatives of the Hidden imam and a structure of religious notables not unlike that of the Sunni ulama. From the middle of the tenth to the middle of the eleventh centuries, Twelver Shi'ism gained important political footings from time to time, especially during the reign of the Buyid princes (945–1055), most of whom adopted Shi'i religious and political expectations. Some of the greatest Shi'i theologians (*mutakallimun*) lived during this period; they helped to construct a Shi'i theology in dialogue with the Mutazilite mutakallimun. The Safavid Persian Empire that arose in the sixteenth century was Shi'i, and the present state of Iran is populated predominantly by Twelver Shi'a, with significant Shi'i populations also found in Iraq, Syria, and Lebanon.

Fiver (Zaydi) Shi'a

Tension within the early Shi'i community resulted in divided loyalties and differences of opinion about the succession of the twelve imams. In the eighth century, some claimed that a certain Zayd, a grandson of Husayn who was not in the succession accepted by the majority, was the real imam. The Zaydis, as his followers were called, established strong communities south of the Caspian; a Zaydi state survived in the Yemen until the mid-twentieth century. Although some Zaydis believed that in theory the imam must back his claim to office by force if necessary, they were considered the moderate branch of the Shi'a while they flourished in the Middle Ages. Many of their political figures were accomplished religious leaders and theologians who, like the Twelver (Ithna Ashari) Shi'a, articulated their doctrines in dialogue and dispute with Mu'tazili mutakallimun.

Sevener (Isma'ili) Shi'a

The more revolutionary Sevener or Isma'ili Shi'a trace their spiritual heritage to Isma'il, a son of the sixth imam. The Isma'ilis contest the legitimacy of the other son, the seventh imam in the Twelver line, Musa al-Kazim. The Isma'ili Shi'a believed that Isma'il did not die but went into occultation. More aggressive than the other Shi'a, the Isma'ilis believed that their imam was the spiritual leader of all of Islam. As a result, after Isma'il's death late in the eighth century, his living representatives sent missionaries, known as *da'is*, throughout the Islamic world, challenging the religious leadership of the Sunni ulama. Basic to the teachings of the Isma'ili missionaries was the assertion that the genuine truths of religion were derived from the esoteric wisdom of God. The main symbols of the Shari'a, the Qur'an and the Sunna, are merely exterior forms of knowledge for the masses. The true interior meaning of religion was in the possession of the Isma'ili imams and their representatives and missionaries. For a while the Isma'ilis presented a revolutionary force within Islam, attacking Sunni strongholds, sometimes with deadly consequences. For example, in the late eleventh century a sect of Isma'ilis arose, known as the Assassins. From a mountain fortress in Alamut, Persia, they conducted suicidal raids on the leadership of Islam, killing many important political and religious figures. Along with other Isma'ili bands, they helped check the advance of Christian Crusaders in Syria. Eastern Arabia was for a time under the political control of the Isma'ilis. Also a branch of the Isma'ilis known as the Fatimids established its own caliphate in Egypt and North Africa in the tenth to twelfth centuries. Today in India, East Africa, and Yemen there are still Isma'ili communities. Ironically, the descendants of the Assassins and other subversive Isma'ilis from the Middle Ages are today businessmen whose religious activities are nonviolent, including such programs as providing relief to the needy and endowing advanced work in Islamic studies and architecture at major universities in Europe and the United States.

CULTURAL BOUNDARIES

Although the first four caliphs had established an empire inspired by the Prophet's message of the unity of God and the equality of all believers, the texture of Islamic civilization was richly variegated with many ethnic and religious groups. As conquerors, the Arabs at first dominated other peoples. Arabic was the sacred language in the worship of the conquerors, centered in the liturgical recitation of the Qur'an. But Arabic did not significantly replace the languages of the conquered peoples for several decades after the Arab conquests. Certain literate classes of functionaries, such as the professional record keepers in the rabbinical academies, the Christian churches, and the Sassanian Persian chanceries, became indispensable civil servants in the bureaucracy of the Islamic Empire. The Jews and Christians could preserve their confessional status by paying a special poll tax called the *jizya*. As noted earlier, they were known as dhimmis. Although these People of the Book enjoyed a special status in Islamic sacred history, social tensions occasionally arose among Muslims, dhimmis, and other religious subgroups within the Islamic Empire.

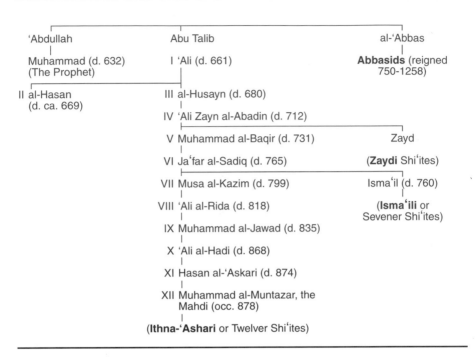

FIGURE 5.1   The Shi'i imams.

Another important class of people was comprised of non-Arabs who chose to convert to Islam. Because the clan structure of social organization among the Arabs was still functional after the rise of Islam, those who converted to Islam were regarded as *mawali* (singular, *mawla*) or "clients" of a particular tribe that absorbed them after their conversion. Note the cultural symbolism: For the first few centuries in the Islamic heartland, one came to Islam through identificfation with an Arab tribe. Many of the mawali were soon heard to complain of being second-class citizens, possessing less than equal rights with Arab Muslims. By virtue of their traditionally important roles in Middle Eastern public life, the limits of their integration into the Arab social structures presented a serious impediment to the achievement of social and political equilibrium.[2]

The Shu'ubi, or People's Movement

Among the dhimmis, and among the mawali in particular, there were signs of cultural resistance to the privileged place held by the Arab Muslims within Islamic society. One movement became a form of counterculture, waging war with the Arab intelligentsia in the field of *belles-lettres*. It was known as the Shu'ubi, or People's Movement. Originally Shu'ubi was a term indicating that no tribe or race among Islamic peoples was superior to any other; all were to enjoy equal status under the Shari'a. By the eighth and ninth centuries, Shu'ubi came to designate the anti-Arab slurs of non-Arab peoples living in the Abode of Islam, including mawali converts. Within the vast caliphal bureaucracy were many Persian mawali, a class of scribal functionaries which had for centuries been masters of courtly literature and etiquette. In view of the enormous pride the Arabs had in their language, the claim of Persians and other mawali to be able to become more lettered in Arabic than even the Arabs was defiantly provocative.

By the end of the Umayyad and the beginning of the Abbasid caliphates (eighth and ninth centuries), the Islamic Empire had produced two classes of literati. The ulama consisted largely of Muslims, including many Arabs, who were devoted to the elaboration of religious sciences. These included the study of the Qur'an and the Sunna, Islamic law, and Arabic grammar and lexicography. The other class of lettered professionals, the court secretaries employed by Islamic officialdom, were drawn largely from the social class of Persian mawali. Around the beginning of the eighth century, Arabic was made the official language of the Empire. Persians and other mawali scribes learned it as a second, official language. There was no comparable class of professionals among the native-speaking Arabs, although some Arabs did serve within the secretariat of the government. Though mostly Muslim, some of the mawali secretaries held thinly disguised contempt for the Arabian prophet and his religion. The ensuing conflict was waged on paper, which was itself introduced from China at about this time. Paper mills were soon built in Baghdad, providing inexpensive material means for the circulation of books. The Shu'ubi movement among the Persian secretaries now produced works in Arabic that were not religious in character. New genres of literature focused on manners and culture, not religious truths. Some Arabs responded by recording their age-old love of poetry and public oratory in writing. The urbane and romantic themes of Bedouin Arab poets were embellished to provide a literature of entertainment.

At the base of all this there seems to have been a fundamental conflict between Arabic and Persian cultural traditions. Although the Islamic religion and the Arabic language were the predominant cultural vehicles of the Abode of Islam by the middle of the Umayyad Age, tensions between the Arab aristocracy and the mawali intelligentsia were abundantly evident. In a battle of words, the Arabs praised generosity and the simpler virtues of their tribal origins. Finding these qualities to be primitive, the Shu'ubi literati esteemed high culture and courtly etiquette. Arabs viewed Persians as niggardly and haughty; Persians regarded Arabs as crude and uncultured. Culture wars are not uncommon in pluralistic societies; it would not be difficult to think of examples of this sort of cultural conflict in other times and societies, including twentieth-century America.

The mood of the Shu'ubi Muslims is typified in the following verse by the Persian poet and satirist Abu Said al-Rustami:

> *The Arabs boast of being master of the world and commanders of peoples.*
> *Why do they not rather boast of being skilful sheep and camel herders?*[3]

Another poet, Mu'bad, could be even more outspoken about his longing for the return of bygone days of Persian empire:

> *I am a noble of the Tribe of Jam—he called in the name of the nation—and I*
>   *demand the inheritance of the Persian kings.*
> *Tell all the sons of Hashim [the Arabs]: submit yourselves before the hour of regret*
>   *arrives.*
> *Retreat to the Hijaz [in Arabia] and resume eating lizards and herd your cattle*
> *While I seat myself on the throne of the kings supported by the sharpness of my*
>   *blade [heroism] and the point of my pen [science].*[4]

Commenting on the import of this literary manifestation of dissent, one scholar has said:

> The dangers of the shuubi movement. . .lay not so much in its crude anti-Arab propaganda (in spite of its appeal to the still lively hostility to the Arabs amongst the lower classes in Iraq and Persia) as in the more refined scepticism which it fostered among the literate classes. The old Perso-Aramaean culture of Iraq, the centre of Manichaeism, still carried the germs of that kind of free thinking which was called *zandaqa* [i.e., the antireligious views of Zindiqs], and which showed itself not only by the survival of dualist ideas in religion, but still more by that frivolity and cynicism in regard to all moral systems which is designated by the term *mujun*.[5]

The Arabs were hardly unequal to the challenge. In addition to pious contempt and religious condemnation, expressed by the ulama and tradition-minded Muslims, many Arabs gave vent to cultural pride in ways that were more artistic and literary. A ninth-century writer whose devastating humor was expressed at the expense of mawali, dhimmis, and others who made light of Arab Muslims was a theologian and man of letters named al-Jahiz (777–869). In his several books that have survived, Jahiz ranges beyond the discussion of mere dogma to show himself to be a shrewd moralizer and keen observer of the manners and customs of virtually every ethnic and political subgroup within the Abode of Islam. In one passage he noted with irony:

> . . . this is what the non-Arabs have come to, what with the Shu'ubiyya and their doctrines and the *mawali* with their claims to superiority over the Arabs. . . . What could be more vexing than to find your slave claiming that he is nobler than you, while in the same breath admitting that he acquired this nobility when you emancipated him![6]

The cultural symbiosis Islam was able to achieve within its borders is all the more remarkable because such movements as the Shu'ubi were bound to arise, and did from time to time. But Islam is ideally a brotherhood of believers, not a melting pot of ethnic groups. Thus the cultural boundaries that existed and still exist in Islam have presented the umma with the ongoing task of ameliorating culture wars with the ideal of religious unity. No society can boast of existing without these conflicts, but few can boast of meeting them with more success over the centuries than Muslims have.

BOUNDARIES OF BELIEF

Ibn al-Rawandi

The most infamous atheist in Islam was Abu l-Husayn ibn al-Rawandi. So hated is his memory among orthodox Muslim thinkers that an accurate historical biography is difficult to reconstruct. Even the determination of when he flourished is difficult. Some sources say he died or was killed around 900, but an earlier date—around 850—is just as plausible, according to others. Information about him comes mainly from those who labored to refute his arguments. Their concern was with the greatness of his impiety and the sharpness of his biting attacks on their beliefs, and thus their accounts of him well reflect the boundaries that the orthodox community felt to be most threatened by the likes of Ibn al-Rawandi.

Basic to the Islamic notion of human creatureliness is that man ought to be *shakir*, that is, in a posture of gratitude for Creation and for the divine blessings contained therein. The opposite, *kafir* (ingratitude toward the Creator), is often translated "unbeliever." But it is especially in the sense of "defiant ingratitude" that Ibn al-Rawandi was held by subsequent generations to be one of the most dangerous kafirs in Islamic history.

One feature of the Sunni version of Ibn al-Rawandi's life that clearly emerges is his alleged association with Jews, Christians, and Zoroastrians. Christian and Jewish polemics against Muslims (and vice versa) were particularly intense in the ninth century. Muslim thinkers usually attributed expressions of religious error to non-Islamic influences. Some said Ibn al-Rawandi's family was Jewish. Others said the Jews hid him from the police in their homes. His sharpest critics accused him of hiring out to Jews and Christians to write damning critiques of Islam for them. The image of an intellectual Judas appears throughout Sunni biographical remarks about him.

Ibn al-Rawandi apparently spent his early life in the eastern Islamic province of Khurasan, where religious ideas had always been more adventuresome than in capitals such as Medina, Baghdad, and Damascus. Gnostic dualism, Manichaeisim, Buddhism, and Hinduism were among the many religions that had settled in Khurasan in earlier times, leaving their traces in the Islamic era. Also in ninth-century Khurasan, a Jewish arch-heretic named Hiwi became notorious for his devastating critiques of pious Jewish belief in the Torah and the prophethood of Moses. Perhaps there was something of a model or paradigm of ultra-atheism being played out in the traditional accounts of figures such as Hiwi and Ibn al-Rawandi.

Ibn al-Rawandi studied Islamic theology in the school of rationalism known as the Mu'tazila, about which we will have more to say in Chapter 7. He learned well their defensive arguments against Islam's critics. At some point he appeared in the Islamic capital, Baghdad, and for reasons that are not entirely clear, the Mu'tazilites there snubbed him. In retaliation, he joined their Shi'i adversaries. In the name of the Shi'a, he wrote several treatises in which he argued that belief in the Qur'an and the prophethood of Muhammad was the height of mental weakness. This was an extreme view which the majority of the Shi'a did not avow.

One of his most interesting ploys was apparently a literary fiction in which he attributed some of his most damning criticisms to the Brahmins, the priestly caste of intellectuals in Hinduism. The basis of the so-called Brahmin critique was a logical dilemma between reason and revelation: If the truths of revelation can be known by reason, then revelation is unnecessary; if they cannot, then revelation is irrational and thus unworthy of human credence. The first horn of the dilemma was directed against the rationalist Mu'tazilite theologians. The other was aimed at blind Sunni piety, like that associated with Ahmad ibn Hanbal and the Traditionalists. Taken together, the dilemma attacked the cornerstone of all three monotheistic religions—Judaism, Christianity, and Islam—making belief in God, prophets, and scriptures a source of ridicule for rational human beings.

Along with others accused of impiety, Ibn al-Rawandi attempted to silence orthodox theologians with a technique called "the equivalency of proofs." Taking the theologians' arguments for God's existence, for the authority of scripture, and for the Prophet's mission, he showed the contrary of each to be equally logical. In effect, through these antimonies of reason, he was trying to demonstrate that if both the pro and con arguments for any article of faith are equally valid, they are ineffectual demonstrations of truth. He also delighted in pointing out contradictions in scriptures, especially the Qur'an, though the Bible was shown to be just as vulnerable. The chief Islamic test of Muhammad's prophethood was the Qur'an itself, a miracle in the eyes of Muslims for its inimitable Arabic linguistic qualities. Islamic dogma asserts that like the miracles of Moses and Jesus, such as dividing the Red Sea and raising the dead, the inimitable Qur'an is a supernatural sign of Muhammad's prophethood. Ibn al-Rawandi countered that if this were the case, then Euclid's *Geometry* and Ptolemy's *Almagest* (on astronomy), which were admired as incomparable books of learning in those fields, must be miracles; hence, their authors must be prophets from God. This tactic of forcing an opponent to absurd conclusions with his own arguments was widely practiced among Muslim theologians.

Later literature has attested that Ibn al-Rawandi ended his life a hunted and despised man, some say killed by government agents. The Mu'tazilites claimed that he recanted late in life and that he wrote works refuting his earlier atheism, perhaps in vindication of being sullied by his attacks on the Mu'tazilites. It is even possible to see him as much abused and misunderstood in his own lifetime, and to say that what he was trying to do was to show that the so-called rationalism of the theologians was a weak disservice to Islamic faith because it attempted to prove the unprovable. Be that as it may, his life and writings had the effect of focusing Islamic attention on some of the most critical problems of belief. Whether in fact or in fiction, he was truly a paradigmatic figure in Islamic intellectual history. Through the refutation of his pungent criticisms, Muslim theologians were better able to achieve a more articulate understanding of the intellectual boundaries that guarded the religious life against dangerous forces of disunity.

BOUNDARIES OF PIETY

In the early days of the Islamic conquests, many Muslims developed an inherent distaste for the corrupting influence of the personal wealth these wars had brought. From this more simple expression of faith arose an ascetic form of piety, that is, a life of devotion to the teachings of the Qur'an and the Sunna, unmarred by quest for worldly gain. The life of the Prophet lent itself to this interpretation: his frequent retreats into the hills to meditate; his total trust in God through many years of hardship and oppression; and the utter simplicity of his house and possessions. Among those who preferred more ascetic forms of piety were some known as "People of the Bench," because they used to spend their time in prayer and devotion on benches near the Prophet's house in Medina. They believed that the riches of God were accessible only through a life of poverty and abstention. Many ascetics adopted the custom of other Middle Eastern holy men of wearing unostentatious white garments made of wool (suf). This may be the origin of the term "Sufi" that is widely applied to the mystics of Islam.

The Sufis sought to discover the interior meanings of the Qur'an and the Sunna. Their interpretation of scripture and their performances of prayer and other religious duties were noticeably at variance with the popular consensus on these matters. The mystics' rejection of the worldly life and the outward forms of piety practiced within the orthodox community brought mistrust and alienation. The struggle against the mainstream of Islam earned oppression and even martyrdom for many Sufis. Such negative reactions, however, usually came from the orthodox ulama, who considered them-

FIGURE 5.2 Portrait of a Sufi Mendicant (Qalandar), Timurid, late fifteenth century. (Courtesy of the Metropolitan Museum of Art, Cora Timken Burnett Collection of Persian Miniatures and Other Persian Art Objects, Bequest of Cora Timken Burnett, 1956.)

selves to be elites (*al-khawass* in Arabic social discourse). In contrast, many Sufis were quite popular among the masses (*al-'awwam*). Ironically, many of the Sufi masters were respected scholars in the religious sciences.

Sufism is not properly a sect of Islam; most Sufis regard themselves as Sunni or Shi'i Muslims. But through their mystical orientations, they express a mode of piety that distinguishes them from the larger community. This mode of piety is still to be found among Muslims, and it has had some appeal outside the Islamic world as well. Non-Muslim Sufi groups have formed in Europe and the United States. Such groups are eclectic, drawing much more on mystical lore from other religions than from the Qur'an and the Sunna of Islam.

The Prophet Muhammad and other early figures became important models of piety in the saintly biographies the Sufis used for their spiritual edification. A Sufi of the ninth century could say of the Rashidun:

When Abu Bakr succeeded to the leadership, and the world in its entirety came to him in abasement, he did not lift up his head on that account, or make any pretensions; he wore a single garment, which he used to pin together, so that he was known as the "man of the two pins." 'Umar b. al-Khattab, who also ruled the world in its entirety, lived on bread and olive-oil; his clothes were patched in a dozen places, some of the patches being of leather; and yet there were opened unto him the treasure of Chosroes and Caesar. As for 'Uthman, he was like one of his slaves in dress and appearance; of him it is related that he was seen coming out of his gardens with a faggot of firewood on his shoulders, and when questioned on the matter he said, "I wanted to see whether my soul would refuse." When 'Ali succeeded to the rule, he bought a waistband for four dirhams and a shirt for five dirhams; finding the sleeve of his garment too long, he went to a cobbler and taking his knife cut off the sleeve level at the tips of his fingers; yet this same man divided the world right and left.[5]

These statements about the Rashidun may seem surprising in view of what was said in Chapter 4 about their involvement in the fitna, civil strife. The Sufis in particular, however, developed an important genre of literature known as the "Lives of Saints." In these anthologies about their spiritual founders, pious and sometimes even miraculous legends served important instructional purposes. In this way, earthy and much maligned figures were transformed into saintly personalities.

Sufi leadership and social organization differed somewhat from the orthodox communities of Sunnis and Shi'a. A spiritual master known as the *shaykh* was the focal point of the Sufi orders that developed widely in the Middle Ages. Muslim aspirants would present themselves to a shaykh and ask to receive his spiritual guidance. Often the shaykh presided over a compound of buildings, known as *zawiyas*, within whose walls several disciples were led in spiritual exercises by the shaykh. The several spiritual devotions or "stations" to which each disciple was assigned included private experiences, such as the constant repetition of the divine name, Allah, over long periods of time. Some Sufi orders also had public liturgical orations in which poetry and dancing served to create ecstatic feelings of nearness to God. Those who practiced piety in this manner were known as the "intoxicated" Sufis—that is, they were drunk on the spirit of God. For all Sufis, the desired goal was to achieve nearness or union (tawhid) with God. Most Sufis have held that *God is the only reality*. Thus their exaggerated forms of poverty, their prayerful ritual remembrances or *dhikrs* of the divine name, and their ecstatic and sometimes erotic love poetry all sprang from the single purpose of striving for union with God.

Abu Yazid of Bistiam

Bistam in northeastern Persia is the site of a shrine to which pilgrims have streamed for more than a thousand years. The hamlet of Bistam was the home of Tayfur ibn 'Isa, known as Abu Yazid, the son of a Zoroastrian convert to Islam. Except for occasional ambiguous statements about a pilgrimage to Mecca and Medina, it seems that Abu Yazid led a life of seclusion in his hometown. He died there in 874. Yet the fame of this spiritual recluse has spread far and wide. The shrine in Bistam that commemorates this celebrated Sufi saint is not unique in the Abode of Islam; hundreds were built in those lands to which Islam spread in the centuries following the death of the Prophet. They were the tombs of Muslim saints, many of whom were barely known outside their immediate locales. Sufis called them "friends of God" (singular, *wali*). The people who have visited these shrines over the centuries have done so hoping to receive *baraka*, a divine blessing richly associated with the saint both in life and in death. Abu Yazid differs from the majority of the other saints only in the extent of his fame. That branch of Sufism known as the Intoxicated Sufis traces its heritage to the recluse of Bistam. His story illustrates important boundaries of piety within Islam.

Abu Yazid was intensely devoted to God, so much so that he labored to extinguish any expression of a "self" separate from God. Yet the path to God was through self-realization, shorn of all external distractions. Consider the following anecdote:

> A man came to the door of Abu Yazid and called out.
> "Whom are you seeking?" asked Abu Yazid.
> "Abu Yazid," replied the man.
> "Poor wretch!" said Abu Yazid. "I have been seeking Abu Yazid for thirty years, and cannot find any trace or token of him."[6]

The search for self *is* the search for God. Yet, ironically, to find God is to lose one's *self*. Abu Yazid's paradox of self-*annihilation* (*fana'*) was later elaborated in theory and technique along different lines in the various schools of Sufism. Abu Yazid's intense preoccupation with the central content of Islamic faith—God—was accompanied by occasional and notorious disregard for the standard forms of expressing that faith, including the obligatory prayers, pilgrimage, and fasting. This earned him a reputation for madness in the orthodox community. Some have said he was a flagrant heretic. But his biography, like those of other Sufi saints, contains solid credentials in the study of the Sunni roots of the Shari'a. This aspect of his story is as essential to his place in Islam as is his irreverence, for as Jesus quarreled with the Pharisees (a term Abu Yazid used on occasion), the saint from Bistam said outward forms of piety are not enough. They may even act as a shield against the interior experience of the God they are prescribed to serve.

Sacred biographies of Sufi saints report that once when Abu Yazid was returning to Bistam from a pilgrimage to the holy city of Medina he was greeted by throngs of townsmen eager to see the now famous Sufi shaykh from their town. It was during Ramadan, the month of the obligatory fast. As they approached, Abu Yazid pulled out a loaf of bread and defiantly devoured it before their astonished eyes. The crowd shrank away in horror and disgust. On another occasion:

> "A man encountered me on the road," Abu Yazid recalled.
> "Where are you going?" he demanded.

"On the pilgrimage," I replied.
"How much have you got?"
"Two hundred dirhams."
"Come, give them to me," the man demanded. "I am a man with a family. Circle round me seven times. That is your pilgrimage."
"I did so, and returned home."[7]

The many stories about the shaykh's notorious lack of piety serve as insights into a man deeply concerned not to let the outward forms of piety build up his own ego to the eclipse of God. The reputation for madness this earned him is itself significant. We need only recall that the Arabs of Quraysh in Mecca had accused the Prophet of madness and of poetic enthusiasm. He was also said to be poor and illiterate. But madness, poetic enthusiasm (ecstasy), poverty, and illiteracy did not become extolled as Islamic virtues in the Sunna of the Prophet. The contrast between Muhammad as pagan Arabia saw him and Muhammad as model for his community (umma) indicates the ironies of his sacred biography. The illiterate Muhammad had been chosen to recite the incomparable linguistic masterpiece, the Qur'an. The poor orphan of Mecca had become Prophet of God and the inspiration for a new political order. The mad, poetic-like utterances of this oft-rejected Prophet had become the rationale for a new world religion.

So, too, with Abu Yazid we find no effort to expunge from his life story the signs of madness and alienation from the community in which he lived. His stance over and against the norms of the Islamic umma was a message to later Sufis. It was also an explicit declaration of boundaries of piety that existed within Islam. Sunni Islam could not accept Abu Yazid's flagrant abuse of normal religious practice, and Abu Yazid could not find in the external forms of worship a final introduction into the mystery of God's being. Both the orthodox ulama *and* the Sufis relied upon the Qur'an and the Sunna as sources of religious piety. There came into focus a distinction between external, observable forms and internal, secret meanings. For the orthodox umma, these were one and the same. For the Sufis, the outer forms were ciphers. One must start there but must go on to penetrate inner meanings. For many, such as Abu Yazid, this called for the rejection of external forms of worship, at least as a provocation to jolt the masses out of the slumber of their pious formalities.

Ultimate truth for Abu Yazid was God. God is the All, and union (tawhid) with God is total. Willing as they were to dismiss most of his antics as madness, later generations of the Sunni ulama could not forgive Abu Yazid's infamous declaration: "Glory be to Me!" The gloria in Arabic is restricted solely to God. Applied to one's self, it amounted to self-deification, and a heinous denial of God. For Abu Yazid, only the annihilated self could so praise God. For the many who saw only blasphemy in this phrase, only one who ceased to be Muslim could declare such sacrilege. Between the polarities that were thereby highlighted, the Sufi shaykhs, the orthodox ulama, and the masses of spiritually motivated Muslims have struggled to define the boundaries of piety appropriate to the mandate of the Shari'a.

In this chapter we have seen some of the ways in which Islamic world views express notions of religious and cultural boundaries—convictions and practices that separate self from other. In the next chapter we will consider how Islamic world views are articulated more formally in thought and doctrine.

NOTES

1. Frederik Barth, ed., *Ethnic Groups and Boundaries: The Social Organization of Culture Difference* (Boston: Little, Brown and Company, 1969), p. 15.
2. A good discussion of the problem the non-Arab converts in eastern Islam had in integrating into Arab/Umayyad society is found in Wilferd Madelung, "The Murji'a and Sunnite Traditionalism," in idem, *Religious Trends in Early Islamic Iran*, Columbia Lectures on Iranian Studies 4 (Albany, N.Y.: Bibliotheca Persica, 1988), pp. 13–25.
3. Ignaz Goldziher, *Muslim Studies*, ed. S. M. Stern, trans. C. R. Barbar and S. M. Stern, Vol. I (Chicago: Aldine Publishing Co., 1967), p. 150.
4. Goldziher, *Muslim Studies*, vol. l, pp. 151–52.
5. Hamilton A. R. Gibb, *Studies on the Civilization of Islam*, ed. Stanford J. Shaw and William R. Polk (Boston: Beacon Press, 1962), p. 69.
6. Charles Pellat, *The Life and Works of Jahiz* (Berkeley: University of California Press, 1969), pp. 85–86.
7. Cited in A. J. Arberry, *Sufism, an Account of the Mystics of Islam* (London: George Allen & Unwin Ltd, 1956), p. 32.

PART III ISLAMIC WORLD VIEWS: RELIGIOUS THOUGHT AND AESTHETICS

6

Cosmology

and

Belief

DIVINE UNITY

I witness that there is no God But Allah. We have seen in Chapter 1 that these words form the basis of the fundamental Muslim creed known as the shahada, and that they are invariably followed by a second affirmation: *I witness that Muhammad is his Apostle.* Muslims utter this simple declaration of faith often. Some express its words many times each day. What does it mean and why is it so important? The answer lies in part in pre-Islamic constructions of religion and reality. In seventh-century Arabia there were other gods besides Allah to be worshipped, in what the Qur'an calls *shirk* (polytheism). In addition, the Middle Eastern milieu had produced many prophets and holy men. These two background elements, the pagan culture and language of Arabia and the monotheistic traditions of the Middle East, stimulated each other in Islam, giving profound meaning to the First Pillar of faith, the shahada. The achievement of Islam can be appreciated all the more if we consider that the religious cosmologies inherent in Arabian culture on the one hand, and in the monotheism of Judaism and Christianity on the other, were quite different, if not incompatible, until the rise of Islam.

From Many Gods to One

As we have seen, Arabia in Muhammad's time was polytheistic in its conception of the cosmos and tribal in its social structure. Each tribe had its own god(s) and goddess(es), which were manifest in the forms of idols, stones, trees, or stars in the sky. We know something about the pagan divinities of pre-Islamic Arabia—the period that Muslims call "jahiliyya" (see below)—both from Greek historians as well as early Muslim authors who wrote about the *asnam* (idols) worshipped up to Muhammad's time. In Mecca, three great goddesses dominated worship among the Quraysh: al-Lat, al-'Uzza, and Manat. The first two are thought to be manifestations of the planet Venus, the evening and morning star. Manat seems to have been a goddess of destiny, a reflex on the fatalism of Arab culture. A male deity, "Allah," appears in pre-Islamic Arabia as well.[1]

The Qur'an as well as other sources suggest that until Muhammad's time, Allah was thought to be a supreme god, but much more attention was paid to local deities and spirits.[2] At special locales throughout central Arabia, gods were enshrined in sacral surroundings. During the sacred months each year, nomadic tribesmen made pilgrimages to these shrines to pay homage to their gods. Within the sacred territories of the gods there could be no killing of anything—plants, animals, or human beings. These sacred times and spaces were coordinated with commercial and other cultural activities. Festive fairs at or near the shrines provided occasions for celebration, for the sale and exchange of goods, and for social intercourse. Poetry and skillful oratory, the pride of Bedouin culture, often took the form of tribal contests between distinguished bards. In pre-Islamic times, the Plain of Arafat outside Mecca had been the site of important annual fairs. Within Mecca were enshrined the idols of some of the most important gods in Arabian culture. The Ka'ba, which housed these idols, was distinguished by a black stone, itself thought to be extremely sacred by pagan worshippers.

RELIGIONS OF THE AXIAL AGE

About a thousand years before Muhammad appeared in Arabia, other prophets were challenging the religions of antiquity in China, India, and the Middle East. In China, it was Confucius and Lao-tze; in India, the Buddha and Mahavira. In the Middle East, the ancient Persian religion was challenged and reformed by the prophet Zoroaster. In Israel, the Hebrew prophets preached messages about the one God, Yahweh, and the religion of Judaism evolved from their moral demand that the people honor an ancient covenant of faith with Him. All of these prophets and reformers inspired the rise of religious traditions that have survived now for 2500 years. The philosopher Karl Jaspers has referred to the original period of this prophetic activity as the *Axial Age,* a time between 800 and 200 B.C. when civilizations arose along the great river valleys of China, India, and the Middle East (the Nile and Tigris-Euphrates), based upon an agrarian economy.

In the Middle East, Zoroaster and the Hebrew prophets had warned their people that God was just and righteous, and that He demanded morality and obedience. These prophetic warnings were regarded as messages from God, and the prophets' words were cherished as scriptures. The scriptures also contained laws (for example, the Torah of the Hebrew Bible), and these laws, regarded as divinely sent, became the fundamental bases of new religious civilizations. The Ten Commandments encapsulate the law of ethical monotheism that was promulgated in the Middle East during the Axial Age. Between the Axial Age and the rise of Islam, the religions of Judaism, Christianity, and several other offshoots of ethical monotheism had become well established in the lands the Muslims would later conquer.[3]

The sociologist S. N. Eisenstadt argues that the religious cosmologies of the civilizations that arose during the Axial Age developed concepts of a chasm between heaven and earth, the "transcendental and mundane." Recalling the theories of the German sociologist Max Weber, Eisenstadt points out that the teachers and prophets in China, India, and the Middle East who preached this moral order found various ways to solve the problem their teachings had created. For by announcing a chasm between the transcendental order and the mundane (the divine and the human), Confucius, the Buddha, Zoroaster and the biblical prophets had to show their followers how to bridge that chasm and bring the realm of the human back into concord with the divine. Using a Christian term and concept, Weber (and Eisenstadt) use the category of salvation (soteriology) to describe this cosmic restoration.

Soteriology in the various religious civilizations of Asia and the Middle East called for, among other things, the accountability of rulers to the mandates of the heavens and the god(s); it established law and individual rights, even if divinely derived, as an autonomous activity of the mundane sphere. Speaking of the social tension caused by the reconstitution of the social order as separate from but reflective of the divine order, Eisenstadt says that

> the quest to overcome this tension generates an awareness of a great range of possibilities. . . . Moreover such institutionalization [of this quest] was never a simple, peaceful process; it has been usually connected with a continuous struggle and competition among many groups and among their respective visions.[4]

The Pharisees, Sadducees, Essenes, and Christians are examples of this struggle and competition in the first century of the Common Era. The early separation between Shi'i and Sunni expressions of Islam is an example more to the point of this book. In the case of Islam, a distinct cosmology emerged in the very beginning. The quranic cosmology was described and analyzed in Chapter 3.

One of the characteristics of the Axial Age civilizations in China, India, the Middle East, and the Mediterranean is that they extended over large territories, both politically and economically; hence, their religions were not limited to local shrines and tribal units, like the religion of the ancient Canaanites or the pre-Islamic Arabs. In the Middle East, distinctive socioreligious ideas characterized the religions of the region, which Marshall Hodgson has summarized as follows:

> As in other areas, it was concern with the private individual as personal, as independent in some degree from the group of which he formed a part, that increasingly exercised the great prophets who arose in the Axial Age, notably Zarathustra [Zoroaster] in Iran and the Biblical prophets among the Hebrews. The prophets spoke to human beings in the name of a supreme and unique God, not reducible within any image, visible or mental, but expressing a moral dimension in the cosmos; they demanded unconditional allegiance from each person to the transcendent vision. . . . On the personal level, the individual's duty was to be expressed in purity of life; on the social level, in maintaining a just balance among agrarian social classes. The Hebrew prophets, in Palestine and later in Babylonia, called men and women to the love of a Creator-god elevated above any nation, who would exact unusually severe standards precisely of those he most favoured, but promised them in the end compassion and fulfillment, when they should be prepared to worship him in full moral purity. These prophets founded strong literary traditions. . .expressing and developing their visions.[5]

Although Islam and Christianity arose in history after the Axial Age proper, it is easy to identify the social and religious characteristics of Axial Age religions with each tradition.

High God Universalism

In order to understand the import of Muhammad's prophetic role as Apostle of God in Arabia during the seventh century, it might be useful to refer to a theory recently advanced in another context by a scholar of religions, Robin Horton. An anthropologist, Horton has sought to explain why African peoples have converted in large numbers from tribal polytheism to the monotheistic religions of Christianity and Islam during the past century. Most of Africa has held traditional polytheistic world views, very similar to those of Canaanites prior to the rise of Judaism, and to those of the Arabians prior to the rise of Islam. *Local gods* and spirits command the attention of the Africans in their sacred rituals, even in their less ceremonial, everyday concerns. More remote, usually, is a *high god*, who is always there but who seldom functions in the rituals and concerns of everyday life. Horton has noticed that as these local African tribes come more into contact with other societies and peoples (through warfare, trading, migrations to natural resources, and incursions from the outside world), the high god comes more into focus. At the same time the local gods and spirits function less explicitly, and they may even be abandoned for all practical purposes. In other words, as tribal societies become absorbed and drawn into communication with other civilizations, a more universal god who rules and orders the cosmos becomes more functional and meaningful in concept and worship. Conversely, if the situation reverses itself and a group should become culturally isolated from the rest of the tradition, we should expect local gods and spirits to regain parochial importance.[6]

Arabian culture in the seventh century is pertinent to Horton's discussion of traditional African cosmologies. The Arabs were Semitic people who worshipped many gods. Like the Africans, the Bedouin people of Arabia had lived for centuries in tribal social groupings, fairly well isolated from the rest of Middle Eastern civilization. When the Byzantine and Sassanian Empires sought to exert military and economic influence over Arabia, success was only partial. In the desert, foreign armies were at the mercy of Bedouin raiders. Caravan routes bringing the spices and exotica of India to markets in the Mediterranean, and Byzantine products back to the East, were in the effective control of the Arabs.

The eventual impact of the outside world upon Arabia was nonetheless inevitable. Men, goods, and ideas from faraway urban civilizations began to circulate in Arabian market towns. Monotheism and, perhaps more significantly, a cosmology that presented a unified world view, began to appeal more to those Arabs affected by these social, economic, and political changes. The message of Allah delivered by Muhammad developed into a system of thought that proved to be appropriate to the growing international awareness felt by the Arabs.

Of course, many Arabs in Muhammad's time were not eager to abandon their local gods and religious customs. Many of the tribal leaders of Mecca, who were devoted to established pagan polytheistic beliefs, resisted such changes, as happened among the Africans. We saw in Chapter 3 that Muhammad's role as Prophet/Warner among the Quraysh was deeply troubled by old tribal resistance. The Qur'an classified tribal polytheism and the culture this entailed as *jahiliyya*, "Time of Ignorance (of God)"—that is, a time in which the original pure monotheism of Abraham had been forgotten. The tribesmen living in distant regions of the central Arabian desert were the most remote from the changing world views of Meccan traders and caravan merchants. It was precisely these tribes that most fiercely resisted accepting Islam. During the early years of the caliphate in Medina, "Wars of Apostasy" were waged by Muslim troops against these recalcitrant tribesmen. Eventually, however, the tribesmen were settled by the expansion of Islam into lands outside of Arabia. Soon they, too, were persuaded by the Islamic doctrine of one all-powerful God, the creator of an all-encompassing cosmos.

These remarks about the changing social, economic, and political situation in Arabia in the seventh century place in perspective the cardinal concept of Islamic belief mentioned in Chapter 1, the doctrine of God's unity, tawhid. Among the monotheistic Western religious traditions, Islam has most insistently asserted the unity and oneness of God. As Islam spread into other Middle Eastern lands, the doctrine of tawhid, at first articulated against tribal world views among the Arabs, contributed to a rigorous monotheistic world view that challenged the dualism of Zoroastrianism and the tri-theism of Christianity. The theological writings of Muslims have usually begun with carefully reasoned chapters on tawhid, God's unity.

ONE GOD, MANY WORLDS AND BEINGS

We have already gained some sense of the Islamic experience of the cosmos. Its structure is compelling in its simplicity, created and governed by the one God, Allah. The cosmos is geographically centered around the sacred Ka'ba, the directional focus or Qibla of the canonical prayers that are performed each day at prescribed times. The annual pilgrimage to the Meccan Ka'ba brings Muslims from every direction around the world to this focal point of Islamic religious consciousness. The sacred center of Islam has persisted in spite of the fact that the political capitals of the Islamic world have located at such far-flung places as Baghdad, Istanbul, Delhi, and Cordoba. As the political fortunes of Islamic civilization have fragmented and shifted, the sacred center in Mecca has persisted as a powerful symbol of the unity of Islam.

Islam affirms the Judeo-Christian doctrine of the divine creation of the world out of nothing, *creatio ex nihilo*. It affirms that the earth is filled with the fullness and goodness of Allah's creative act. Adam, the first man, was a special creature, but humans were not the only beings created to inhabit the cosmos in obedience to Allah. The first sura of the Qur'an, entitled "The Opener," begins with the phrase, "Praise be to God, Lord of the Worlds." The plural, worlds, does not refer to other planets and stars as we think of them but rather to other sacred realms of angels and unseen spiritual beings. The most important of the angels is *Jibril* (Gabriel), whose function it was to convey the message of Allah to Muhammad, who in turn recited it to the Arabs. Jibril is sometimes called the "Faithful Spirit"; he occupies an important place within the Islamic conception of cosmos.

Among the angels was also the figure of *Iblis*, who, as in other Near Eastern traditions about the Devil, had fallen through disobedience into disrepute among the heavenly host. According to the Qur'an, the cause of Iblis' fall was his refusal to pay homage to Adam, the first man:

> *And when We [Allah] said unto the angels:*
> *Prostrate yourselves before Adam,*
> *They all fell prostrate except Iblis.*
> *He demurred through his pride,*
> *and so he became an unbeliever (kafir). (Sura of the Cow, Qur'an 2:34)*

Iblis and his legion of seducers were granted a reprieve from punishment until the Day of Judgment, at which time they will be cast into the fiery pit of hell. In the meantime it is within the power divinely granted to Iblis to lead astray those who do not believe in Allah. The paradigm example of this seductive power is the quranic story of Iblis tempting Adam and Eve to eat of the forbidden tree of immortality and power (Sura Ta Ha, Qur'an 20:116–122).

Other angels appear in Islamic cosmology. Michael, Israfil, and Azrael were mentioned in Chapter 1. Others appear with special functions. Harut and Marut were thought to have possessed the secret knowledge of ancient Babylonian magic. In the myths of earlier Near Eastern peoples, including the Hebrews, human knowledge about the secrets of nature and the use of civilized tools was communicated to humankind through divinely sent sages and kings (cf. Genesis 4:17–22). Harut and Marut also possessed the means of creating disharmony between men and women (Qur'an 2:102). Here again the student of religion notices a correspondence between cosmological views and social realities. In Chapter 14 we will encounter Munkar and Nakir, the angels who interrogate the dead in the grave. Thus the pursuit of a life of faithful obedience to Allah is seen as a cosmic drama that engages the many realms, visible and invisible, that are felt to impinge upon the phenomenal world of reality and social experience.

Early Muslims inhabited a world felt to be filled with other unseen creatures of God. Angels played an important role in the mythic times of origins and in the revelation of Allah's word to humankind. The Arabic term for angel, *malak*, means "messenger." Other unseen creatures included the *jinn* (known in the West as "genies"). Along with humankind and the angels, the jinn appear in the Islamic tradition as intelligent beings who, like humankind, are subject to being led astray or saved. They are usually defined as imperceptible creatures, made of fiery substance, although they have the power to assume visible, creative form from time to time. Muhammad's role as Messenger/Warner to humankind was to the jinn as well, for the salvation of the Last Day comprehends the many realms of Allah's lordship. Thus some of the early Islamic juristic works entertained a number of questions regarding legal status in matters of property and marriage between humankind and jinn. Islamic folklore has associated the jinn with fabled performances of magic. Many of the stories in the popular romances of the *Thousand and One Nights* portray jinn as agents of marvelous feats of magic. Related to the jinn are the *shayatin* (singular *shaytan*—that is, Satan). They appear in the Qur'an as proud and rebellious demons who, through their disobedience, will suffer punishment in hellfire. The Qur'an (Sura of the Poets, Qu'ran 26) had suggested that the poets and other Arab contemporaries of Muhammad who persisted in the cultural and religious attitudes of the "Time of Ignorance" were inspired to go astray by the satans.

Another aspect to the Islamic conception of the cosmos is the notion that the Word of God is inscribed on a Heavenly Tablet, sometimes referred to as the "Mother of the Book." The Qur'an, and the earlier scriptures of the Christians and Jews, are spoken of as having been "sent down" to humankind through angels to prophets. The prophets mentioned in the Qur'an are mostly figures that appear in the Old and New Testaments of the Bible. Thus the original Torah, Gospel, and the Qur'an are all believed to be revealed scriptures in the Islamic world view. On the historic occasions with which the prophecies of Moses, Jesus, and Muhammad are associated, the Islamic view is that Allah's heavenly inscribed word was sent down to select human civilizations. These recipients of Allah's Word through His messengers are the People of the Book. The obvious cultural and religious affinities among Judaism, Christianity, and Islam have their religious bases for Muslims in such cosmological doctrines as that of the Heavenly Tablet.

PROPHETIC RELIGION AND THE QURANIC VIEW OF HUMANKIND

Humankind's purpose in the world, according to Islamic religious thought, is to receive Allah's messengers and to obey His commands and prohibitions, as we saw in Chapter 3. Human beings are created with the faculty of reason, which is sufficiently developed at the age of puberty for one to be held "accountable" (the Arabic theological term is *mukallaf*) for his or her obedience to Allah and His messengers. This raised the issue of whether, if humans are morally responsible for their acts, God can be held to be omnipotent. We will look more closely at this debate in early Islam in Chapter 7.

In traditional Islamic society, formal education beyond rote memorization of the Qur'an began at about the age of eleven or twelve. (In modern times elementary education begins for children at a much earlier age.) A child was first instructed in the Qur'an and taught how to recite it properly. Later the student learned the Prophet's hadith, the roots of Islamic law, and other religious sciences. In all of this, the human faculty of reason ('aql) is held in high esteem by most Muslim thinkers. According to some Muslim thinkers, reason complements knowledge gained through revelation. *Reason* teaches humankind in general to be thankful to God, and it teaches the general moral precepts and practical matters that are essential to a good life. *Revelation* teaches the specific ways of expressing grateful obedience to Allah, such as the five prayers daily, the fast during Ramadan, pilgrimage to Mecca, and so on. Thus the basis of the Islamic view of humanity is that men and women are under obligation to live lives of faithful obedience. The Islamic emphasis on revelation *and* reason implies the importance of education and learning in both spiritual and worldly affairs. It also raises the issue, known also to medieval Jewish and Christian thinkers, of the conflict between reason and revelation, which we will examine further in the next chapter.

FIGURE 6.1 The mosque is a place of worship and learning. (Courtesy of the United Nations.)

Although Islam teaches that Muhammad and all prophets were fully human and in no way divine, the figure of the Prophet plays an important role in Islamic humanism. The Qur'an says, "Truly you have a good example in the Messenger of Allah for those who regard Allah and the Day of Judgment, and remember Allah often" (Sura of the Parties, Qur'an 33:21). Believed to be the most noble of humankind, the Prophet Muhammad possessed all the human qualities that should be emulated by his community (umma). Those who had the closest contact with the Prophet, known as Companions, became revered sources of his Sunna, or path. Along with the next two generations of followers, these Muslims of the first century of Islam were largely responsible for shaping the subsequent Islamic idea of humanity, based as it was on the formation of a living tradition about the Prophet's Sunna.

From the hadith literature and other aspects of the Shari'a, there emerges a total way of life for Muslims. It touches upon religious duties as well as secular responsibilities. Indeed the Shari'a does not recognize a distinction between these two realms. In modern times, many Muslim countries have instituted civil law courts, but the religious Shari'a courts have remained a force, especially in the lives of pious Muslims and those who seek a revival of Islam in public life. One's duty to Allah and His Messengers extends to government, neighbors, and family. A well-known hadith of the Prophet has it that a man's responsibility to take care of his family is just as much a religious duty as prayer. Thus even in the sphere of social and political ideals, the experience of God's unity, tawhid, is strongly felt: Ideally, Islam presses for unity at every level.

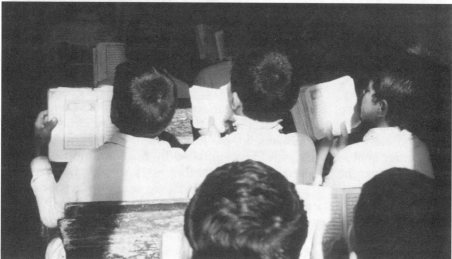

FIGURE 6.2 Children reciting the Qur'an. (Photos by the author.)

The question of sex, marriage, family, and the role of women is of interest in contemporary scholarship. It should be remembered that Islamic society arose out of kinship patterns characterized by extended families. This was typical of the tribal structure of Arabia and elsewhere in the Middle East in the seventh century. The effect of the Prophet's teaching was to emphasize the importance of the family while at the same time replacing tribal loyalties with loyalty to the cohesive notion of an Islamic umma. This task required an ordered sense of humanity and society. The Prophet's example, his Sunna as recorded in hadith, is a major source of Islamic conceptions of humanity and society. We will consider the importance of gender roles in Islamic societies in a later chapter.

This brief introduction to the cosmological and social backgrounds of Islamic world views has focused once again on the quranic cosmology, stressing the themes of divine unity and the powerful forces that operate in the divine and human realms. Many of these same ideas arose in other world religions of the Axial Age, as we have seen. The notions of divine unity, prophetic mission, and human obedience to God are central themes in Islamic world views and are basic to Islamic belief systems. The next chapter will construct a narrative of the early development of Islamic religious thought.

NOTES

1. On pre-Islamic Arabian religion, see Joseph Henninger, "Pre-Islamic Bedouin Religion," in *Studies on Islam*, ed. and trans. Merlin L. Swartz (New York and Oxford: Oxford University Press, 1981), pp. 3–22.
2. See the articles "Allah" in *The Encyclopaedia of Islam*, 2nd ed. and "Nabi" in *The Shorter Encyclopaedia of Islam*.
3. The importance of the Axial Age to the rise of Islam within the Middle Eastern environment is discussed by Marshall G. S. Hodgson in *The Venture of Islam*, 3 vols. (Chicago: University of Chicago Press, 1974), 1:103–45.
4. S. N. Eisenstadt, "Religion and the Civilizational Dimensions of Politics," in *The Political Dimensions of Religion*, ed. Said Amir Arjomand (Albany, N.Y.: State University of New York Press, 1993), p. 15.
5. Hodgson, *Venture of Islam*, 1:115.
6. Robin Horton, "On the Rationality of Conversion," *Africa*, 45/3 (1975):219–35, and 45/5 (1975):373–99.

7

The Formation of Islamic Religious Thought

GOING BEYOND SCRIPTURE

Scripture serves the needs of basic beliefs. Sacred texts like the Qur'an indicate how a community comes into being and receives a prophet, and what purpose the community serves in the cosmos. Scripture informs the liturgical rituals of worship and the legal modes of social behavior. The Qur'an thus served its proper function in the early Islamic community. With the expansion of Islam into lands already settled by Jews, Christians, Zoroastrians, and other religious communities, the simple enunciation of scripture proved to be insufficient for the discussion of Islam, both among Muslims and by Muslims with non-Muslims. With the help of Greek philosophy and established rhetorical traditions, Jewish and Christian thinkers developed systematic articulations of their beliefs as well as arguments against the beliefs of rival traditions. Thus, by the time Islam appeared in the seventh century, Jews and Christians had already engaged in sophisticated polemics with each other in attempts to prove the truth of one tradition against the claims of the other. In this environment of theological controversy, which flourished in the towns and cities conquered by the Arab armies, Muslim intellectuals found themselves drawn to respond in kind.[1]

Islamic thought had another, more intrinsic impulse, in the view of many scholars. The two sources of the Qur'an and the Sunna required considerable interpretation for each generation of Muslims after the Prophet, and inevitably, differences of opinion occurred. The expanded Muslim community in the newly conquered lands of the Middle East experienced numerous threats of internal disruption. The sectarian groups of Shi'a, Khawarij, and Murji'a, described in Chapter 5, sought to define and clarify the meaning of crucial concepts such as faith, sin, and the nature of human freedom and ability to act independently of divine empowerment. From these early disputes came schools of thought that in time produced important theologians and theological works. Islamic thought, then, centers around theological issues that sprang from the historical circumstances of early Islam. The chief language of discourse during the early centuries—Arabic—was soon adapted to the theological and philosophical discussions of contemporary Christian, Jewish, and other religious thinkers. The result has been a rich literary history of religious thought, which we shall survey briefly.

KALAM: DISPUTING DIFFERENCES

Those who formulate religious beliefs into doctrines are called theologians in Western parlance. In classical Islam they were called *mutakallimun*, and their activity—a term derived from the same Arabic root (*k-l-m*)—was called *kalam* or, more formally, *'ilm al-kalam*, the discipline or science of kalam. What, then, is kalam? Quite literally it means "speech," or "talking." The mutakallimun were specialists in speaking about the "fundamentals of religion," the *usul al-din* It is tempting to translate kalam as "theology" and the mutakallimun as "theologians," as was implied in the first two sentences of this paragraph. The differences between kalam and theology are interesting and important to note, however. The term theology is derived from two familiar Greek words, *theos* (god) and *logos* (reason, rational speech). Among the Greeks, *theologein* meant "to discourse about the gods." In early and medieval Christian civilization, theology came to mean "the study of God and His relation to humankind." In Western Christendom, after several centuries of determining religious doctrine by grand councils of bishops, universities began to appear in Paris, Bologna, Oxford, and elsewhere. Theology emerged as an authoritative discipline, often in conflict with the church hierarchy, to become "queen of the sciences" within the university. The matter was otherwise in early and medieval Islam.[2]

Caliphs and wealthy patrons in the first centuries of Islam frequently gave audience to Muslims of various points of view as well as Christians, Jews, philosophers and others, letting them dispute their doctrines openly. These disputations, called *munazarat* (singular, *munazara*) were a cultural product of

Islamicate society from the very beginning. They took place in virtually every discipline of the Islamic religious sciences, especially in *fiqh* (the study of the roots of the Shari'a) and kalam. But these disputations—even the ones sanctioned by caliphs—never attained the degree of magnitude or magisterial authority of the church councils called by the Emperor Constantine and his Byzantine successors, beginning with the Council of Nicea in the fourth century. Whereas the church councils of medieval Christendom were convened by Christian emperors to settle doctrinal disputes, Muslim lawyers and theologians engaged in a continual process of disputation to resolve questions of religious practice and belief as they arose. Disputation was a normal cultural process for finding peaceful settlement of divisive religious issues.

The earliest function of the mutakallimun may have been as military missionaries during the Umayyad period (661–750), serving as "spokesmen" for Islam (or Islam as the Umayyad caliphs and regional governors and Arab generals understood it) on the frontiers of territory just under, or not yet under, Islamic rule. In the next section, we will review the chief issues in dispute during the first few generations of Muslims, for these became the foundation issues of *'ilm al-kalam*. The reader will recall that the earliest issues in dispute were related to the experiences and conflicts (fitnas) that occurred in the formation of Islamicate society in the periods of the Rashidun and Umayyad caliphs.

EARLY THEOLOGICAL PROBLEMS

The monotheistic religious traditions—Islam, Judaism, and Christianity—have each wrestled with a common set of theological problems. For example, the problem of evil has occupied the minds of religious thinkers in all three traditions. God is described as good and all-powerful in the creeds of all three faiths. The question then arises: Given the nature of God, is there a source of evil in the cosmos other than God? If not, why is there suffering?

Another problem that divided early Muslim thinkers was the seeming contradiction between free will and predestination. In this case, not only the nature of God but the nature of man was at issue.[3] The problem that drew the most attention was free will versus predestination, to which we shall turn our attention briefly.

God's Determination of Events

During the Umayyad Age (661–750), many mutakallimun attempted to define God's "power" to determine events. The real problem arose when it came to defining acts done by human beings. To what extent is God involved in the doings of humankind? Who is the efficient cause or agent of, say, an act of murder, or of saving a life? One group of thinkers took the position that God is all-powerful and thus the ultimate source of the power behind all events in the cosmos; humans act under the compulsion of God's power. This group of predestinarians was known as the "Compulsionist" party (*mujbira*). Another group argued that human morality would be thereby undercut; thus humans must be held responsible for their own acts. This latter group became known as the "Free Will" party (*qadiriyya*).

These early theological debates did not take place in a historical vacuum. They were related to claims, especially of the later Umayyad rulers, that their control and conduct of the caliphate was divinely willed, that is, a matter of God's power, not man's. Many Muslim thinkers, regardless of their personal offense and distaste for the impiety and secular interests of several of the Umayyad caliphs, defended the current state of political affairs and thus accepted the Umayyad caliphate on theological grounds. The others, the Free Will party, held the Umayyads accountable on the ground that human beings (including the caliph) are responsible for their own acts. The Free Will party of the Umayyad Age, then, was political as well as theological in its opposition to the mainstream of thought. Many of them paid for their stubborn resistance by imprisonment and even execution.

Both the Free Will party and the Predestination party claimed that the Qur'an and the sayings (hadiths) of the prophet supported their views, and in this claim each was correct, for passages from the Qur'an could be found that supported each position. Islamic theology, like Christian and Jewish theology, accepts scripture and tradition as authoritative sources on which to build decisive arguments. The problem is that scripture and tradition can be read in more than one way on most theological problems that divide the religious community. The Qur'an, like the Bible, is not a systematic theological or philosophical treatise.

Many passages of the Qur'an suggest that whatever befalls a man or woman in life, there is nothing that person can do; only God can do an undo what happens in the universe. Consider the following passage from the Sura of Jonah (Qur'an 10): "If God afflicts you with some hurt no one can remove it except Him; and if He desires some good [for you] no one can repel his goodness." The role of the book and of writing in Islamic cosmology is made clear in this regard in the Sura of Hud (Qur'an 11:6): "And there is not a beast in the earth whose sustenance does not depend upon Allah. He knows their habitation and reserve. All is in a clear book."

Other passages appear to say that humankind is to be held accountable for its sins on the Last Day, with the obvious implication that human beings are masters of their own acts. The Sura of Ya Sin (Qur'an 36:54) puts the matter this way: "On the Day [of Resurrection] no one is wronged for anything, nor is he recompensed, except for what you have been doing." The eschatological significance of free will is confirmed by the following passage from the Sura of the Cave (Qur'an 18:29–30):

> *Say: "The truth is from your Lord, so, whosoever wills let him believe and whoso-*
> *ever wills let him disbelieve. Truly, We have prepared Hellfire for*
> *disbelievers. . . ."*
>
> *Lo: As for those who believe and do good works, We do not allow to go lost the*
> *reward of any who do good deeds.*

Thus, although theological disputants sought to rest their cases on the war-
rants of scripture, the matter could not be decided on scripture and tradition
alone. The process of theological argumentation, already highly developed
by Christian thinkers who used Greek philosophy to support their claims,
was soon adopted by Muslim thinkers. On the other hand, internal political
problems led to sectarianism in early Islam and thus provided an urgent
need for theological reflection.

The Circle of Hasan al-Basri

During the Umayyad period, there lived a pious, reflective and somewhat
ascetic man named al-Hasan al-Basri (Hasan of Basra, d. 728). Born in 642,
just ten years after the death of the Prophet Muhammad, Hasan came from a
Persian family living in Iraq at the time of the Muslim conquests. His father
had converted to Islam, which made him a mawla, a Muslim by virtue of
being a client of the Arab family that had converted him. Hasan himself was
born a freed man. As a young man he participated in the continuing conquests of lands beyond Persia in what is now called Afghanistan. Later he
became secretary to the governor of Khurasan. He returned to live in the
Iraqi garrison town (one of the amsar) of Basra around 680. There he soon
formed around him a circle of students with whom he debated the theological implications and interpretations of the political events of the day. These
were quite tumultuous, as this was the period of the great fitnas or sectarian
uprisings, which were described in Chapter 5.

Among the issues that Hasan debated was the one raised by the Khawarij
who, as we have seen, argued that the Muslims had a duty, established in the
Qur'an, to punish sinners (like the caliph 'Uthman, whom they alleged had
ruled in violation of quranic precepts). Against this view, Hasan argued
"that a Kharijite who tries to right a wrong (*munkar*) commits a greater
wrong." By this he meant that the social order of the Muslim umma is only
made worse when wrongs are met with self-righteous acts of reprisal.[4]
Hasan also attacked the Khawarij for their insistence that a grave sinner is an
unbeliever, a kafir, who must be excluded from the Muslim umma, by
putting him to death if necessary. On the other side, Hasan rejected the position of the Murji'a, who argued that the fate of the grave sinner was in the
hands of God, and thus action against such a person must be postponed
until the Day of Judgment, because even a grave sinner must be regarded as
a believer, a *mu'min*. Invoking the quranic notion of "backslider" (*munafiq*)
against both positions, Hasan argued that sinners, even grave sinners, were

hypocrites, subject to punishment as provided by the Shari'a. Nonetheless, they were still Muslims and should not be excommunicated from the Muslim umma. In rejecting both the Khariji and Murji'i positions on the matter of the communal status of the grave sinner, Hasan was said to have taken up the "intermediate position" (al-manzila bayn al-manzilatayn).

We shall meet up with this doctrine again when we discuss the Mu'tazila, who adopted it. Indeed, even the earliest Arabic sources are in conflict over whether Hasan took this position or whether one of his disciples, Wasil ibn 'Ata (d. 748), did. According to the standard account of the origin of the Mu'tazili movement (which we shall consider in more detail below), during one of the sessions someone asked Hasan of Basra whether the grave sinner should be regarded as a believer or unbeliever. Hasan is reported to have hesitated, at which Wasil jumped up and said that the grave sinner was neither, but rather in an intermediate position. W. M. Watt recounts this version as follows: Wasil "then withdrew to another pillar of the mosque, followed by a number of those in [al- Hasan al-Basri's] circle, whereupon al-Hasan al-Basri remarked 'Wasil has withdrawn (i'tazala) from us.' From this remark came the name Mu'tazila."[5]

On another matter of grave concern to the early Muslim umma, Hasan took a stand that was to be debated throughout the early centuries of Islam. This was the problem of the antinomy between free will and predestination, the problem dealt with above. The Muslim predestinarians, who came to be called the "Compulsionists" (al-mujbira) argued that all that happens in the world, including human acts, is determined by God's decree (qadar). Opposing this view were early mutakallimun, who ironically were labeled the "Qadariyya." In effect, the Qadarites were those who contended that God's decree (qadar) does not override the human capacity to act and, more important, it does not obviate people's moral responsibility for their own actions.

There is some debate among scholars as to how much al-Hasan al-Basri deserves to be called a Qadarite. That he shared some of their views is made clear in an exchange of correspondence with the Umayyad caliph 'Abd al-Malik (reg. 685–705), attributed to al-Hasan al-Basri. We begin with a few lines from the caliph, to give the reader a sense of the literary formalities and style of religious discourse in translation (which loses the effect of the wordplay and zest of the original):

> From 'Abd al-Malik ibn Marwan, Commander of the Faithful, to al-Hasan ibn Abi al-Hasan al-Basri. Greetings to you! May the only God who exists commend you. The Commander of the Faithful [caliph] has heard your views on qadar, hearing the like of which he has never heard before. Nor has the Commander of the Faithful heard of any of the companions of Muhammad talk about [this] matter. . . . So write to him about your position on this matter. . .explaining whether this is on the basis of transmissions from the companions of the Prophet [i.e., hadith about Muhammad's Sunna], or according to your own view of things, or on the basis of truth which is known from the Qur'an. We shall listen to no other disputant nor intelligent person on this topic until we hear from you.[6]

Note the caliph's reference to the two sources of religious authority we discussed in Chapter 1 above, the Sunna of the Prophet and the Qur'an. 'Abd al-Malik mentions a third source, Hasan's "own view of things": what early Muslim jurists such as Abu Hanifa (d. 767) called "legal opinion" (ra'y) and later jurists called "independent reasoning" (ijtihad). The legitimate role of the individual scholar, in applying his considered judgment to the interpretation of the Qur'an and the Sunna, has been much debated throughout Islamic history. Those Muslims who have insisted on a literal reading and understanding of the roots of religion and law, excluding reason as an acceptable or even valid method of determining belief and practice, have always been critical of intellectual enterprises like that of kalam. Both the scholars of kalam (the mutakallimun) and the scholars of law or "fiqh" (the fuqaha) differentiated into schools (madhabs), some of which were more rationalist, while others were insistent on reliance on fundamental sources (the usul), such as the Qur'an and the Sunna. Interestingly, in his reply to Caliph 'Abd al-Malik, Hasan does not cite the Sunna of the Prophet; he relies mainly on proof texts from the Qur'an, and very little on independent rational argument. We quote a small but indicative portion toward the middle of Hasan's letter.

> Consider also, O Commander of the Faithful, the statements of God in Qur'an 26:99: *Only the evil-doers led us astray,* and 20:85: *The Samaritan led them astray,* and 17:53: *Satan is an obvious enemy for people,* and 41:17: *As for Thamud, We guided them but they preferred blindness over guidance because of what they had earned.* So, the beginning of guidance was from God but the beginning of their deserving blindness was in their erroneous opinions. My statements and my letter do not demand a lot from you, O Commander of the faithful, for the proofs are quite clear in them for whoever's soul is free of guilt. . . .[7]
> [The predestinarians] also dispute about Qur'an 11:105: *Some of them will be unfortunate, others fortunate.* They interpret this such that God created people in their mothers' wombs either fortunate or unfortunate so there is no way for whoever is fortunate to become unfortunate nor is there a way for the unfortunate to become fortunate. . . . God has said. . .in Qur'an 11:105: *A day comes; no soul shall speak except with His permission. Some of them will be unfortunate, other fortunate.* The fortunate ones on that day will be those who hold fast to the command of God while the unfortunate will be those who scornfully neglect the command of God about His religion [din].[8]

Hasan al-Basri's letter indicates that the predestinarians also based their arguments on passages from the Qur'an. Interpretation (or "exegesis" as textual commentary is called in religious studies) then turns on disputing the meaning of one passage by bringing other verses to bear on the meaning one wishes to impute. The meaning of one passage in the text is to be found elsewhere in the same text. There were two reactions to this manner of quranic argument. One came from Wasil ibn 'Ata and his followers, who "withdrew" from Hasan's circle (or at least from reliance solely on quranic proof texts) to

FIGURE 7.1   Traditional circle of Muslim scholars, mosque in Egypt. (Photo by author.)

found the "madhhab" or movement known as the Mu'tazila. The other came from the early jurists, the fuqaha, who vested great authority in the practice of the Prophet Muhammad as a second source of information about Muslim faith and practice besides the Qur'an. We turn, now, to consider further intellectual disputes among the mutkallimun.

THE CLASSIC SCHOOLS OF ISLAMIC THOUGHT

By the middle of the eighth century, when the Abbasid caliphs came to power in Baghdad, Islam was entering its golden age. Baghdad became an intellectual marketplace for many new ideas, religious and secular. The Free Will party was no longer politically suppressed. Shi'i theologians more openly argued their claims that 'Ali, not the first three rightly guided caliphs, was the true successor to the Prophet. Christians, Jews, Manichaeans, and even atheists with schooling in Greek philosophy gained established reputations in the Abbasid court, as we have seen. During the eighth through the early eleventh century, the various theological trends in Islam produced noteworthy figures who gathered many pupils around them in Baghdad and elsewhere. In the next chapter we will look at the main Sunni madhhab of kalam today, the Ash'rites. In this chapter the focus is more on the Mu'tazili madhhab and their early opponents, the Traditionalists, the Shi'a, and the philosophers.

The Mu'tazila

One of the most powerful theological movements in the early Islamic Middle Ages was known as the Mu'tazila. The origin of this school in the circle of al-Hasan al-Basri was discussed above. In reality, the Mu'tazila were not a unified school at all, but rather various groups of intellectuals with common but not identical sets of views. In a sense, the Mu'tazila were the continuation of the Free Will party, and like that party, they soon ran afoul of both the religious and the political establishment. Yet in the teachings of the early Mu'tazila, much of which has been cited in later works we now possess, we find these theologians to be extremely sophisticated in their articulation of Islamic thought. They were among the first Muslims to challenge heretics and non-Muslim thinkers. Their attempt to systematize Islamic thought in a way that was intellectually defensible had the effect of identifying the most essential doctrines of the Islamic religion.

In an eleventh-century commentary on a work by one of the last great Mu'tazili thinkers, Qadi 'Abd al-Jabbar (d. 1024), the following postulate of Mu'tazili kalam is set forth:

> The Chief Magistrate Abu l-Hasan 'Abd al-Jabbar. . .began his commentary with a question about the five fundamental principles, saying: "If a questioner asks 'what is the first thing God imposes on you,' say to him, 'speculative reason [nazar] that leads to knowledge of God Almighty, because He is not known intuitively, nor empirically, so we must know him through thinking and speculative reason.'"[9]

The Mu'tazila organized their discussions around five fundamental principles. First was the doctrine of tawhid, God's unity. Most Mu'tazili mutakallimun denied any resemblance between God and His creatures. Against more popular conceptions, the Mu'tazila argued that God could not be conceived in human terms; that is, they "deanthropomorphized" the notion of God in order to be more clear about His unity and uniqueness. This view had implications for quranic interpretation as well. In one famous passage of the Qur'an, God is described as sitting on the throne of Heaven. In this and all such passages, the Mu'tazila argued, it is best to give the verse an allegorical interpretation, for it could not be an accurate literal description of God. The early Mu'tazila developed their understanding of tawhid particularly in arguments against the Zoroastrians and Manichaeans, who held dualist notions of the godhead. But their arguments were also a challenge to those Muslims who read the Qur'an literally and thus understood God in anthropomorphic terms. Thus we see how early mythical world views of monotheism versus pagan polytheism were translated and developed into a sophisticated theological doctrine.

Second was the doctrine of 'adl, divine justice. In Western theological terms, 'adl has to do with the problem of *theodicy*. Given the existence of evil in the world, how can the notion of an all-powerful, good God be justified? Here the Mu'tazila carried the arguments of the Free Will party further, asking about the implications of the doctrine of qadar for the ethical nature of God's being. The basic premise of the Mu'tazila under the doctrine of 'adl is that God is just, and therefore He must do what is best for His creation. It also means that God, though all-powerful, cannot (or does not) do evil or require human beings to do what is evil. Human beings, then, are responsible for their own acts, which they commit under their own power.

The third fundamental doctrine of the Mu'tazila was *al wa'd wa l wa'id,,* the Promise and the Threat. Under this heading, theologians discussed religious beliefs concerning the Last Day or Day of Judgment. In Western religious thought this is the problem of *eschatology.* The fourth fundamental Mu'tazilite principle was *al-manzila bayn al-manzilatayn,* literally "the position between the two positions." This position was first attributed to al-Hasan al-Basri, as we saw above. Under this category came the discussion of what we might call *political theology.* The Arabic phrase refers to the early period of conflict, when many of the Mu'tazila adopted a middle position between the extremes of the Khawarij on the one hand and the Murji'a on the other. All questions concerning the caliphate and imamate were discussed here, as well as the nature of the Islamic state or community, that is, the umma.

The fifth and final principle was *al-amr bi l-ma'ruf wa l-nahy 'an al-munkar,* roughly "commanding the known (good) and prohibiting evil." It is a quranic phrase that all Muslim jurists and theologians have regarded as a religious impetus to spread Islam. Here the missionary enterprise of spreading the faith came under discussion. Islam first grew under the impulse not just to conquer, but to spread the faith. The Mu'tazila had been especially active helping the Abbasid family overthrow the Umayyads in the first half of the eighth century. This they did through their interpretation of Islam, which denied the predestinarian views supported by the Umayyads. Mu'tazilite political and missionary doctrines were especially popular in the Abbasid court until the middle of the ninth century. Mu'tazili mutakallimun continued to be influential in Iraq and in Eastern Islam until the eleventh century. When the Seljuq Turks took possession of the Abbasid caliphate, more conservative religious sensibilities took hold of the intellectual ethos of Islam. Mu'tazilism had by then run its course. The appeal of rationalism in theology remained dormant in Islam for many centuries until the twentieth century, when modernists such as the Egyptian Muhammad 'Abduh (d. 1905) revived interest in the spirit of Mu'tazilism, but not in the five fundamental principles.

These five fundamental principles—the doctrines of God, theodicy, eschatology, political theology, and missions—nonetheless formed the five subdivisions of most early works on theology. Even the opponents of the Mu'tazila adopted these categories, if only to refute the main arguments. Before long, however, opposing trends of thought became powerful enough to challenge the schools of the Mu'tazila in Baghdad, Basra, eastern Persia, and elsewhere.[10] One of the most powerful Sunni countermovements came from the Traditionists, often called the People of Hadith. Their strength in early Islam can be attributed to the popular teacher, jurist, and collector of hadith Ahmad ibn Hanbal.

Ahmad ibn Hanbal (780–855)

There is hardly any aspect of the religion of Islam upon which the stamp of Ibn Hanbal's name and influence does not appear, either positively or negatively.[11] His collection of hadith, known as the *Musnad*, is still widely used in the Muslim world. But Ibn Hanbal was more than a Traditionist (*muhaddith*, one who collected and taught prophetic traditions); he was also a Traditionalist. By this latter term we mean those Muslims who insist that religion is founded on revelation and prophetic example, not on speculative theology and reason. As a jurist he offered penetrating insights that drew a large following, and the Hanbalite school of Islamic law became one of the four orthodox branches of religious jurisprudence in Sunni Islam. Ibn Hanbal also became a legend in his own time by refusing to subscribe to the Abbasid court's official pronouncements on Islamic doctrine. As a Traditionalist, Ibn Hanbal held views that were much closer to those of the pious masses of Sunni Muslims, and soon his heroic resistance and refusal to recant his views, even in prison and under physical punishment, forced the government to release him and eventually to condemn his theological opponents. Throughout the Middle Ages the term "Hanbalite" was practically synonymous with the English term "Traditionalist," as defined above. A revival of Hanbalism in the fourteenth century was headed by Ibn Taymiya, as noted in Chapter 1. The religious monarchy in Saudi Arabia traces its spiritual heritage to Ahmad ibn Hanbal, as do many Islamic revival movements in modern times.

Ibn Hanbal's family had descended from a prominent Arab clan. His grandfather and father had participated in the conquest and pacification of Iraq and Persia. By the time of Ibn Hanbal's birth in 780, the family had settled in the recently built city of the Abbasids, Baghdad. The social and intellectual climate of the Abbasid capital must have been quite stimulating for the bright young son of a retired military figure. Most of the great religious teachers of the day found their way to Baghdad, and Ibn Hanbal was to become the pupil or teacher of many of them.

The main focus of his education was the collection and study of the hadiths attributed to the Prophet Muhammad. Until Ibn Hanbal's time, these had been preserved mainly by oral tradition. The early Abbasid period, however, produced an environment in which Islamic religious knowledge turned increasingly to literary forms. Such scholars as Ibn Hanbal were still known for their extensive memories and wide travels to gain comprehensive command of the thousands of sayings attributed to the Prophet. With the expansion of Islamic civilization came the growing need for an established literature about the Prophet's Sunna. Judges, lawyers, teachers, and other religious writers were to profit greatly from the work of Ibn Hanbal and others in classifying and writing down the prophetic sayings that played such an important role in the life of the Islamic umma. In this activity, Ibn Hanbal came to adopt a theological position that ran directly counter to the Mu'tazilites of his day.

The Uncreated Qur'an. The divinely given message of the Islamic way of life, contained in the Qur'an and the Sunna and known as the Shari'a, was viewed in a very particular way by the Traditionalists, who were known more broadly as the *ahl al-sunna wa l-jama'a*, "the People of the Sunna and the Community." Against the Mu'tazilite theologians and others, the People of the Sunna argued that innovations through reasoning and individual judgments had no part in religious matters. The Shari'a prescribed a total way of life. To thinkers like Ibn Hanbal, it was not necessary to go beyond the Qur'an and the Sunna to establish the Islamic way of life. This is why Ibn Hanbal was so extremely popular among the common people, and less so among Muslim and non-Muslim intellectuals who were not ready to accept the Qur'an and the Sunna as the sole authoritative sources of belief. Thus, as we have seen, tradition and reason emerged as two different, sometimes incompatible, sources of religious knowledge.

The conflict surfaced during Ibn Hanbal's lifetime, creating a whirlwind of controversy that swept the entire sociopolitical structure of the intelligentsia of Baghdad into the eye of its storm. The caliphs, their large staffs of civil servants, famous Mu'tazilite teachers, eminent philosophers, and many others became involved. Fortunes and reputations were gained and lost almost overnight. At the center of the storm stood two men of immense public stature: Caliph al-Ma'mum (reg. 813–833) and the Traditionist (and Traditionalist) Ibn Hanbal. Both men claimed deep commitment to the Islamic religion. The confrontation between them was a poignant reminder that religious ideas do not just inhabit the minds of pious recluses; the controversy over right belief (orthodoxy) can affect the whole social and political order.

The theological issue that brought Ibn Hanbal and al-Ma'mum into public conflict had political and social dimensions, but it was the Qur'an that stood at the center of the controversy. Al-Ma'mun, in addition to the matters of state for which he was directly responsible, took a personal interest in 'ilm al-kalam, the study of theology. He gathered around him many of the eminent Mu'tazili mutakallimun of the day. He even wrote several treatises on theology that were decidedly influenced by Mu'tazili arguments. He thus came to favor the Mu'tazili view that the Qur'an was God's revelation to man, created and recited to the Arabs in their own language at a particular and finite moment in history. The Mu'tazilites had further argued that the notion of God's unity, tawhid, would be compromised if the Qur'an were regarded, as it was in the popular view, as an eternal, preexistent document inscribed in Heaven. The question that exercised so many minds, then, was this: Is the Qur'an eternal or created? The Mu'tazilites, whom Caliph al-

Ma'mun supported, said that it was created and that it could not be otherwise. The Traditionalists and People of the Sunna, whom Ibn Hanbal supported, said that the Qur'an was the eternal, uncreated Word of God. The arguments that raged back and forth were sometimes subtle and elusive, but the social and political effects were not.

Al-Ma'mun took decisive steps to implement the Mu'tazili views as state policy. He required his chief civil servants to state publicly that the Qur'an was created. Many were willing to submit to this imperial meddling in matters of belief in order to save their jobs, despite their own convictions to the contrary. Along with a few others, Ibn Hanbal chose imprisonment over subversion of religious conviction. The rounding up and conviction of dissenters was known as the inquisition (*mihna*).[12] Outside the Baghdad prison in which Ibn Hanbal was incarcerated, the streets filled with common folk who supported his resistance to the caliph. Most of them were devoted to the popular belief in the uncreated, eternal Qur'an. Soon afterward Caliph al-Ma'mun died, and under his successors, Ibn Hanbal was held in prison for a few more years. During that time the additional measures of scourging could not persuade him to accept the doctrine of the created Qur'an. And so he was released on his own recognizance to live in retirement in his own home. There he remained in seclusion until the accession of Caliph al-Mutawakkil in 847, when Ibn Hanbal was able to resume his lectures on Traditions. Five years later Ibn Hanbal was invited to the new royal palace in Samarra, a town not far up the Tigris River from Baghdad. In the royal compound he tutored the caliph's son and, in sharp contrast to much of his public career in Baghdad, Ibn Hanbal enjoyed the last years of his life as something of a celebrity in the highest echelons of government, where he was guaranteed independence of thought. He died at the age of seventy-five in 855, and his body was interred in a cemetery near one of the main four gates of the city of Baghdad. Thousands of Muslims mourned at his graveside, and for generations his grave was a shrine for the large segment of Sunni Islam that in law and orthodox interpretations of the Shari'a goes by the name Hanbalite.

Ahmad ibn Hanbal's legacy in the Abode of Islam has been considerable. As a personality, he is remembered in history and legend as a heroic resister of doctrinal innovations and of rationalism, where these appeared to threaten popular, Traditionalist notions about the Qur'an and the Sunna. In theology, the widely accepted view that the Qur'an is the eternal, literal word of God found its most popular champion in Ibn Hanbal. Throughout the Middle Ages, many of the Ash'arite theologians defended such Hanbalite doctrines, although not all Ash'arites followed or studied the Hanbalite branch of Sunni law; and to many Hanbalites, the Ash'arites erred on the side of rationalism as opposed to Tradition. Historically, the Hanbalites have reappeared from time to time as the inspiration behind religio-political attempts to reform Islam. The terms "fundamentalist" and "puritan" are often applied to the Hanbalites and to Ahmad ibn Hanbal himself. Accurate as these terms may be, it would be unfortunate if such terms were taken to mean that a great religious and theological figure such as Ahmad ibn Hanbal (and his followers) should be overlooked in the intellectual history of Islam.

The Shi'a

During the eighth and ninth centuries, as the Traditionalists, Mu'tazila, and Ash'ariyya (see next chapter) were striving to clarify Sunni Islamic religious doctrines, the Shi'a were also engaged in theological reflection. Like the Mu'tazila, the Shi'a were motivated by political considerations. At first the Abbasid court had seemed much more friendly toward Shi'i groups than had the Umayyad court. Against the prevailing view of the Abbasids and of Sunni Islam, however, Shi'i theologians argued that 'Ali, not the first three rightly guided caliphs (Abu Bakr, 'Umar, and 'Uthman), had been the right-ful successor to the Prophet, designated by Muhammad himself. The Shi'a preferred the term "imam" to "caliph," and their religious thought sprang from the twelve (five or seven) imams whose teachings were regarded as sources of inspiration along with the Qur'an and the Sunna. Most of the early Mu'tazili and Ash'ari writings contained refutations of the political and reli-gious views of the Ithna Ash'ari (Twelver) Shi'a in particular. For their part, the Shi'a were not silent. Many of them wrote important theological and philosophical treatises about the various Shi'i world views and doctrines.

The terms each group used for the others were seldom polite and often extremely deprecating. The Isma'ili branch of the Shi'a spread esoteric doc-trines throughout Islamicate society, using highly trained missionaries known as da'is, as we have already seen. Thus during the classical period of Islam, theologians of all branches formed a class of intellectual elites whose function it was to articulate interpretations of Islam commensurate with dis-tinct religious and political groups within the Abode of Islam. Looking back-ward into those turbulent moments of intellectual history, we see that the categories of heresy and atheism, bandied about with emotion and convic-tion, were related to the articulated political convictions that each group of Muslims established for itself.[13]

Nasir al-Din al-Tusi (1201–1274). One of the most important Shi'i thinkers of the late classical period was Nasir al-Din al-Tusi. Born in Tus, Per-sia, Tusi managed to gain a solid education in the religious, philosophical, and physical sciences before the destructive armies of the Mongols marched across the Islamic East. In his early professional career he served as an astrologer to an Isma'ili prince, but when the Mongol invasions posed a threat to libraries and academies, he gained the confidence of the famed Mongol lord, Hulagu. Tusi was thereby able to save many libraries contain-ing intellectual treasures of the past. Much of the Mongol "loot" of this type was brought to Azerbaijan, where, with the support of Hulagu, Tusi founded an important institution that housed an observatory, library, and academy of scholars. Tusi's keen analytic mind ranged over a variety of subjects about which he wrote more than one hundred books. He is best known in the West for his work in astronomy and mathematics. In the Islamic world, particularly among the Shi'a, Tusi's works (written in Arabic and Persian) in theology, philosophy, ethics, and logic mark an important stage in intellectual history. Not only did Tusi save books and libraries from extinction, but he revived the achievements of philosophers such as Avicenna from the intellectual decline of the thirteenth century.

FALSAFA

The last group of intellectuals to be considered in this chapter is those who followed the Greek and Hellenistic traditions of *falsafa*, an Arabic loan word from the Greek *philosophia*, "love of wisdom" or philosophy. Greek philosophy—in particular, that of the Stoics, the Academy of Plato, Neoplatonism, and the Peripatetic tradition of Aristotle—played an important role in medieval thought. Among the Jewish philosophers, Philo (fl. circa 39 C.E.) and Moses Maimonides (d. 1204) interpreted and explained the Torah and Jewish beliefs with arguments drawn from Greek philosophy. Maimonides lived, wrote, and taught in Islamicate society (Islamic Spain and Egypt), where he had considerable contact with Muslim intellectuals. So, too, the Fathers of early Christianity and the Schoolmen of the Middle Ages employed Stoic, Platonic, Neo-Platonic, and especially Aristotelian philosophy to elaborate on Christian doctrine. We have already seen that in Islamicate society during the early Abbasid Age, there was much interest among Muslim rulers and intellectuals in translating the works of Greek philosophy into Arabic. This produced Islamic interpretations and elaborations of the Greek classical intellectual heritage, which Muslim intellectuals generally referred to as *rum*, (pronounced "room") "Rome."

In this regard, it is important to note that Western civilization is not the only intellectual inheritor of ancient Greece. The Greek heritage also played an important role in Islamic intellectual life in the Middle Ages. Indeed, Islamicate society was host, as just mentioned, to Jewish, Christian and Muslim philosophical traditions that relied on Greek thought.

The Philosophers

Al-Kindi (d. circa 866). Abu Yusuf Ya'qub ibn Ishaq al-Kindi was a younger contemporary of Ahmad ibn Hanbal; like the latter, he was born of pure Arab lineage. Nonetheless, al-Kindi, as we shall call him, was a man of completely different intellectual temperament than Traditionalists like Ibn Hanbal. Al-Kindi was involved in the translation movement, referred to previously in this chapter and in Chapter 4. Although he was probably not the translator of Greek works into Arabic, as some historians have claimed, as a philosopher he rephrased earlier translations in order to make more rational sense out of the texts. Like several Mu'tazili mutakallimun of his day, al-Kindi received patronage from Caliph al-Ma'mun (reg. 813–833) and his two successors. Indeed, there is some indication that al-Kindi was sympathetic with some of the doctrines supported by the Mu'tazila. One of his books, on the justice of God's actions, recalls the Mu'tazili doctrine of theodicy. His association with the Mu'tazila is also suggested by the fact that in 847, when an anti-Mu'tazilite, al-Mutawakkil, became caliph, al-Kindi lost favor with the court and his personal library was confiscated. Al-Mutawakkil was the same caliph who liberated Ahmad ibn Hanbal from prison and exonerated him publicly.

Ya'qub ibn Ishaq al-Kindi wrote many works, some of which have survived to the present day. Some of these works seem more theological in scope. Others are decidedly philosophical, reflecting Aristotelian and Platonic approaches to metaphysics. Philosophers like al-Kindi were able to find value in the intellectual contributions of the ancient civilizations of the Greeks, Chinese, Indians, and others, whereas Traditionalists like Ahmad ibn Hanbal sought to restrict knowledge to that which is known from the Qur'an and the Sunna. The following passage illustrates al-Kindi's appreciation of the ancient philosophers:

> We owe great thanks to those who have imparted to us even a small measure of truth, let alone those who have taught us more, since they have given us a share in the fruits of their reflection and simplified the complex questions bearing on the nature of reality. If they had not provided us with those premises that pave the way to truth, we would have been unable, despite our assiduous lifelong investigations, to find those true primary principles from which the conclusions of our obscure inquiries have resulted, and which have taken generation upon generation to come to light heretofore.[14]

Reasoning from first principles rather than starting from quranic teachings, al-Kindi sought nonetheless to establish the truths of religion on rational grounds. That he found himself in conflict with Traditionalist Muslims should not surprise students of early and medieval Christianity, where the same conflict between reason and revelation occurred.

Al-Farabi (d. 950).   Abu Nasr Muhammad ibn Tarkhan al-Farabi, a Turk, studied and wrote in the Abbasid capital, Baghdad, though he journeyed also to Egypt and Syria. Farabi studied logic from the masters of his day, in which field he showed himself to be of more subtle mind than al-Kindi. Baghdad in the tenth century was home to many scholars, some of them Christians, in logic and in related sciences, such as rhetoric. Again, we discover in philosophers such as al-Kindi and al-Farabi intellectual interests that transcended Islamic religion or, rather, that sought to integrate Islamic beliefs with other metaphysical systems. For example, in the field of political philosophy, Farabi wrote about Plato's Republic, in which he substituted the Islamic notion of prophet as ruler in place of Plato's philosopher-king. Farabi also gave the emanationist philosophy of Neo-Platonism much place in his own evolving system, as did many other Muslim, Jewish, and Christian philosophers in the Middle Ages.

Ibn Sina (d. 1037). Abu 'Ali Husayn ibn Sina is known in the West as Avicenna. He was born near Bukhara, in Khurasan. Like all Muslims, Ibn Sina began his studies in the Islamic disciplines. In typical fashion for him, he tells us with no attempt at modesty, "I had completed the study of the Qu'ran and a major part of Arabic letters [*adab*], so much so that people wondered at my attainments."[15] He is even more pointed in recounting how quickly and thoroughly he surpassed his teachers in logic, metaphysics, and other philosophical subjects. More of his works than those of al-Kindi and al-Farabi were translated into Latin. One modern biographer has counted nearly 300 works or fragments of works in print or in manuscript. In the Middle Ages in Europe, Ibn Sina was known both as a philosopher and as a physician. His best known work, the *Kitab al-shifa'*, "Book of Healing," was widely read among Latin and Arab Christian thinkers. Like most of the philosophers in Islamicate society, Ibn Sina was attacked by Sunni jurists and theologians for his heterodox religious views. In the next chapter we will mention one such attack, from the great thinker of the Islamic Middle Ages, al-Ghazali (d. 1111).

FIGURE 7.2 Al-Razi (left), ninth century, and Avicenna, eleventh century. Two noted philosopher/physicians.

In addition to the Greek philosophical tradition, Ibn Sina was greatly influenced by the illuminationist tradition in Sufism, a form of theosophical reflection called *ishraqi* philosophy in Islam. These latter works, few in number, contain a much different discourse than commentaries on the Greek tradition, like the *Kitab al-shifa'*. Also of interest to Ibn Sina was the Neo-Platonist tradition, expounded in a treatise that had been composed by Isma'ili Shi'i authors, titled *Epistles of the Brethren of Purity*.

Ibn Rushd (d. 1198). Abu l-Walid Muhammad ibn Ahmad ibn Rushd, known in the West as Averroes, lived and wrote in Muslim Spain. Like Ibn Sina, his education began in the traditional way, with study of the Qur'an, hadith, and fiqh (jurisprudence). And like Ibn Sina and many other philosophers in the Middle Ages, Ibn Rushd studied medicine, which he practiced along with his duties as a teacher and a qadi (judge). He was recognized as a master commentator on the works of Aristotle by his Jewish contemporary, Moses Maimonides (d. 1204), and later by the great Latin Christian Aristotelian, St. Thomas Aquinas (d. 1274). Al-Ghazali's attack on the philosophy of Ibn Sina, titled *Incoherence of the Philosophers*, drew a reply from Ibn Rushd, titled *Incoherence of the Incoherence*. It is a carefully reasoned work that faults al-Ghazali, not for his reading of earlier Muslim philosophers like Ibn Sina, but rather for his understanding of Aristotelian philosophy.[16] Ibn Rushd's works were translated into Latin and enjoyed wide reading, comment, and refutation in the late European Middle Ages. Today numerous analytical translations of his Arabic works have been made into English and European languages.

Brethren of Purity. Along with the writings of Plato and Aristotle on logic, physics, metaphysics, politics and ethics, more esoteric Greek writings on Pythagoreanism and Neo-Platonism were translated into Arabic, where they enjoyed considerable reading and influence. Among the Islamic religious world views that favored esoteric interpretations of texts was that of the Isma'ili Shi'a. It will be recalled from Chapter 5 that the more radical Isma'ilis were propagandists who sought to subvert the Sunni Abbasid regime. During the Buyid Age of the tenth century, when Shi'i warlords ruled eastern Islam, and an Isma'ili regime, the Fatimids, ruled in North Africa and Egypt, Isma'ili *da'wa*, "propaganda," activities became more intense. The most violent of these were the so-called Assassins. However, the Isma'ili Shi'a, then as now, were also philosophers and thinkers of merit.

In Basra during the tenth century, a secret society was formed, called the *Ikhwan al-Safa*, "Brethren of Purity." It was a fraternal society of philosophers committed to a common search for truth and a way of life bent on avoiding the pitfalls of this world. Its members were later exposed as being Isma'ili religious philosophers. They nonetheless produced a work of considerable interest at the time, called *Epistles of the Brethren of Purity*. We have seen that Aristotelian philosophers like Ibn Sina were influenced by this work, despite its different tenor from the Greek philosophical heritage. It consisted of fifty-two epistles and was eclectic in the scope of knowledge it sought to integrate with the teachings of the Qur'an, the Prophet, and the Isma'ili imams. In one passage from *Epistles*, the society's members are described as pledging

> to shun no science, scorn any book, or to cling fanatically to no single creed. For [their] own creed encompasses all others and comprehends all the sciences generally. This creed is the consideration of all existing things, both sensible and intelligible, from beginning to end, whether hidden or overt, manifest or obscure. . .in so far as they all derive from a single principle, a single cause, a single world, and a single Soul.[17]

The emanationst philosophies of Islamic Neo-Platonism and Isma'ili Shi'i sm were part of the varied intellectual landscape of medieval Islam. At once more eclectic and inclusive than the Sunni or other Shi'i madhhabs, the Isma'ilis were driven underground to conduct their intellectual activities. Eventually they thrived in places like India, where religious pluralism has been the norm. Today, the Isma'ili Shi'a remain a small but vital part of the world of Islam.

The formation of Islamic religious thought during the first few centuries produced a number of madhhabs and trends now considered to be heterodox, outside the mainstream of Sunni (or Twelver Shi'i) Islam. It is best, perhaps, to think of Islam today as a dynamic and varied theological and ritual system that was forged out of these different trends. Today, some of these early trends, like the Traditionalism of Ahmad ibn Hanbal, are more influential than others, like that of that of the rationalist Mu'tazila. Nonetheless, they are all still there in the historical consciousness of Muslims. Our next task is to look more closely at the orthodox movements and thinkers that emerged from intellectual dramas of these early centuries.

NOTES

1. For an account of Christian-Jewish polemics in fourth-century Syria, see Robert L. Wilken, *John Chrysostom and the Jews: Rhetoric and Reality in the Late 4th Century* (Berkeley: University of California Press, 1983).
2. On the institutional comparson of universities and theology in Islam and in the West, see George Makdisi, *The Rise of Humanism in Classical Islam and the Christian West: With Special Reference to Scholasticism* (Edinburgh: University Press, 1990), esp. Ch. 1.
3. An excellent history of the early period of Islamic thought is W. Montgomery Watt, *The Formative Period of Islamic Thought* (Edinburgh: Edinburgh University Press, 1973).
4. Watt, *Formative Period*, p. 80.
5. Watt, *Formative Period*, p. 209.
6. Translated in *Textual Sources for the Study of Islam*, ed. and trans. Andrew Rippin and Jan Knappert (Manchester: Manchester University Press, 1986), p. 115.

7. *Textual Sources*, pp. 118–19.
8. *Textual Sources*, p. 120–21.
9. 'Abd al-Jabbar, *Sharh al-usul al-khamsa* [Commentary on the five fundamentals (of religion)], ed. 'Abd al-Karim 'Uthman (Cairo: Maktabat al-Wahba, 1965), p. 39.
10. For more on the Mu'tazila, see Watt, *Formative Period*, pp. 209–50.
11. *Encyclopaedia of Islam*, 2nd ed., s.v. "Ahmad b. Hanbal."
12. On the Mihna and Ibn Hanbal's role in it, see *Encyclopaedia of Islam*, 2nd ed., s.v. "Mihna."
13. On the Shi'i theologians in early Islam, see Watt, *Formative Period*, pp. 252–78, and Abdulaziz Abdulhussein Sachedina, *Islamic Messianism: The Idea of the Mahdi in Twelver Shi'ism* (Albany, N.Y.: State University of New York Press, 1981).
14. Quoted by Majid Fakhry, *A History of Islamic Philosophy* (New York and London: Columbia University Press, 1970), p. 87.
15. Quoted by Fakhry, *Islamic Philosophy*, p. 149.
16. Fakhry, *Islamic Philosophy*, p. 308.
17. Quoted by Fakhry, *Islamic Philosophy*, p. 187.

8

Sunni

Islamic

Thought

RELIGIOUS AUTHORITY

It has been observed earlier that the word *islam* connotes religious practice rather than beliefs. A Muslim, then, is one who follows "orthoprax" behavior (right practice) in performing religious duties. The term "orthodoxy" (right belief) relates more to *iman*, "belief, faith." A believer is a *mu'min*, from the same root as iman. We have seen that Islam is structured institutionally in such a way that the contents of iman are supplied by: (1) a book, the Qur'an; (2) prophetic example, the Sunna; and (3) for Shi'i Muslims, the teachings of the imams (an extended sense of the Sunna and hadith not recognized by Sunni Muslims). An important question lies behind the history of Islamic thought, which we began to explore in the previous chapter: What religious institution defines and preserves right belief in Islamic societies? For Christians, the answer is "the church" in some sense of the word: the papacy for Roman Catholics; and councils and synods for Orthodox and much of Protestant Christianity.

Models of Ritual and Doctrinal Authority

Shi'i Islam, as we have seen, recognized a central institutional authority for defining and preserving right belief and practice after the death of the Prophet, the office of the imamate. This central symbol of authority differed from the Roman papacy, which also vests authority in an infallible religious leader, insofar as the Shi'i imams after the early centuries of Islam have led their communities in absentia, in occultation (*ghayba*), expected to return to this world to defeat God's enemies and restore God's teachings and justice. This is the doctrine of the *mahdi*, which forms a distinctive doctrine of messianism in Islam. Also, neither Shi'i nor Sunni ulama perform sacraments—rituals of divine power that ordinary Muslims cannot perform.

Sunni Islam, which shares a majority of its beliefs and practices with Shi'i Muslims, evolved a different structure of authority. We will speak more about the institution of the ulama in Chapter 13 below. Here the main point to note is that neither a single infallible religious authority, such as the Pope in Roman Catholicism, nor councils of higher clergy, such as the Church Councils of Orthodox Christianity and councils of monks in early Buddhism, characterize Islamic patterns of religious authority. The Christian and Buddhist councils acted to canonize scripture and other sacred texts, construct creeds, define religious doctrine, and deal with deviations from "orthodoxy." How did the main body of Muslims, Sunni Islam, form a tradition of religious orthodoxy without imams, popes, or councils of clergy?

A closer model of Sunni authority and doctrinal orthodoxy is found in rabbinical Judaism. Oral Torah, later written down and called Mishna in Judaism, established from the beginning a dialectical process of disputation among teachers, generation after generation, on the interpretation of Written Torah, the Pentateuch. In Islam during the early centuries, the *ahl al-sunna wa l-jama'a*, "People of the Sunna and the Community," adopted similar dialectical processes for resolving questions about Islamic belief and practice. Questions about law and ritual were brought before the fuqaha (jurists), and questions about doctrine were disputed among mutakallimun (theologians), as we saw in the previous chapter. Trends in legal interpretation arose geographically behind the names of early jurists (Abu Hanifa, Ibn Hanbal, al-Shafi'i, and Malik ibn Anas), and trends in religious doctrine formed around the names of certain mutakallimun—al-Ash'ari and al-Maturidi in particular, about whom more will be said in this chapter. These trends in interpretation, which take the name madhhab in Arabic, were written down and taught from one generation to the next. No central office or council guaranteed the authority of al-Shafi'i or al-Ash'ari, however. It was the process of disputation and interpretation itself that was constant.

The Gate of Ijtihad

The Islamic processual model of deriving authoritative interpretations of ritual and creed had, in the absence of infallible leaders of councils, another doctrine that guaranteed the unity of Islamic practice and belief. In the tenth century, at the close of the age of the great collections of hadith and the founding of the major madhhabs in jurisprudence (some say as late as the twelfth or thirteenth century), jurists propounded the doctrine of the *Closing of the Gate of Ijtihad*. Ijtihad, as we have seen, is the technical term for independent reasoning. From the beginning, Sunni Islam has expressed a strong distaste for innovation (*bid'a*) in ritual practice and doctrinal belief. And, as we saw in Caliph al-Ma'mun's *mihna*, "inquisition," of civil servants who would not subscribe to the Mu'tazili doctrine of the created Qur'an (see Chapter 7), Islamic society resisted not only innovation in creed, but any attempt to articulate and enforce public creeds at all.

What the ulama declared to be Islamic orthopraxy and orthodoxy was not so much an inviolable code of ritual practice or creed as it was four interpretive roots of legal reasoning, the *usul al-fiqh*: the Qur'an, the Sunna, Consensus, and Analogical Reasoning. The doctrine of the four usul al-fiqh was more important than drawing up an authoritative statement of what they contained. Divergences of interpretation were allowed among the four Sunni madhhabs. The overall unity of information and teaching derived from the Qur'an and the Sunna was held in check, at least in theory, by the legal conceit of the Gate of Ijtihad. It was also a doctrine that valued the interpretations of earlier authorities, the *salaf*, over the generations of jurists after the central caliphate lost its authority to rule to the Buyid warlords (945). Independent reasoning was no longer necessary, according to this doctrine.

By the tenth century, the companions of the Prophet, their followers, and the founders of the major hadith collections and legal madhhabs had constructed orthodox Islamic belief and practice. In other words, the Qur'an and the Sunna *meant* what the earliest generations concluded they meant. The consensus of the Muslim umma, especially its ulama, was also acceptable, particularly the agreements among the earliest authorities. Interpretive arguments drawn by analogy were acceptable, but again, the arguments made by earlier authorities were felt by many to be sufficient.

Of course, what has been described as a legal conceit was just that. Muslim jurists did not stop thinking, or think only in ancient patterns, after the ulama declared the Gate of Ijtihad closed in the tenth century. The reasoning and considered opinions of the ulama continued to be the driving force of Sunni intellectualism and world views, as Islamic historical circumstances changed dramatically, century after century. Nonetheless, it is the framework of the usul al-fiqh that best characterizes Sunni world views. Therefore, it is important to consider the jurist most responsible for establishing the four usul al-fiqh as they are understood today: Muhammad al-Shafi'i.

Muhammad al-Shafi'i (d. 820)

Abu 'Abdallah Muhammad ibn Idris al-Shafi'i died just thirteen years before Caliph al-Ma'mun publicly favored the theological teachings of the Mu'tazili mutakallimun. This is important to note, because in the evolving struggle between the political authority (caliphate) and religious authority (ulama), the early Abbasid caliphs intervened in religious affairs openly. As we saw in the last chapter, Ahmad ibn Hanbal was responsible for successfully challenging caliphal authority to meddle in determining religious practice and doctrine. Muhammad al-Shafi'i was the scholar who laid the intellectual foundations for the Sunni ulama and the world view they propounded after the ninth century.

Al-Shafi'i was a Meccan Arab of the tribe of Quraysh. He first studied law in Mecca and Medina, the "home of tradition" (hadith), as one scholar has pointed out.[1] In the Hijaz (Arabia), he studied with Malik ibn Anas, the founder of another legal madhhab. Political intrigue got him sent in chains to Iraq, where he was brought before Caliph Harun al-Rashid. In Iraq he came into contact with Muhammad al-Shaybani (d. 805), the pupil of the founder of yet another legal madhhab, that of Abu Hanifa. In Iraq, under the influence of al-Shaybani's legal mindset, al-Shafi'i decided to give up politics (with good reason) and take up the study of hadith and fiqh for the rest of his life.

Soon al-Shafi'i and al-Shaybani fell into conflict over points of legal reasoning. This occurred in the form of disputations (munazarat), not so much between the two scholars as between their pupils, as was often the case when legal and theological madhhabs engaged in public disputations. The Hanafi madhhab espoused by Shaybani recognized the considered legal opinion (ra'y) of the individual scholar more than other madhhabs were willing to do. The Mu'tazili mutakallimun were predominantly Hanafite in fiqh. Al-Shafi'i decided to leave Baghdad and return to Mecca, where he met yet another founder of a legal madhhab, Ahmad ibn Hanbal, with whom he got on well. After teaching for a while in Mecca and later again in Iraq, he left in 814 for Egypt, where he spent the rest of his life.

Al-Shafi'i wrote numerous works on Islamic jurisprudence. Perhaps the best known is his Risala, a systematic treatise on the sources (usul) of legal reasoning.[2] In the Risala, al-Shafi'i set forth his doctrine of the importance of hadith, along with the Qur'an, as a textual authoritative source in Islam. He also began a discourse that was in the next generations to establish the four usul al-fiqh (Qur'an, Sunna, consensus, and analogy) as Sunni doctrine. As with hadith, he set strict limits on legitimate consensus and reasoning by analogy. In his disputes in Iraq with Hanafi jurists, and in his close association with Malik and Ibn Hanbal in Mecca, al-Shafi'i was disposed to distance himself from the rationalism of the Mu'tazila.

Muhammad al-Junayd (d. 910)

Abu l-Qasim Muhammad al-Junayd was born in Iran and moved to Baghdad, where, a century after Muhammad al-Shafi'i, he studied the legal teachings of the latter, along with the other religious sciences. Junayd's life indicates another form of religious authority and guidance in the history of Sunni Islam, that of mysticism (Sufism). The Sufi world view of the so-called "sober" [serious] madhhab of Junayd was in sharp contrast to that of the "intoxicated" Sufism of al-Bistami (see Chapter 5). The sober form of Sufism was well expressed by al-Qurayshi: "We did not take Sufism from talk and words, but from hunger and renunciation of the world and cutting off the things to which we were accustomed and which we found agreeable."[3] The point to be made here about Sufism is that the master/disciple relationship, which Sufism came to epitomize, was another pattern of authority that many Muslims found congenial. Many (but not all) Sufis like al-Junayd became recognized members of the ulama for their mastery of the Qur'an, Qur'an commentary, hadith, kalam, and the other religious sciences. Nonetheless, although they were often accused of teaching heterodox ideas, the Sufi orders saw themselves as providing spiritual environments and methods for getting inside the Qur'an and the Sunna to discover their internal secrets and have more direct communion with the divine. Sunni Islam in Egypt and North Africa, Turkey, South Asia, and Indonesia has been strongly influenced by the mystical teachings of Junayd and other Sufis.

SUNNI KALAM

The Mu'tazili mutakallimun, as we saw in the preceding chapter, lost political favor and public sympathy, owing in part to the doctrines and excessive rationalism that men like Muhammad al-Shafi'i and Ahmad ibn Hanbal found reprehensible. Nonetheless, the intellectual pursuit of kalam was not dead. Two generations after Ibn Hanbal's heroic stand against Mu'tazili teachings, another mutakallim stepped forward to champion a theological discourse that reflected the religious ideas of men like al-Shafi'i and Ibn Hanbal. That mutakallim was Abu l-Hasan al-Ash'ari.

Abu l-Hasan al-Ash'ari (d. 935)

Toward the end of the ninth century, Abu l-Hasan al-Ash'ari was born in Basra, the earliest center of kalam studies. He began his career as a brilliant student of one of the leading Mu'tazili theologians of the day, Abu 'Ali al-Jubba'i (d. 915). Later biographers report that one night al-Ash'ari had a dream in which he was advised of the errors of Mu'tazili thinking and interpretation. Henceforth he left his Mu'tazili mentor and founded the school that would be named after him, the Ash'ariyya, which came to be regarded as the main orthodox school of kalam in Sunni Islam. Al-Ash'ari died in 935.

Until al-Ash'ari's time, the main opponents of the Mu'tazila had been a pious group of thinkers among the ulama known as the "Hadith People," or Traditionists. Their mindset we have called "Traditionalism." Traditionalists like Ahmad ibn Hanbal (d. 855) greatly distrusted the use of independent

reasoning and reliance upon thought—methods that were characteristic of the mutakallimun. The Traditionalists insisted on a literal interpretation of the Qur'an (including its anthropomorphic passages) and on the authority of the Prophet's Sunna; these, they argued, must be the sole sources of religious knowledge *bila kayf*, "without (asking) how." The opposition between the Traditionalists and the Mu'tazila raised the very important question of the relation between reason and tradition as sources of religious knowledge. In the West, this problem is usually comprehended as reason versus revelation. In both Islam and Christianity during the Middle Ages, the problem was very much the same.

Al-Ash'ari and the mutakallimun who followed him accepted reason as a legitimate tool or instrument in understanding the sources of Islamic faith. But the Ash'ariyya were more careful to defend and explain popular Islamic beliefs—that is, tradition— rather than subject these matters to rational criticism. Whereas the Mu'tazila had fallen into political disfavor with the Abbasid court, the Ash'ariyya became for the next few centuries the leading thinkers of Sunni Islam. Most of the leading Ash'arite mutakallimun were Shafi'i in fiqh. This association of Ash'ari kalam and Shafi'i fiqh, though not rigid, has lasted down to the present day.[4]

Abu Mansur al-Maturidi (d. 944)

In Transoxiana (Central Asia), far from the Iraqi intellectual circles of Basra and Baghdad, the teachings of al-Shafi'i and al-Ash'ari were not very influential. The Hanafi madhhab in fiqh was much stronger in the northeastern regions of Islam. Although Mu'tazili mutakallimun established teaching circles in these regions, orthodox kalam came to be identified with the teachings of Abu Mansur al-Maturidi, a contemporary (but not an acquaintance) of Abu l-Hasan al-Ash'ari. Little is known about the life of al-Maturidi. The kalam madhhab that goes by his name, the "Maturidiyya," was more rationalist than the Ash'ariyya. It was not until several centuries after al-Maturidi that Turkish conquerors, the Seljuqs and Ottomans, promoted Maturidi kalam widely, perhaps as a foil to the influence of Ash'ari kalam and Shafi'i fiqh in Iraq. In addition, the teachings of al-Maturidi in kalam are found today in Southeast Asia, where they are considered Sunni orthodoxy along with the teachings of al-Ash'ari.

The Maturidi mutakallimun taught that iman "faith" consists in the inner consent of the heart when one confesses his or her faith; the Ash'ariyya, on the other side, held that iman consists in word *and* deed (e.g., performance of the religious duties), and hence one's faith can be judged by other human beings. The Ash'ariyya rejected the Mu'tazili doctrine of free will (qadar), as we have seen, whereas the Maturidiyya accepted the notion that a person's belief or unbelief (iman or kufr) is a matter of free will, not predestination. In

some other doctrines, the Maturidi school was closer to the Ash'ariyya than to the Mu'tazila.[5]

ABU HAMID AL-GHAZALI (1058–1111)

Ninth-century questions regarding free will and predestination, the problem of good and evil, and the proper form of Islamic government were, by the eleventh century, answered according to definite systems of thought by Sunni and Shi'i theologians. This produced what historians of thought refer to as *scholasticism*. Schools of thought became doctrinaire in posture, abstract in modes of expression. The religious and the nonreligious sciences became much too sophisticated for the average Muslim to grasp. By the eleventh century, most Traditionalists and some mutakallimun believed that it was harmful to the faith of the average person to study theology. Others believed that religious knowledge and secular knowledge were incompatible. The average Muslim regarded the abstract study of most of these sciences, secular *and* religious, as irrelevant to his or her personal spiritual life. By the eleventh century, the time had arrived for a religious and intellectual synthesis of these repellent trends. Abu Hamid al-Ghazali (1058–1111) looms large in Islamic intellectual history for providing such a synthesis.[6]

Ghazali was born in Tus, near the modern city of Meshed in northeastern Iran. Like most Muslim boys, he obtained his early education with a shaykh at a mosque, where he learned to recite the Qur'an by rote memory. Later he was sent to the college at the provincial capital of Nishapur. There he advanced through the usual religious curriculum of Qur'an, Traditions, and Law. His greatest teacher was an Ash'arite theologian at Nishapur, Imam al-Haramayn al-Juwayni. By this time the Ash'ari school was the leading school of theology in Sunni Islam, and the Mu'tazilites were less influential than they had been a century earlier.

Al-Ghazali wrote numerous books, many of which have survived and have been translated into Western languages. One of the most interesting was his autobiography, *Deliverance from Error*. Reading through it, we gain glimpses of a searching, often deeply troubled quest for peace of mind on religious matters. Al-Ghazali's lifelong scholarly pursuit of an intellectual grasp of the truths of religion reminds us of the great Christian theologian Saint Augustine. Like Augustine, al-Ghazali as a young man found his religious faith severely tested by the conflicting intellectual currents of his day. In the eleventh century, orthodox Sunni and Shi'i religious thought were by no means the only religious world views circulating in the Abode of Islam. Many Muslims were being drawn into the "errors" of rival and heretical religious groups. The more devout Sunni Muslims remained persuaded of the Traditionalist path of accepting the authority of the Qur'an and the Sunna

"without asking how," that is, on faith alone. Others were persuaded by the arguments of non-Muslim and radical Muslim heresies.

The Case Against the Esoterists

As with Augustine's intellectual odyssey, al-Ghazali was drawn for a while into the semi-philosophic movement known as Skepticism. Both in Augustine's and in al-Ghazali's times, the Skeptics advanced arguments that seemed to shatter religious and scientific assumptions. In the West, Skepticism had originated in Plato's Academy. In the East, a similar philosophical trend of thought had flourished in the Sassanian court of the Persians. By al-Ghazali's time, the radical Isma'ili Shi'a had assumed many of the doctrines of the Skeptics, especially their political tactics, mentioned in previous chapters. These radical Isma'ili Shi'a were known as the *Batiniyya*, which means "esoterists." As a philosophical movement, Skepticism raised serious questions about the reliability of reason and sense perception for determining knowledge and truth. As a religious movement, Skepticism substituted absolute faith in the teachings of a charismatic leader for the more usual reliance of the faithful upon the face value of tradition and the teachings of the ulama. As a political movement, Skepticism created cadres of propagandists and missionaries devoted to the subversion of the established government and their supporters, the leading figures of the Sunni ulama.

One of al-Ghazali's early works was a treatise against the Batiniyya. The Batiniyya claimed that their teachings came from the Qur'an and the Sunna of the Prophet. But *batin* means "secret," or "gnostic." The literal meaning of the Qur'an and the Sunna urged by the Traditionalists, and the more abstract meanings argued by the Mu'tazila and other theologians, were replaced by the Batiniyya with secret meanings that bore no literal or obvious rational relation to the actual words of the texts. The imam or semi-divine head of the Batiniyya assumed absolute authority to interpret the sacred texts of Islam in ways that the average Muslim, the trained members of the ulama, and the rational arguments of the theologians could not refute. Appealing to the emotional devotion of the masses to the Qur'an and the Sunna, the Batiniyya fomented social and political anarchy with secret teachings. Whether seen as an attack from without or within the Islamic umma, the effect upon the political and intellectual stability within the Abode of Islam was profound.

For this reason, in 1094 the caliph in Baghdad commissioned al-Ghazali to write a refutation of the Batinites. In this and several books written much later, including *Deliverance from Error*, we see the complexity of issues—religious, theological, and political—that the Isma'ili Shi'a stirred up within the Abode of Islam. Al-Ghazali recognized that at the level of the simplest minds, he would have to show that the Qur'an urges humankind to follow logical principles in clarifying religious truths, not the illogic of secret teachings. In another line of attack (or polemic) against the Batiniyya, al-Ghazali argued against the general Shi'i notion of a charismatic leader in the imam, by pointing out that Islam has such a leader in Muhammad. The Sunna of the Prophet is, along with the Qur'an and the Consensus of the ulama, a sufficient source of charismatic leadership, said al-Ghazali. It seems that he was trying to restore the intellectual appeal of Sunni Islam by showing that in the traditional sources and in the Prophet himself, Islam has a spiritual source and figure par excellence.

The Case Against the Philosophers

In 1091, al-Ghazali received an appointment to a theological college, or *madrasa*, in Baghdad known as the Nizamiya. It was named after the famed Sunni Muslim statesman Nizam al-Mulk. The college opened in 1067, and its faculty was dominated by theologians of the Ash'ari school and legal theorists of the Shafi'i madhhab in fiqh. The more conservative Traditionists and Hanbalite legal theorists resented its opening, but the real target of Nizamiya faculty teachings, especially after al-Ghazali arrived, were the philosophers and the Batiniyya. Resuming our comparison of al-Ghazali with Saint Augustine, we may note that both men were attracted to the intellectual discipline of philosophy. The Neo-Platonism that was so prevalent in the Mediterranean world in Augustine's lifetime (354–430) was still influential in the eleventh and twelfth centuries, when al-Ghazali lived. Unlike Aristotle's philosophy, which had first inspired the philosophical movement in Islam, Neo-Platonism was more conducive to religious systems. For this reason, many of the Muslim philosophers, such as al-Kindi (ca. 800–873) and Ibn Sina (Avicenna, 980–1037), combined the more logical characteristics of Aristotle's philosophy with the religious doctrines of Neo-Platonism. Thus, for example, Aristotle had held that matter, the basic substance of the world, was eternal and indestructible. This view was difficult to reconcile with the monotheistic doctrine of creation out of nothing. The Neo-Platonists, on the other hand, held that the cosmos was made up of a succession of grades or realms of being, from matter to pure spirit. The world of human experience was the result of emanations downward from the One (pure spirit) into the corruptible many in the realm of matter. But the process reverses itself as the many seek to escape the corruption of the realm of matter and return to the One. Thus Neo-Platonism offered a philosophical (and highly abstract) way of rationalizing the monotheistic doctrines of creation and salvation.

Although Traditionists and Hanbalites would accept only the literal concepts of creation and salvation articulated in the Qur'an and the Sunna, philosophers argued that scriptures such as the Qur'an were allegorical explanations of divine, philosophic truths, aimed at simpler minds. Only philosophers understand the full rational truth of God's revelation to humankind (scripture). Prophets, in the view of Muslim philosophers like

Avicenna, are the most perfect philosophers, for they comprehend both the rational truths of the divine mind and the simpler expression of those same truths in the stories and allegories of scripture. The Muslim philosophers in the Middle Ages believed, with Plato's *Republic*, which had been translated into Arabic, that the best founders and rulers of society were philosopher-kings (prophets). Prophets, then, in the view of many Muslim philosophers, were conceived of as Plato had conceived of kings in the *Republic*.

Al-Ghazali carefully read and considered the works of Muslim philosophers such as Ibn Sina, whom we met previously, as well as the works of Greek philosophers translated into Arabic. He was not unmindful of the lack of intellectual sophistication that a religion may have when truths and beliefs are claimed without justification. Philosophers attempt to be systematic and logical in their treatment of thought. One thing troubled him about philosophy, however. Even those philosophers who claimed to be Muslims, such as al-Kindi and Ibn Sina, were accused of not explaining, but of explaining away Islamic beliefs. While he was teaching at the Nizamiya in Baghdad, al-Ghazali wrote *The Incoherence of the Philosophers*, a point-by-point refutation of several inconsistencies he found in the writings of Ibn Sina. His basic argument was that reason, so highly exalted by the philosophers, works very well in disciplines such as logic and mathematics, but when philosophers attempt to rationalize divine truths and metaphysics, their arguments are filled with confusions and inconsistencies. In a word, they become unphilosophical. Thus al-Ghazali did not deprecate rational thought, as the Traditionalists and some theologians were accused of doing, but he carefully restricted the limits of reason in apprehending divine truth. As we saw in the last chapter also, a century later in Islamic Spain al-Ghazali's *Incoherence of the Philosophers* was refuted by Ibn Rushd in a work called *The Incoherence of the Incoherence*.

Influence of Sufism

Toward the end of his teaching career in Baghdad, al-Ghazali underwent a severe period of mental and emotional unrest, brought about in part by his inability to find intellectual peace of mind in any of the disciplines and movements to which other scholars were devoted. Even the theology of the Ash'ari theologians he found spiritually bankrupt and intellectually stagnant. Moreover, his worldly success as a famed teacher, to whom the caliphs turned for professorial guidance, was distasteful to him. In a work that was given the English title of *Faith and Practice*, al-Ghazali reflects on the final moments of despair before he turned to the mystical understanding of Islam that was professed and practiced by the Sufis. Al-Ghazali's own words speak best at this point.

> Lastly I turned to the way of the mystics. I knew that in their path there has to be both knowledge and activity, and that the object of the latter is to purify the self

from vices and faults of character. Knowledge was easier for me than activity. I began by reading their books. . .and obtained a thorough intellectual understanding of their principles. Then I realized that what is most distinctive of them can be attained only by personal experience ("taste"–*dhawq*), ecstasy and a change of character. . . . I saw clearly that the mystics were men of personal experience not of words, and that I had gone as far as possible by way of study and intellectual application, so that only personal experience and walking in the mystic way were left.[7]

The moment in his life to which al-Ghazali referred occurred about 1095. He reports that some days he was so disturbed that he couldn't even utter words during his lectures, and soon his health declined so far as to require physicians. But there could be no physical antidote for a malady that was psychological and spiritual. Finally, in a drastic move inspired by Sufism, he resigned his teaching post, made arrangements for the maintenance of his family, and left Baghdad for Syria. He spent two years in Damascus exploring mystical doctrine and ways of life. He received much criticism from the ulama, for here was one of the most famous intellectuals of the day shirking his duties and responsibilities as a professor, husband, and father, in order to retire to the suspect life of the mystic. What did al-Ghazali hope to find in "the Path" of Sufism? Sufism, to which we have referred in earlier chapters and to which we shall return below and again in Chapter 15, promised a certainty of faith, but not through reason, theology, or philosophy. It drew Muslims from all walks of life into practices and states of mind that produced the felt experience of nearness or union with God. The Qur'an, the Sunna of the Prophet, and the obligatory duties of worship, as understood in Sufism, had special mystical meanings. Tawhid, the cornerstone on which Islamic theology is laid, meant for Sufis the *experience* of union with God. The Sufis who sought this experience found it either as solitary wanderers or as disciples, gathered in special communities that were directed by a renowned "Friend of God" (*wali*) or saint. In both cases—on the road or gathered in communities—the Sufis withdrew from the open society of war, commerce, and politics. They felt that society, even at best when structured according to the demands of the Shari'a, causes one to forget God. Al-Ghazali finally realized that even a highly honored calling in society—teaching in a respected theological academy—was pulling him in the wrong direction. And so he took up the Path.

After some years with Sufism, al-Ghazali finally resumed a state-appointed teaching post, this time in Nishapur, where he had first studied with al-Juwayni. Shortly before he died in 1111, he retired to his hometown of Tus, where he continued to write until the end.

Al-Ghazali's Achievement

Scholars, both Muslim and non-Muslim, have argued the overall achievement of al-Ghazali in Islamic intellectual history. Some have found him rather overbearing in his frequent statements of self-esteem, a quality he seems to have shared with other philosophers, such as Ibn Sina. Others have doubted the sincerity of his conversion to Sufism or the extent to which he actually adopted its path and discipline. But almost all historians agree that he had a profound effect upon the history of thought in Islam, and many would say that the spiritual dimension of Islam as a living faith was revived by al-Ghazali. In what is perhaps his greatest work, *Revivification of the Sciences of Religion*, al-Ghazali carefully worked out both the rational and spiritual bases of the Islamic religion. The work is a magnificent achievement in the history of religious thought. It has been cited by Muslim intellectuals and common folk alike down to this day.

THE LATE MIDDLE AGES

Despite the efforts of Nasir al-Din al-Tusi (see previous chapter) and others to preserve the rich heritage of the classical period and to build upon it, the Mongol invasion and the destruction of the caliphate proved to be a moment of decisive intellectual as well as political change in Islam. Major theological schools and philosophical movements either declined and vanished or simply perpetuated the more creative achievements of the past. An important exception to this trend was Sufism. Among the most important "speculative" sufis were Shihab al-Din Suhrawardi (d. 1191), Jalal al-Din al-Rumi (d. 1273), and Ibn al-'Arabi (d. 1240). The lives and works of these figures belonged to a new trend in Muslim thought known as "Illuminationism," from the Arabic term *ishraqi*, meaning "eastern." Illuminationist philosophy had already been expounded by such important figures as Ibn Sina (Avicenna). Iluminationism was infused with the symbolism of light, which had traditionally played an important role in Persian reflections on the nature of the divine. Another strong influence on this trend of thought was Neo-Platonic philosophy which, as we have seen, conceived of the cosmos in gradations of being from the most perfect and abstract (God) to the material, corruptible realm of earthly existence.

The most important orthodox Sunni thinker of the late medieval period was Taqi al-Din Ibn Taymiya (1263–1328). Ibn Taymiya's intellectual heritage came not from the prevailing Sunni school of theology, the Ash'ariyya, but rather from the more conservative Traditionalists inspired by the Hanbalites. Against the Traditionalists, however, he argued that individual Muslims must follow the teachings of the Qur'an and the Sunna with reason (*ijtihad*), not in blind acceptance of the authority of the ulama (*taqlid*). He also accepted the Mu'tazilite teaching that moral responsibility for human acts must be accepted by each person and not relegated to God alone. Unlike the majority of the Sunni ulama, Ibn Taymiya did not condemn outright the popular teachings of the Sufis of his day, although he did criticize them on many points. While recognizing the importance of the Sufi focus upon the spiritual reality, *al-haqq*, of God, he also faulted the Sufis for what he saw as their moral laxity when they claimed that the ideal of union with God placed them beyond the ritual requirements of the Shari'a.

Despite such figures as Ibn al-'Arabi and Ibn Taymiya, some non-Muslim and Sunni Muslim scholars have characterized the period from the thirteenth through the eighteenth centuries as the "dark age" of Islam. This is perhaps a misconception, due to the predisposition of both groups to appreciate more readily the intellectual achievements of the classical period of the caliphate. The specter of stagnation during the late Middle Ages is raised by the ongoing conflict between the Sunni ulama and Sufism. The sultans, lords, and princes who ruled the various regional empires during this period often gave less support and authority to the ulama. Sufi orders and brotherhoods, on the other hand, gained popular support throughout the Abode of Islam. The ulama often bickered with Sufis when the latter defied orthodox interpretations of the requirements and restrictions of the Shari'a. Illuminationism and Sufism were "inward" religious trends of thought and practice, which during this phase of Islamic history found ready acceptance by great numbers of Muslims.

THE MODERN PERIOD

Islamic thought experienced a "revival" of classical interests in the nineteenth century. Two main reasons are usually given for this revival. First, as we have seen, the dominance of Sufism during the late Middle Ages had led to what many orthodox Muslims regarded as a drifting away from the teachings of the Shari'a. Second, the West, once overshadowed by the unity and power of the Muslim world, was now attempting to control it. The answer to both trends for many Muslim intellectuals was to recapture the vital force of the Islamic past. Like the Humanists of the late Middle Ages in Europe, nineteenth-century Muslim reformers sought to rediscover their true heritage as they believed it had been during the classical ages of the Rashidun and Abbasids.

Many of the reformers, such as Jamal al-Din al-Afghani (1838–1897), Sir Muhammad Iqbal of India (1876–1938), and Muhammad 'Abduh of Egypt (1845–1905), had received traditional Muslim educations as well as training in Western thought. Al-Afghani traveled widely throughout the Muslin world giving speeches and writing pamphlets that urged Muslims to reform their educational curricula and take their Islamic heritage with intellectual seriousness. Iqbal and 'Abduh argued in their influential writings for modernist reforms through the cultivation of science and reason. Both men agreed that Islam, not the West, had been the champion of philosophy and

Reason vs Text!

science when other civilizations had been in decline. Both men argued, in different ways, that the Qur'an and the Muslim world view encourage the use of reason. To put it differently, reason and faith are complementary requisites to the life prescribed by the Shari'a. Also, both men were deeply suspicious of the influence of Western, materialistic values upon the Islamic world.[8]

Islamic thought in the twentieth century has been dominated by social and political concerns. Political and economic control of the regional empires of the late Middle Ages was in the hands of Western powers in the modern period, and as each "colonial possession" has sought and gained its independence, the struggle to retain or regain "Islamic" identity has intensified. Four distinct approaches are often identified. *Modernist* reformers like Iqbal and 'Abduh have argued that Islamic society can recover its past greatness by seeking educational reforms, including modernizing the religious curriculum and educating women. 'Abduh believed that Islam and modernity are not incompatible. In this respect, modernists have often been accused by other Muslims of being "neo-Mu'tazilites," that is, rationalists who do not accept the sole authority of the Qur'an and the Sunna in the modern world. *Revivalist* Islamist reformers like Sayyid Qutb (see Chapter 1) have stressed returning to the traditions of the fathers, the first three generations of Muslims, because of their historical proximity to the time of the Prophet and because they are relatively unsullied by non-Muslim influences. Earlier in the twentieth century, the Islamists were known as the "Salafiyya," that is, the upholders of the traditions of the fathers. In a tradition that goes back to Ibn Taymiya and before, the Islamists have stressed independent reasoning (ijtihad) rather than blind reliance (taqlid) on the teachings of Muslims belonging to the next category, the ulama. *Traditionist* ulama, such as the regional grand muftis and the Shaykh of al Azhar in Egypt, on down to local jurists and other specialists in the religious sciences, often function as the conservative element, struggling to retain their control over the interpretation of the Qur'an and the Sunna in Islamic society. Traditionist ulama in countries where Sunni Islam prevails are often close to the councils of government, and thus quietist in their involvement in domestic politics. *Secularist* Muslims, such as Taha Hussein of Egypt, argued that the religious world view (islam) should be separated from the science and technology of the modern world; islam, in this interpretation, should be an individual and private spiritual matter, protected by the state, but having no direct influence on the public sector.

Sunni Islamic thought, as we have seen, has had a rich and varied history. This and the preceding chapter have tried to show that Sunni Islam cannot be understood without a comparative study of intellectual movements that vied with the Sunni ulama for authority over the minds of ordinary Muslims. Islam today reflects the influence of all these movements, which have waxed and waned over the centuries, but which still live in the Islamic historical consciousness. We conclude this section on Islamic world views with a chapter on Islamic expressions of form and beauty.

NOTES

1. Majid Khadduri, trans., *Islamic Jurisprudence: Shafi'i's Risala* (Baltimore: Johns Hopkins Press, 1961), p. 8.
2. Translated and introduced by Khadduri, *Islamic Jurisprudence*.
3. Cited by Annemarie Schimmel, *Mystical Dimenstions of Islam* (Chapel Hill, N.C.: University of North Carolina Press, 1975), p. 58.
4. See W. Montgomery Watt, *The Formative Period of Islamic Thought* (Edinburgh: Edinburgh University Press, 1973), pp. 279–318.
5. On the comparison of the Ash'ariyya and Maturidiyya, see Watt, *Formative Period*, pp. 312-16.
6. A useful historical and intellectual biography of al-Ghazali is W. Montgomery Watt, *Muslim Intellectual: A Study of Al-Ghazali* (Edinburgh: Edinburgh University Press, 1963).
7. Cited in Watt, *Muslim Intellectual*, p. 135.
8. Muhammad 'Abduh's thought can be studied in the translation of his *Risala fi tawhid*. See Muhammad 'Abduh, *The Theology of Unity*, trans. Ishaq Musa'ad and Kenneth Craqq (New York: Books for Libraries, 1980).

9

Islamic Expressions of Form and Beauty

THE LIMITATIONS OF LANGUAGE

Muslims often ask their Western acquaintances who have read the Qur'an (usually in translation) whether or not they liked it or were persuaded by it. The question is perfectly natural, but those who read a scripture as outsiders to the language and culture in which it was originally expressed have little reason to appreciate it, and they may find it unappealing without intending disrespect. If the initial assignment is not to read the Qur'an in translation, but to listen to the melodic Arabic chant of a trained reciter, or to look at the beautiful pages of the Qur'an in stylized calligraphy, the reaction can be quite different. Calligraphy and chant greet the senses, leaving an artistic rather than an pedantic impression. Art rises above the limitations of specific languages and captures the eye or ear of any beholder or listener. Full appreciation of another religion and culture cannot come from painting, concerts, recordings—in short, not from art through the senses alone. But, as one writer on art and religion has said, artistic expression "opens up the possibility of communication between people who are separated by distances of space and time."[1] Without requiring us first to learn another language, art offers us insight into how others have seen the world—what kind of world created the artist and what kind of world he or she was creating through a specific medium of expression.

In previous chapters we reflected upon many of the diverse elements that come together to form the mosaic of the Islamicate society. The diversity of artistic traditions found within the Abode of Islam is no less varied than other customs and traditions, and yet there exist some distinctive Islamic art styles that articulate the vast cultural unity formed by Islamic peoples.

THE UNIFYING FACTORS OF ART

Several unifying forces contribute to form art styles found in Islamic civilization. The most important of these is the Islamic religion itself. Islam as religion serves as a common foundation upon which other aspects of culture are built. The bond of a common faith creates a certain attitude and a certain world view which are to be found throughout the centuries and the regions of the Islamic world. Common expressions of belief, ritual, and social pattern are in turn reflected in the arts, giving rise to "Islamic" forms of architecture, visual art, and music. Arabic, the language of the Qur'an and the Sunna, becomes a major vehicle for expression in poetry and prose, and its script becomes the medium of the arts of the calligraphers throughout the Islamic world. Another unifying factor was the high mobility of the population. Trade between peoples of diverse cultures brought them into contact with one another. We have seen how population mobility played an important role in the rise of Islam. A ritual process that had enormous social and economic implications for the circulation of goods and ideas was the annual pilgrimage to Mecca from all parts of the Islamic world. The pilgrimage will be studied in full in Chapter 12. Through social contact and a common religious faith, an Islamic art style arose that served to embody these attitudes and beliefs in concrete form. The sense Muslims shared in the ultimate meaning of their world found expression in the arts, and the specific beliefs unique to Islam actually gave rise to a distinctive art style. Such traits as the extensive use of calligraphy and the use of intricate interwoven linear designs can be seen to have been influenced by the importance Islam has placed upon the written word and by the reluctance of Islamic artists to render realistic human and animal forms. In this chapter we will discuss the various arts in the Islamic world, paying special attention to the roles of religious belief and cultural traditions in shaping each particular art form.

THE VISUAL ARTS

Arabesque

The viewer of the arts in Islam becomes immediately aware of the importance given to patterns of abstract design. By avoiding representational motifs, a purely abstract design succeeds in breaking ties with the concrete world. There are no figures or other recognizable forms that relate to one's everyday environment. There is no sense of three dimensions—only an intricate pattern on a flat plane. By seeking to avoid realistic representations of the world around us, which Islamic doctrine forbids, abstract art becomes especially suited to symbolize the quranic world view. By this means, in the case of Islam, abstract art approaches the true reality—the sacred dimension of the spirit—more closely than could any representational artwork. This notion is related to the fact that the rise of Islam also necessitated the rejection of the previously existing nature cults and their pagan mythologies. The art of the nature cults relied heavily upon works depicting natural phenomena, and therefore, with the Islamic rejection of pagan cults, artistic representations of nature also fell from favor. Those attitudes, in combination with a precedent of abstract design in earlier, Byzantine art, partially account for the preference in Islamic art for abstract design.

Abstract designs find their expression in two different yet compatible modes—the straight line and the *arabesque*. The straight line is used in creating geometric patterns. Closed, static forms composed of straight lines represent what is fixed and stable. The geometric forms in their mathematical regularity exhibit clarity and a sense of order. The arabesque, on the other hand, represents growth and change. The curving, interwoven lines of the arabesque call to mind the rampant and vivacious growth of an ivy plant; spreading, twisting, and branching off in numerous directions. Geometric and arabesque patterns of line are often used together, the designs overlapping and interlacing into a complex of intricate configurations that dazzle the imagination as well as the eye. The two modes complement each other, giving a sense of growth and life within a framework of order. The student of religions finds an analogy in arabesque with the order that Islamic teachings provide in directing what would otherwise be a random existence. In art as in religion, human beings create a *cosmos* that yields meaning to their lives.

A precedent for the arabesque can be found in the marginal page illuminations of pre-Islamic Coptic (Egyptian) and Sassanian (Persian) art. In these earlier cultures, vegetal design patterns were used, and the interweaving of stems and leaves for a decorative effect eventually gave way to more abstract forms extended over entire surfaces. Found on mosque and shrine walls and facades, arabesque is frequently used in combination with another basically linear art form that gained supreme importance in the Islamic world, calligraphy.

CALLIGRAPHY

Calligraphy is considered the ultimate achievement in the Islamic arts, for it has the power to render the spoken word in a concrete form. The religions of the Middle East have placed high importance upon the power of the *word*. The Qur'an echoes the biblical and ancient Mesopotamian and Egyptian

FIGURE 9.1　Arabesque panels, al-Aqsa Mosque, Jerusalem. (Courtesy of Cresswell.)

mythical notions of divine creation by words of command. The sending of prophets, so essential to the sacred histories of the monotheistic traditions, was the divine mode of communicating the word to humankind. In earlier chapters we saw how important the revelation of the Qur'an through Muhammad is to Muslims; its revelation forms a sacred time in history, a "time out of time," to repeat Eliade's phrase referred to in Chapter 3. Through the spoken word of Allah, communicated through Muhammad, revelation was rendered visible and preserved in the Arabic script. Since Muhammad claimed only to be a messenger of God, an ordinary human being, the miracle of the Qur'an takes a position of primary importance that touches religious belief, literature, and art, as well as calligraphy itself. For in the artistic modes of quranic recitation and calligraphy, the supernatural role in the historical appearance of Islam is borne witness.

The skillful copying of the sacred words of the Qur'an became a highly cherished talent; the exercise of writing the words themselves became a sacred occupation that required years of patient apprenticeship with a noted shaykh or master. Often words from the Qur'an are elaborated in calligraphy to the point where, like the arabesque, they become abstract patterns interwoven and interlapped into ciphers whose meaning requires careful study to discover. Also, like the arabesque, calligraphy is nonfigural, and thus it is better suited to express the spiritual, nonmaterial side of humankind declared in the message of Islam.

An interesting characteristic of Arabic calligraphy, then, is that it is often difficult to read. We have already mentioned the elaboration of script into abstract design. Consider also that calligraphy may be painted or carved high up on a wall or dome of a mosque, where the viewer on the ground, even with sharp eyesight, has visual difficulty resolving the lines into a script of words. Thus calligraphy, both in design and distance, is neither blatant nor obvious, but subtle, requiring thoughtful reflection. As with the message of God and the Messenger who brought it, it is believed that some will hear it and pay no heed, see it and fail to understand its sense. Rather than detracting from the meaning of the Word by making it appear to be illegible, calligraphy enhances the symbolic quality of the Word. The Word becomes elusive and mysterious. These qualities reinforce the Islamic belief that the true and total meaning of the Qur'an is known only to God.

Calligraphy was also used for more straightforward purposes, such as copying nonquranic manuscripts and decorating buildings and mosques with inscriptions. In the case of literary and scientific works, legibility was of course important. In such works the calligraphy was stylized and artistic, but rendered more obvious to the reader. Inscriptions on buildings were often written in the more angular and difficult Kufic script. Reminding worshippers who enter, quranic inscriptions grace the border facades around the large gates and doors leading into mosques.

FIGURE 9.2 Quranic calligraphy, Kufic style. (Courtesy of Staatlische Museen, Berlin.)

FIGURE 9.3 *Left:* "Allah" in abstract calligraphy. *Right:* "Allah" in normal calligraphy. Can you detect the abstract form of "Allah" in the octagonal rendering?

ARCHITECTURE

Although secular forms of architecture abound in the Islamic world, as elsewhere, the mosque (*masjid*) stands as the example par excellence of an architectural form created to serve religious functions. There is really no standard form of the Islamic mosque, because different regions have developed different forms. Forms common to each region reflect in large part pre-Islamic and local customs. Artistic expression, like language itself, varies from region to region. Different people have different ways of "saying" the same things.

The general mode for the mosque in most Arabic countries is based upon the form of the prophet's house in Medina. Tradition teaches that Muhammad's house was a square building with wide arches and a courtyard, much like the typical houses of Baghdad described in Chapter 4. One functional consideration produced a change over time. The wall that faced in the direction of Mecca, known as the qibla wall, was itself faced by worshippers standing tightly shoulder to shoulder during the prayer. The broader shape of a rectangle better served the function of worship, and in time many mosques, especially in the Arab world, assumed a rectangular shape.

The great mosque of Córdoba, Spain, exemplifies many features of mosques throughout the Arab world. Inside the mosque, in the wall facing Mecca (the qibla wall) is a small niche known as the *mihrab*, which forms the focal point of the mosque. The mihrab is cut into the center of the wall. As in all mosques, it is highly decorated in the styles customary in the geographic region in which it was built. Near the mihrab there is an area set aside for royalty or aristocracy, covered by a canopy. Inside the mosque the limits of the inner space are obscured by rows of columns, by elaborate decoration that uses calligraphy and arabesque designs, and by carvings and stucco decorations. The effect is that one cannot clearly define the space within the mosque. Therefore the space appears possibly limitless, and this adds to the feeling of mystery.

In front of the main building of the mosque is a courtyard, where there is a large fountain for the worshipper to perform ablutions *(wudu')*, the ritual cleansing before the prayer. The courtyard is large in order to serve as a central gathering place for the community. Famous teachers have met their students in this area, or met and disputed points of theology and law in front of their students. The mosque as a whole is a focal point of communication.

Outside most mosques there are one or more minaret towers. Like the church bells tolling from a steeple, the call of the muezzin from the minaret beckons Muslims to the prayer five times each day. Minarets vary greatly in style throughout the Islamic world. Squares, spirals, and tapering cylinders grace skylines in different regions. Some rise up from the mosque building itself; others are freestanding. In the absence of a minaret, a platform located on the roof of the mosque can serve the same purpose.

The main mosque in each city is known as a *jami'*, that is, a cathedral or "Friday" mosque. Often it is the largest mosque in town, more elaborately

FIGURE 9.4   Minbar (pulpit) of mosque in Egypt (Courtesy of Elizabeth Gottschalk.)

decorated than the others. Each Friday the leading religious figure climbs the stairs of the *minbar*, an elevated pulpit structure that stands in front of the qibla wall facing the worshippers, to deliver a sermon.

In Iran, mosques have acquired features somewhat different from those of the Arab type just described. In the courtyard of Iranian mosques are features derived from the style of courtyards in the traditional Persian home. Each wall of the mosque's courtyard has at its center a high *eyvan*, which is a deep hallway, the opening of which is a large niche-shaped chamber that may be decorated with elaborate honeycombed vaults. One eyvan leads into the courtyard itself, one leads to the prayer hall, and the two side eyvans lead to other halls. The Iranian courtyards became more elaborate as the style developed, culminating in mosques such as the Masjid-i-Jum'a (Friday mosque) in Isfahan.

Also characteristic of the Iranian mosque is the brilliant blue color of the ceramic tile. The blue of the mosque contrasts sharply with the stark surrounding desert environment, and it gives the mosque a sense of cool restfulness.

The Turkish mosques may have had a domestic precedent in the domed tent, which seems to have served as a model for the Anatolian domed prayer hall. The style was further developed when the Ottomans captured Constantinople and were impressed by the architecture of the Byzantine church, Hagia Sophia. In the sixteenth century, an architect by the name of Sinan further developed the Turkish style, creating a mosque dominated by a great dome and flanked by half-domes. The half-domes functioned as supports for the main dome, thus making the usual maze of columns beneath unnecessary. The interior space of the Turkish mosque therefore had a different visual effect; the mihrab was visible to all, pointing more boldly toward Mecca. The mosque known as Iskele Jami' at Uskudar exemplifies this style.

PAINTING AND SCULPTURE

It has already been established that Islamic art proliferated in vegetal and geometric designs, shunning representation, especially of human figures. Not only was nonrepresentational art considered suitable for portraying the spirit, but the portrayal of figures was at times even suppressed. When Muhammad returned to Mecca in 632 and took over the Ka'ba, he removed the idols and destroyed them in condemnation of idolatry. The idols were statues, and the Qur'an specifically mentions statues of idols among the works of Satan. But what about other kinds of statues and figures in paintings? The Qur'an did not specifically mention these. In popular religious feeling, statues of any kind were abominated, but early Islamic art contained images of animals and even nonfigural Hellenistic landscapes were used as

FIGURE 9.5 Minaret of Badhshahi Mosque, Cairo. (Photo by the author.)

wall decorations in mosques. Sassanian Persian styles in art also influenced the Mosque, and eventually there arose a school of painting in Islam. Sculpture, however, is almost totally lacking from Islamic art.

We might reflect for a moment on why Islamic art was generally nonrepresentational, and yet in certain periods and regions, human and animal figures came to dominate the exquisite miniature paintings, especially in Persia. Robert Ellwood, a historian of religions, has defined religion from two essentially different perspectives, the *temple-oriented* and the *prophet-oriented* perspectives.

> The first approach is basically cultural, starting with an awareness of society's art, architecture, music, poetry, rites, and philosophy. . . . The second—the "marketplace" or "prophet"—approach is more related to that side of human nature which makes words, which argues, which sees the separateness of man from man and of man from God. It is highly aware of the conflict between what one is and what one thinks one ought to be. It is less interested in the religion of esthetic expression, or of feelings of bliss, than in faith for moments of crisis and decision, in the inner agonies of guilt and anxiety and moral choice.[2]

Ellwood's description of the prophet-oriented religion of the marketplace aptly characterizes the original Arabian impetus of Islam. The social context was a market economy. The moral demand conveyed by the Prophet Muhammad was a verbal delivery, in keeping with the highly prized oratorical and poetic skills of the Arabs. And, as we have seen already, the primary visual art form of early Islam was calligraphy. Again, the "word" was the best expression of the divine. However, both the Byzantine and Sassanian cultures, whose lands and peoples fell largely into Muslim hands, were what Ellwood would call temple-oriented. Art for art's sake commingled with religion in the churches of Eastern Christianity and of Zoroastrianism. Thus in time, Islam brought religion into the Persian marketplace (the bazaar), but the temple-oriented aspect of Persian culture brought into Islam expression in the visual arts. The most noteworthy effect was in painting.

From circa 800 onward, strict injunctions against representational art appeared in Islamic religious literature. Behind such injunctions lay not a deprecation of works of art themselves so much as fear that the artist would create images of living things. In Islam, the creative act is one reserved for God alone; God's power can not be usurped by man; this is a doctrinal matter. The Sunna of the Prophet, written down in the hadith collections, reinforced this concept. In one such hadith, it is said that on the Day of Judgment, an artist who had dared to create images of living creatures would be enjoined to breathe life into them. If he failed, as he surely would, he would be condemned by God.

The ban against representational art was effective against works intended for public display, but in the more private sectors of society, representational art was created and appreciated. Gradually there appeared to be a willingness to permit living things to be artistically represented, so long as they were not shown to cast a shadow (thus not really there), or were applied to objects of daily use, such as carpets, pottery, and other household implements. Human and animal figures also came to be represented in abstract arrangements as a part of decorative patterns so that they carried no more importance than vegetal or geometric ornament. By portraying men and animals in this fashion, the artist proved that he had no intention of creating a replica of a living form.

Very little is known about Islamic painting from the eighth to the thirteenth centuries. Not much has survived from that period, and the only evidence we have comes from literary sources, not the works of art themselves. The minor arts, however, flourished. The nomadic social element of the Abode of Islam preferred ornaments that were portable, such as carpets, pottery, decorated boxes, and the like. The illustration of texts in the margins was another form of minor art of this period. As we saw in Chapter 4, the Muslim world translated and studied Greek and other foreign works on science. Arabic manuscripts with ample margins provided "canvases" for Muslim artists, while often the content of the books only suggested but did not

FIGURE 9.6   Pottery, sixteenth-century Ottoman. (Courtesy Museum of Fine Arts, Boston, and Victoria and Albert Museum, London.)

determine the real subject matter of the illustrations. The information on the page might be Greek in origin, but the illustrating artist might create his own or an Islamic story in the picture he painted.

Illustrations of literary manuscripts were particularly prevalent in Persia from 1300 onward. East of the Arab heartland, the ban against representational art was not felt quite so strongly. Particularly in Persia, the figural paintings of China had a strong impact. Eventually even the painting of religious subjects became acceptable. It is interesting to note that in connection with the production of illuminated manuscripts, the social position of the calligrapher, as a transmitter of words, was very high; the social position of the illustrator painting on the very same text and subject matter was by contrast very low. The artist's craft was considered less honorable and less skilled than that of the calligrapher. The power of the word retained its conceptual importance even in Persia, where painting came to be a form of artistic expression. The calligrapher was thought to transmit not only the form of the word but its inner meaning as well. The artist, through the use of hue and color, merely embellished the scene conveyed. An artisan of words, the calligrapher held the status of a learned man, while the painter was merely a workman. Some theologians argued that the painter was worse than the sculptor of images, to be ranked with money lenders and tattoo artists. It was only during the Mongol rule, beginning in the thirteenth century, that artists gained a measure of social esteem.

The Persian miniatures (taking chiefly the form of manuscript illuminations) of the Timurid dynasty (fourteenth century) carried on the traditions
already established for Islamic art. The Timurids succeeded the Mongols as
rulers of Persia. The figures painted in that period rendered no sense of sub-
stantiality; the artistic goal was still to decorate. All objects appearing in the
picture are equidistant, with a different sense of perspective (see Figure 9.7).
Often the viewpoint changes as one looks from one element in the painting
to another. For example, carpets may appear spread out as if one were looking down on them from above even though the view is otherwise from the
side. The closer side of an object may be shown smaller than the farther side.
An object or person, such as the hero of the scene, may appear much larger
than the other figures in order to give emphasis to that particular figure.
Symbolic gestures may be used to indicate mood. In fact, symbolization and
abstraction are important characterizations of such paintings.

These remarks should not be taken to suggest that the Muslim artists of
this period lacked skill or technique. The artists wanted and were able to create visually pleasing designs while at the same time giving symbolic content
to the objects in the painting. An illustration from Rumi's poem "Mathnawi"
may serve as an example. A group of travelers, after eating an infant elephant (which symbolized righteousness), is trampled to death by the mother
elephant (judgment). It is evident in this painting that the artist did not
intend to portray a gory realistic picture of an elephant trampling human
beings. Instead the artist is concerned with the visual pattern of the illustration and with emphasis on the significance of the mother elephant through
her size and white color.

Despite attempts to suppress representational art, it nonetheless continued to exist, after a fashion. One should note, however, that even figural art
conformed to the influence of Islamic belief, and the figures themselves are
not so much representational as they are decorative and symbolic. Such
paintings still belonged somewhat to the abstract modes of arabesque. Like
arabesque, Islamic painting tended to convey a meaning beyond the surface
appearance of form, and it relied on ornate patterning to present a pleasing
visual effect.

OTHER ART FORMS

Music

The music of the Islamic world is a unique blending of styles from four different sources: Arab Near Eastern, Iranian, North African (Maghrebi), and
Turkish. Because of the widespread use of the Arabic language as a medium
of expression in speech, writing, and poetry, vocal music tends to be preferred over purely instrumental music. Often the rhythmic or melodic struc-

FIGURE 9.7 Fifteenth-century Timurid miniature painting. Note the different means of portraying perspective. (Courtesy of the Iranian Institute.)

ture of a piece is determined by the vocal inflections in the lyrics and is arranged according to the rules of prosody.

The two main types of music in Islam are *folk music* and what we will call *art music.*

"Folk music" arises in a popular environment and is closely associated with the lives of common people and their everyday concerns. The same melody may occur over and over with new words to fit new occasions, which may range from weddings to birthdays to the adventures of a villager on the pilgrimage to Mecca. Folk music is often sung without instruments. With the exception of Central Asia, there is virtually no tradition of a purely instrumental peasant folk music. Even for the dance the music is often purely vocal. Again, this is due to the importance placed upon the word, especially poetry, and to its significance in the social life of the people.

"Art music," on the other hand, is usually performed for the aristocracy, and thus it is more common in urban centers. Unlike folk music, art music requires a trained professional musician for its performance and it adheres to certain melodic and rhythmic rules. The musicians are trained individually by a master until they reach a high level of virtuosity. As with folk music, the singer is foremost in importance. A concert usually consists of a singer accompanied by one instrument—usually never more than just a few.

Islamic music differs greatly from Western music in the manner in which it is performed. In the West, composers write their music down on paper exactly as it is to be played. A great deal of a Western musician's training is aimed toward learning to play music exactly as it is written. In the Islamic world, on the other hand, the key to music virtuosity is the ability of a performer to improvise on a particular melody or rhythm in an innovative way. Several musicians playing the same melodic line will each add their own variations in the tempo or in the ornamentation of the melody. Therefore, the performer is allowed a great deal of freedom as to how a piece will be played. The judging of a performer's artistic ability is based upon the amount of creativity and imagination displayed in the improvisation. A musician is not expected to compose new melodies, but to improve and embellish traditional ones. Even in music, the very concept of Sunna and tradition reminds us of just how Islam was woven into the fabric of culture. Enormous creativity is there, for like the religious scholar who must interpret and apply the Shari'a to ever new situations, the musician working in traditional modes also gives creative self-expression. Art and religion require interpretation in order to bring contemporary meaning.

Islam has not entirely favored music as a legitimate form of expression, especially in the context of worship. Because of its association with the aristocracy, especially in the early days of Islam, music was viewed by some as a frivolous luxury. Women also took part in the performance of music, or in dancing accompanied by music, thereby adding an element of sensuality. Another forbidden activity, the drinking of wine, was associated with music and dancing. The Qur'an and the Sunna, especially under Sunni interpretation, saw each of these elements in association with the other, a threat to one's character. In fact, the Qur'an does not forbid music as such; rather, it is in the Prophet's hadith that music, especially of the aristocracy, is condemned. In orthodox Sunni and Shi'i Islam, music does have some important functions. The call to prayer, for example, certainly resembles chant or music. On certain festivals and holy days, hymns are sung. Even the recitation of the Qur'an is very highly stylized so as to strike the ear as a type of music. This quality enhances both meaning and memorizing.

Outside of orthodox Islam, music and dance play more important roles, especially among the Sufis. Mystical orations called in Arabic *sama'*, meaning "listening," are spiritual exercises done in the mode of music. The oration may include singing, dancing, and instrumental music as aids to the Sufis' attempts to reach higher and higher levels of ecstatic experience of union with God. The music serves both as an aid to heightening the emotions and as a symbol or ritual gesture of transcending the material world. Sufis believe that music can lead to spiritual knowledge by echoing the beauty and the harmony of the universe, urging the worshipper to go beyond the pedestrian feelings and concerns of this life.

Poetry

The supreme example of literature in Islam could be said to be the Qur'an, but the Qur'an actually ranks in a class by itself, as scriptures often do. As revelation, Muslims do not judge the Qur'an along with works by humans. Even to attempt to imitate the literary quality of the Qur'an was a matter of sacrilege. Other prophets had brought miracles, such as Moses dividing the Red Sea and Jesus raising the dead. The evidence of Muhammad's prophetic mission was the inimitable Qur'an. In keeping with the pre-Islamic Bedouin Arab's high appreciation of poetry and skill in spoken eloquence, the miracle of the Qur'an was seen at first in terms of its poetic, oratorical eloquence. The art of proper recitation was from the first days of Islam an important religious calling. Eventually, as the Arabic language passed into the medium of literature, the Qur'an also served as the model or paradigm for establishing rules of literary criticism.

Pre-Islamic poetry falls into two categories. The first is a type of poem composed in preparation for battle and is called the *rajaz*. It contained eloquent insults hurled at the enemy tribe. A more elaborate style is called the *qasida*. The qasida is written according to strict rules of composition and has three parts. The first part is a lament for the tribe of a loved one that has gone away. Part two describes a journey into the desert. Part three offers a eulogy to a person or a tribe that is friendly, or the denunciation of an enemy.

With the rise of Islam, the basic form of the qasida acquired some variations. Instead of the old tribal wars of the desert, the Islamic conquests provided new subject matter. Instead of lamenting a lost loved one, Arab soldiers, taken far from their homeland in battle, remembered poetically the desert that had once been home. Pride in Islamic victory formed another new theme. Political poetry emerged as an expression of conflicts within and between religious communities. Skill in poetic polemics, as earlier in tribal wars of revenge, roused emotions and renewed commitments. Even some philosophers and theologians composed their more academic subject matters in poetic rhymes in order to aid the memory.

Like music, some poetry developed in a frivolous and decadent style. Many poets valued the power of words not only to inform and teach, but also to entertain. Such a precedent was also to be found in a pre-Islamic form. Similar to the first part of the qasida, which lamented the loss of a loved one, some poetry was more arrogant and explicit about sexual exploits. The pleasures of food, wine, and women, which were not topics encouraged by Islamic religious idealism, nonetheless found some expression in poetry. The aristocracy in Islamic cities resurrected interest in this more sensational poetic genre.

Non-Arab parts of the Abode of Islam developed still other forms of Islamic poetry. In Muslim Spain, a type of poem called the *muwashshah* developed. The muwashshah ignored the metrical structures of classic Arabic poetry. Actually, part of the poem is in classical Arabic, part in vernacular

Spanish. The Persians also developed independent forms of poetry in an attempt to break with Arab traditions.

Literature

The term literature normally makes us think not of poetry but prose. Islam also came to regard prose composition highly, even though it lent itself to oratory less dramatically than poetry. In a previous chapter we spoke of al-Jahiz, the great Arab littérateur of the ninth century. The term in classical Arabic meaning worldly knowledge and the witty use of it in composition and conversation, of which al-Jahiz was a master, was *adab*. A man of letters was an *adib*. This was something different from the training of the ulama, which was steeped in the religious sciences. Adab is considered the earliest form of secular Arabic prose writing; it contains fables and treatises of a didactic nature. Al-Jahiz' best remembered work, still read in the Islamic world, is a book entitled (and largely about) *Animals*, but the lines and pages contain lively diversions about the manners of foreigners, love, religion, and a whole host of topics, all very entertaining and informative about the customs of the times. Consider the following anecdote, which offers an amusing comment on gender roles in Islam:

> I was sitting one day with Dawud b. al-Mu'tamir al-Subairi when a beautiful woman went by, dressed in white; she had a lovely face and figure, and wonderful eyes. Dawud got to his feet. . .and since I was sure he was going to follow her, I sent my slave to see what happened. When Dawud came back, I said to him: "I know that you got up to go and speak to her; it is useless to lie, and your denials will not hold water. I merely wish to know how you accosted her and what you said to her" (though I fully expected him to embroider some fantastic exploit for me, as was his wont). "I accosted her," he replied, "with these words: 'Had I not espied in you the stamp of virtue, I should not have followed you.' She burst out laughing, and laughed so much that she had to lean against the wall, then replied: 'So it is the stamp of virtue that gives a man like you the impudence to follow and lust after a woman like me? To say that it is virtue manifest that makes men brazen really is the absolute limit!'" [3]

After the tenth century, another form of prose writing, the *maqama* genre of literature, appeared. It was developed by Badi al-Zaman al-Hamadhani (968–1008). His honorific name means "Wonder of the time from Hamadhan." A maqama tells of imaginary events that involve two principal characters, a hero and a narrator. Through rhyming prose, the narrator relates the adventures of the hero. Al-Hamadhani's hero was a certain Abu l-Fath of Alexandria, whom the narrator represents as a witty "Renaissance Man" of his age; his exploits as told by Hamadhani delighted the reader, whether peasant or professor. Perhaps the best known author of maqama literature was al-Hariri of Basra (1054–1122). His works, known as *al-Maqamat* [the maqamas], had as its hero Abu Zayd of Saruj. The following account, in Hariri's own words, tells of what led him to write about Abu Zayd.

> Abu Zayd of Saruj was an important old beggar, full of eloquence, who came to us in Basra and one day stood up in the mosque of the Banu Haram [the quarter in which Hariri lived] and after pronouncing a greeting begged alms of the people. Some of the magistrates were present, the mosque being crammed with eminent men, and they were charmed with his eloquence and wit and the beautiful phrasing of his speech. On this occasion he related the capture of his daughter by the Greeks, as I have related it in the Maqama called 'Of the Haram.' That same evening a number of the eminent and learned men of Basra were gathered at my house and I told them what I had seen and heard of this beggar and of the elegant style and witty allusiveness which he had employed to effect his purpose. Thereupon every one else there told of how he too had seen this same beggar, each in his own mosque, what I had seen, and how he had heard him deliver on other subjects a discourse even better than the one I had heard, for he used to change his dress and appearance in every mosque and show his skill in all kinds of artifices. They were astonished at the pains he took to gain his object and at the cunning in changing his appearance and at his ingenuity. So I wrote the "Maqama of the Haram" and thereafter constructed upon it the remainder of the Maqamat.'[4]

The primary purpose of Hariri's tales about Abu Zayd was to amuse. Story telling had long been a high art in Middle Eastern cultures. Hariri transformed this form of entertainment into the best remembered works in literature to come out of the Middle Ages. Many editions of his Maqamat were illuminated by Persian miniature paintings, thus preserving in one volume the art of storytelling, a rich literature of entertainment, and treasured paintings from the hands of gifted artists.

Both poetry and prose played a significant role in the traditions of Sufism. The Sufi poets found poetry to be an eloquent mode for expressing the intoxicating joys of experiencing nearness to God. The Sufis orally transmitted narratives and the sayings and events from the sacred biographies of saints and holy men. From the ninth century onward, these narratives were written down and became a type of religious prose. These sacred biographies also included passages from the Qur'an and the hadith of the Prophet, interwoven into the legendary accounts of the saints' lives. Sufi prose literature also contained treatises of a more theological nature that sought to explain mystical doctrine. Another type of literature belonging to this class was the confessional type, with eloquently described individual mystical experiences. Perhaps one of the best examples of mystical prose is the *Mantiq al-Tayr* [*Conference of the Birds*] by Farid al-Din Attar (d. 1230). *Conference of the Birds* describes the allegorical journey of thirty birds in search of the Simurgh. This allegory of the mystical search for God is revealed in the symbolic meaning of Simurgh, which means "thirty." That is to say, their journey was in search of themselves. As we have seen previously, Sufis such as Abu Yazid al-Bistami had taught that the journey to God is an interior one. Sufi literary artists such as Attar explored this abstract notion in memorable literature.

Two important conclusions may be drawn concerning the function of the arts in traditional Islamic culture. First, they served to crystallize the abstract concepts of Islam into concrete form. Second, they integrated these concepts into the daily life of the people. We have suggested that many of the arts attempt to convey the difficult-to-grasp concept of God's transcendence beyond the material world. In the visual arts this concept is emphasized by an avoidance of representational forms. In music the nonmaterial quality of sound itself points to the spiritual experience of man, and that experience is extolled also in the mystical poetry and prose of the Sufis, albeit in a quite different way. Didactic prose, on the other hand, sought to establish morals for everyday life. Calligraphy rendered visible the spoken Word of God.

We have also seen that Islamic principles have done much to formulate the styles of Islamic art. From the unity of the Islamic faith comes a unified purpose to art. Cultural differences from region to region have accounted for differences in taste and style. Thus an important unifier, classical Arabic, finds its way into poetry in vernacular Spanish, on the facades of Persian mosques, and within the biographies of Sufi saints. The unifying force of Islam is felt in many cultural aspects of a Muslim's life, and the arts give evidence to this unity.[5]

Much has been said about the Islamic world view in the past four chapters. How do world views held by Muslims get expressed in society, as manifested in the manner of relationships and behavior preferred by Muslims? The term we used earlier to express this dimension of religion is ethos. We turn now to consider the ethos of Islamic societies.

NOTES

1. James W. Karman, "Art," In *Introduction to the Study of Religion*, ed. T. William Hall (New York: Harper & Row, Publishers, Inc., 1976), p. 110.
2. Robert S. Ellwood, Jr., *Many Peoples, Many Faiths: An Introduction to the Religious Life of Mankind* (Englewood Cliffs, N.J.: Prentice-Hall, Inc., 1976), pp. 8–9.
3. Quoted in Charles Pellat, trans., *The Life and Works of Jahiz: Translations of Selected Texts*, trans from the French by D. M. Hawke (Berkeley and Los Angeles: University of California Press, 1969), pp. 148–49.
4. Cited and translated from Yaqut's *Irshad* by H. A. R. Gibb, *Arabic Literature: An Introduction*, 2nd (revised) ed., (London: Oxford University Press, 1963), p. 124.
5. The following works offer a good introduction to the arts of the Islamic world: Oleg Grabar, *The Formation of Islamic Art* (New Haven, Conn.: Yale University Press, 1973); *Islam and the Arab World*, ed. Bernard Lewis (New York: Alfred A. Knopf, Inc., 1976), especially the chapters on Islamic art and architecture by Richard Ettinghausen, literature by Charles Pellat, and music by A. Shiloah; David Talbot Rice, *Islamic Art* (New York: Praeger Publishers, Inc., 1965).

PART IV ISLAMIC RITUAL AND ETHOS:
RELIGION AND SOCIETY

10

Ritual Contamination

and

Cleansing

THE RITUAL OF PRAYER

It is Friday noon on campus. Students are hurrying to have lunch, to attend class, or to celebrate "T.G.I.F." with friends. This bustling activity, so familiar to American students, highlights a contrast with a different scene. Somewhere on campus or nearby, perhaps at several locations, a number of students—Arabs, Indonesians, South Asians, Americans, and others—are lined up side by side, facing in an easterly direction. In the midst of the Friday noon rush, they bow, kneel, then prostrate themselves. They are Muslims observing *jum'a*, "Friday" (prayer). The canonical prayer performed at noon on that day is the most important prayer ceremonial of the week. Jum'a means "congregation" as well as "Friday"; were they back in their hometowns, these Muslims would join members of their families and neighbors at a *masjid* (mosque) in their neighborhood, often crowded to capacity and overflowing, for the congregational prayer. At universities and businesses, a hallway or empty room may serve as a masjid, a place of prostration in prayer.

Religious practice in the Islamic world might seem strange to non-Muslim Americans. Hymns are not sung, collections are not taken, and children are not baptized. No one equivalent to an ordained priest, rabbi, or pastor serves

FIGURE 10.1　Muslim students performing ablutions (wudu') in preparation for prayer (salat), near Ache, Indonesia. (Photo by author.)

in a sacral capacity, as we have often noted. Having first prepared themselves through ritual cleansing called *wudu'*, worshippers leave their shoes at the door of the masjid. They enter and stand shoulder to shoulder in rows facing the *qibla*, the direction of Mecca. It is the same ritual prayer that is performed five times each day at home, school, places of business, and nearby masjids. On Fridays a religious leader called an imam or *khatib* (preacher) climbs into a pulpit (minbar) to deliver a sermon. On this occasion, the leader may speak about theological, political, or moral issues, or matters of common decency and etiquette. All such matters are appropriate in the Friday sermon.

Religious practice in Islam, as in other religions, is performed according to discernible patterns. These patterns exemplify general religious notions that are essential to the Muslim world view. Some of the patterns are also found in other religions, and some are distinctive to Islam. At specific stages of life—birth, circumcision, puberty, marriage, and death—rituals sanctify an individual's passage from one stage to the next. These are called "rites of passage" by anthropologists, and such rites are found in one form or another in every culture. (We will consider Islamic rites of passage in Chapter 14.)

The lives of Muslims are also religiously ordered by the calendar year. Like Jews and Christians, Muslims celebrate appointed holy days. These are arranged by a calendar that is distinctive to Islam. The notions of "weekdays" and "weekend" are foreign to traditional Islam, although the Islamic week may be said to begin on Saturday and to reach its high point on Friday noon. Five times each day normal concerns are interrupted by the muezzin's call to prayer. A closer look at these patterns of worship is the purpose of the next chapter. In this chapter we will consider the first topic to appear in most Muslim books on religious practice, pollution and purity.

POLLUTION AND PURITY

At the basis of religious ritual are concepts of pollution and purity. Many religions, such as Islam, prescribe acts of spiritual and physical cleansing when contamination occurs. The canonical prayer, *salat*, which will be discussed in more detail in the next chapter, requires that participants not be contaminated by certain acts and substances, such as sexual intercourse, blood, and alcohol. Indeed, in Islam, purity (*tahara*) is primarily a requirement for performing the religious duties, such as prayer and pilgrimage and reciting the Qur'an. In most cultures, there is more to being pure, however, than washing one's body. Tahara is a topic that takes up an entire section within collections of hadith, such of that of Bukhari, as well as in works on fiqh, Islamic jurisprudence (see Chapter 1). Moreover, the topic of tahara always occurs at the beginning of hadith and fiqh works. It is clear from the primacy of tahara in Islamic religious and legal texts that purity, and therefore pollution, are matters of central concern in Islam.

What makes the comparative study of religions interesting and challenging is that there is no general agreement among religions as to which foods, substances, and human activities are polluting and dangerous, and therefore require ritual cleansing of the one who comes into contact with them. Nor do religions agree as to the consequences of pollution. In fact, the specifics and requirements of tahara are among the many religious matters on which the various madhhabs (schools) of legal interpretation in Sunni and Shi'i Islam differ. Eating pork causes pollution for Muslims and Jews but not for Christians. For Muslims, rubbing water or fine sand or dirt on one's body before the prayer if one has recently been to the privy is the subject of much discussion in hadiths that are attributed to Muhammad or his wife Aisha. Yet contact with blood, semen, or wine is more contaminating and hence requires a greater ritual act of cleansing than does pollution encountered at the toilet. Religious legislation, such as the Talmud for Jews and the Shari'a for Muslims, goes into considerable detail on how to avoid and remedy pollution. Finally, it should be recalled from the discussion of Shari'a that the various Sunni and Shi'i madhhabs differ, mostly in small ways, in their interpretations the Qur'an and the Sunna, including rules regarding what acts and substances pollute and what must be done to remove pollution.

A more basic kind of question raised by anthropologists and historians of religion is, Why is this, and not that, polluting to the members of a given religious community? Religious teachings are generally thorough in explaining what is unclean; religious studies analyze *why* some thing or some activity is unclean. Let us consider the example of dietary laws in Judaism briefly by comparison.

Dietary laws are a major aspect of ritual purity in Judaism. The dietary laws are based on the biblical books of Deuteronomy (Chapter 14) and Leviticus (Chapter 11). The well-known Jewish injunction against eating pork, which is also prohibited in Islam, is part of a complex and complicated set of rules. A few verses from Chapter 11 of the Book of Leviticus will do for our comparison.

> 1. And the Lord said to Moses and Aaron, 2. "Say to the people of Israel, These are the living things which you may eat among all the beasts that are on the earth. 3. Whatever parts the hoof and is cloven-footed and chews the cud, among the animals, you may eat. 4. Nevertheless among those that chew the cud or part the hoof, you shall not eat these: The camel, because it chews the cud but does not part the hoof, is unclean to you. 5. And the rock badger, because it chews the cud but does not part the hoof, is unclean to you. 6. And the hare, because it chews the cud but does not part the hoof, is unclean to you. 7. And the swine, because it parts the hoof and is cloven-footed but does not chew the cud, is unclean to you.[1]

The remaining thirty-nine verses in Chapter 11 on dietary restrictions spell out which fish, birds, and insects may be eaten and which not, as well as the prohibition against eating carrion or touching anything that touches carrion. In other words, the Jewish prohibition against eating pork is based on a complex set of distinctions (in this case parted hoof but not cud-chewing) that define what contaminates and what does not, when eaten by humans. But what do these diverse, seemingly arbitrary, distinctions mean? Why have they been so important to one particular religious community, the Jews, for over two thousand years in all parts of the world to which that community has spread?

Mary Douglas on Purity and Pollution

In her famous study of purity and pollution, Mary Douglas mentioned several kinds of explanations often given for the significance of Jewish dietary laws. For example, in the late nineteenth century, it was common among scholars to find a natural rationale. Eating pork in the days before refrigeration, it was argued, was unhealthy and could cause one to suffer from such diseases as trichinosis. Laws of purity and pollution were therefore seen as having a basic hygienic or medical rationale, which had become encrusted with religious symbolism and regulation in premodern world views. Earlier, some Christian theologians had argued that the Jewish dietary laws should be understood allegorically. For example, the various kinds of unclean animals were taken to symbolize unclean or sinful human beings. Douglas offered a different theory, based on the definition of dirt (pollution)

> as matter out of place. . . . It implies two conditions: a set of ordered relations and a contravention of that order. Dirt, then, is never a unique, isolated event. Where there is dirt there is system. Dirt is the by-product of a systematic ordering and classification of matter, in so far as ordering involves rejecting inappropriate elements.[2]

A Theory of Islamic Ritual Purity

What happens if we apply Mary Douglas's notion of purity as a cultural system of ordered relations (things you can and can't eat, touch, do, etc.), and pollution as contraventions of that order—matter out of place—to the Islamic system of tahara? A. Kevin Reinhart has explored this topic and concluded that the definition of purity and pollution just quoted from Douglas applies only partially to Islam. Islamic ritual practices do require purity, and these rituals are invalid if one does them in a condition of defilement and pollution. This implies that Islamic rituals establish a system and maintain order, and forbid that which causes disorder within that culturally constructed system. Nonetheless, Reinhart concludes that in the Islamic system of tahara, there is no lasting "danger" or consequence of pollution from impure activities. Whereas for Douglas the chief characteristic of ritual purity is *order*, Reinhart believes that in Islam the defining element is *control*. Restoration of tahara is required when certain things happen that imply loss of control, such as discharging fluids from the body, sleeping, fainting, or drinking alcohol. Tahara is achieved by performing certain ritual acts of cleansing that remove the contamination and restore control. Let us turn from these more general and theoretical considerations to the specific categories of tahara as defined by fiqh.[3]

THE ISLAMIC SYSTEM OF TAHARA

The scriptural verse that lies at the basis of much legal discussion about the maintenance of tahara is Qur'an 5:6, which reads as follows:

> O you who are faithful, when you stand for the prayer, wash your faces, your hands to the elbows, and rub your heads, and your legs to the ankles; and if you are precluded (*junub*), then cleanse; and if you are sick or traveling, or one of you is coming from defecating or from [sexual] contact with women, and you do not find water, then take good soil and rub your faces and hands with it. God does not want to place a burden on you, but rather He wants to purify you and complete his benefaction for you, so that perhaps you will show your gratitude.[4]

Within the tahara system as discussed in Islamic jurisprudence, there are three terms for that which is impure among humans and which requires ritual purification. These impurities are, in the order of their seriousness: that which is affected (*hadath*); defiled (*najas*); and precluded (*junub*).

Temporary Contamination and Its Removal

Hadath (transient effect) is contamination by *acts* associated with the toilet and sexuality, not by bodily fluids as such—that is, urine, excrement, semen, etc. (The reader will note that "hadath" and "hadith" have quite different meanings.) Al-Bukhari reports a hadith from the Prophet Muhammad, who is reported to have said, "The prayer of a person who does Hadath (passes urine, stool, or wind) is not accepted till he performs (repeats) the [rite of purification]."[5] Elsewhere among hadiths, as well as in books on fiqh, we learn that hadath results from such things as urinating, defecating, sleeping, flatulence, and touching the genitals. Fainting is another form of hadath contamination. All of these forms suggest loss of control, according to the theory of tahara propounded by Reinhart.

When one is so "affected" by one of these acts, an ablution (wudu') must be performed. Wudu' may take two forms: wiping the head, face, hands and feet three times with water or performing the same actions with uncontaminated soil. The alternative of using fine sand or good soil when water is unavailable to rub on one's body is known as *tayammum*. Videos and photographs of Islamic religious practice often show Bedouin and other pastoral Muslims performing tayammum in the desert. Usually, a lone worshipper is shown marking out a place of prostration, literally a masjid on the ground, oriented toward the qibla, the direction of Mecca. Worship in Islam is far more often, however, a corporate, collective ritual performed in a village or city mosque that is equipped with a fountain or water faucets for wudu'. The provision of tayammum in place of water reminds us that Islam arose in the arid desert region of Arabia. Tayammum also reminds us that dirt as such is not necessarily "dirty" in the ritual symbolism of the Islamic world view.

The Sunna of the Prophet regarding tahara, as recorded in several hadiths, provides commentary on Qur'an 5:6 quoted above. In the first hadith on the topic of wudu' "ablution" in Bukhari's collection,

> Abu 'Abdullah said: The Prophet (prayers and peace be upon him) had made clear that it is obligatory (while performing) ablution to wash the [head, face, forearms and feet] once. And the Prophet (prayers and peace be upon him) also did perform the ablution by washing (these) parts twice and thrice, but he never washed them more than three times.[6]

The practice of washing each part three times during wudu' is now standard for most Muslims.

Defilement and Lustration

A person may become defiled (najas) as a result of contamination by fluids and substances that are external to one's person. Reinhart summarizes the hadith and fiqh definitions of najas.

> Nearly anything that has left its proper place within the body is *najas*: pus, vomit, blood [except the blood of martyrs], urine, excreta of all animals (except birds), but not tears or sweat, and so on. Logically, things from the interior of the body, things that have crossed the boundaries of the body, ought not to be outside the body; when they leave their place, they become impure.

As Reinhart notes, we are once again in the company of Mary Douglas's theory that "dirt is matter out of place."[7]

Another type of *najasat* (plural of najas) reminds the student of comparative religions of passages in the biblical books of Numbers and Leviticus, quoted above. This category of najas may be defined as contamination from contact with "pigs, dogs, wine, carrion, corpses, water used by unclean animals, the food left over by an unclean animal, its milk, and so on." In these cases the logic of transient effect (hadath) caused by the act of evacuating fluids from the body is replaced by historically and culturally derived prohibitions involving certain animals, death, alcohol, human corpses, etc. Not just the Jews, but Zoroastrians and pre-Islamic Arabs had similar categories of defilement.[8]

The remedy for najas is *ghusl*, a bathing or lustration of the entire body with water. It is also common practice to perform ghusl before the Friday canonical prayer, jum'a. Al-Bukhari reports on the authority of Abu Sa'id al-Khudri the following hadith: "The prophet said, 'Ghusl . . . on Friday is compulsory for every Muslim reaching the age of puberty.'"[9] Muslims who go on the hajj to Mecca must perform the ghusl before they don the sacred garb and enter the marked precincts (see Chapter 12). Ghusl is also required in the case of a person who is precluded from worship for the following explicit reasons.

Precluded

One is precluded (*junub*) from worship because of defilement that results from sexual intercourse, the emission of semen and vaginal fluids, menstruation, and parturition (the blood caused by childbirth). The last two involve blood and apply uniquely to women. The reason or ground (*'illa*) which makes women in these last two conditions junub is the limiting effect of menstruation and childbirth presumed on performing the physical rites of prayer and hajj, as well as sexual intercourse. When one is junub, he or she may also not even recite the Qur'an, much less touch it (which one may do under the lesser circumstance of a hadath). Finally, Reinhart has concluded that *janaba* (that which causes one to be junub and thus in need of ghusl, a full ritual bath) is not contagious. That is, in Mary Douglas's terms, janaba is not dangerous. People under the polluting effect of a janaba resulting from sexual intercourse or menstruation are excluded from performing prayer, pilgrimage, and Qur'an recitation until they have performed ghusl.[10]

BODY AND COSMOLOGY

This chapter has dealt with tahara, the system of purity that is prescribed in the Qur'an, exemplified in the Sunna of the Prophet, and applied in daily life by Muslims everywhere. A broader aspect of this topic is the symbolism of the body and its orientation within Islamic cosmology. In other words, there is a cosmological dimension to tahara, a brief discussion of which will bring us to the close of this chapter.

Right/Left Symbolism

The topic of "left and right" has to do with politics and is the proper domain of political science. The phrase "right and left" often has an entirely different connotation that belongs more to anthropology and religious studies. The symbolism of right- and left-handed (and -footed) gestures is found in most cultures, and there are remarkable parallel meanings among many cultures about the cultural valences of right and left orientations. Some things, usually negative or polluting things, such as touching the genitals while in the bathroom, are to be done only with the left hand, in many cultures; the right hand is often reserved for more constructive, social activities, such as greeting someone. Some scholars argue that social codes that distinguish right- from left-handed and -footed activities are derived entirely from culture; they are not genetically produced. Others believe that right/left distinctions are physiologically determined, perhaps by the left and right hemispheres of the brain. Whatever the causes, Islamic practice, as recorded in hadith collections and books on jurisprudence, and observed in everyday life, makes important distinctions between right and left. These distinctions vary in different parts of the Muslim world, under the influence of local custom. We will encounter right/left symbolism in the next chapters on religion and society.

In the quranic cosmology, the right and left hands have eschatological significance: that is, the ritual of distinguishing between the right and left hand will be observed on the Day of Judgment. Notice the following scene, predicted dramatically in the sura called The Reality (Qur'an 69):

> 15. Then on that day will the Event take place. 16. And the heaven will split asunder, for on that day it will be frail. 17. And there angels will be on the sides thereof, and eight will uphold the Throne of thy Lord that day, above them.

18. On that day you will be exposed; not a secret of yours will be hidden. 19. Then, as for him who is given his record in his right hand, he will say: Take, read my book. 20. Surely I knew that I should have to meet my reckoning. 21. Then he will be in a blissful state 22. in a high Garden 23. whose fruit shall be easy to reach. 24. (and it will be said to those therein): Eat and drink to your delight on account of that which you did in days past. 25. But as for him who is given his book in his left hand, he will say: Oh, would that I had not been given my book 26. And knew not what my reckoning would be. 27. Oh, would that it had been death.

The "book" (*kitab*) in this case refers not to scripture, as it so often does in the Qur'an, but rather to the reckoning, the account book of all the deeds one has done throughout his or her life. Those who receive their book in their right hand need to know nothing more; they shall go on to Paradise. The left hand symbolizes judgment and punishment. The sura called "The Event" (Qur'an 56) echoes the cosmological significance of left/right symbolism, as do several other passages in the Qur'an.

The practice of the Prophet Muhammad reflected the good and propitious use of the right hand and foot, and the opposite significance of the left. Muslims are enjoined to enter a masjid with the right foot first, but toilets and cemeteries with the left. In this example we can see that right/left symbolism is embedded in pollution and purity ritual practices as well as in the eschatology of Hellfire and Paradise. Similarly, tahara is at the heart of the requirement to touch food with the right hand only, but the genitals while in the toilet only with the left.

The Qibla

By now the term "qibla," the direction or orientation on the Great Mosque in Mecca, is familiar. In prayer, as we shall see in more detail in the next chapter, Muslims first determine, then pray in the direction of the qibla. In a masjid, literally a "place of prostration," a special niche known as a mihrab marks the qibla, the direction in which worshippers, lined up in rows, should pray. We come to a close of this chapter on ritual purity by emphasizing not just the need for cleanliness of the body in prayer, but also its proper physical orientation: the cosmology of prayer, which the concept of qibla entails.

That the qibla orientation during the canonical prayer is associated with tahara is indicated by the following hadith:

Narrated Abu Aiyub al-Ansari: The Prophet (prayers and peace be upon him) said, "while defecating, neither face nor turn your back to the Qibla but face either east or west." Abu Aiyub added. "When we arrived in Sha'm we came across some lavatories facing the Qibla; therefore we turned ourselves while using them and asked for Allah's forgiveness."[11]

Recalling the previous discussion about transient effect (hadath) that must be removed by wudu' before one may perform salat (the canonical prayer), this hadith and others like it indicate the importance of the cosmological dimension of tahara.

Qibla orientation has been compared with other religious cosmologies. The central point of the qibla perspective worldwide is the Ka'ba, the cubical edifice in the center of the Great Mosque in Mecca. The historian of religion, Mircea Eliade compared this to concepts of an *axis mundi*, a center of the world, or of the *omphalos*, the "navel" of the universe, where heaven and earth meet or find their most poignant contact.[12] More recently, the anthropologist Victor Turner, whose work on pilgrimage and drama will be cited in Chapter 12, has reevaluated comparative notions of "center" and "periphery" in religious studies, with special attention to the Islamic pilgrimage to Mecca.

The concept of tahara pervades Islamic world views, perhaps even in ways that are subconscious to many Muslims on such occasions as the Friday prayer, jum'a, described at the beginning of this chapter. We have seen that this involves many aspects: the Qur'an; th : Sunna of the Prophet as recorded in hadith; the rituals, especially of canonical prayer (salat), pilgrimage to Mecca (hajj), and Qur'an recitation; and rituals of ablution and lustration. Having introduced the topic of ritual in terms of tahara, purity and pollution avoidance/removal, we turn now to consider the religious duties (*ibadat*), for most of which the concepts of tahara and qibla are essential.

NOTES

1. *The Oxford Annotated Bible*, Revised Standard Version.
2. Mary Douglas, *Purity and Danger: An Analysis of Concepts of Pollution and Taboo* (London: Pelican Books, 1970), p. 48.
3. A. Kevin Reinhart, "Impurity/No Danger," *History of Religions 30*, no. 1 (1990): 1–24.
4. Following Reinhart's translation of Q. 5:6, "Impurity/No Danger," p. 5.
5. Al-Bukhari, *The Translation of the Meanings of Sahih al-Bukhari: Arabic-English*, trans. Muhammad Muhsin Khan (Chicago: Kazi Publications, 1976), 1:101 (Book IV [Wudu'], Chapter 2, no. 137).
6. Al-Bukhari, *Translation*, 1:101 (Book IV [Wudu'], Chapter 1).
7. Reinhart, "Impurity/No Danger," p. 7 and Note 19. The quote from Douglas is cited in Note 2 above.
8. Reinhart, "Impurity/No Danger," p. 8.
9. Al-Bukhari, *Translation*, 1:453 (Book XII, Chapter 79, nr. 817). See also 2:1-3 (Book XIII [Jum'a], Chapter 1, nos. 1-5).
10. Reinhart, "Impurity/No Danger," pp. 13–16.
11. Al-Bukhari, *Translation*, 1:235 (Book VIII [Salat], Chapter 29, no. 388).
12. Mircea Eliade, *The Myth of the Eternal Return or, Cosmos and History*, trans. Willard R. Trask (Princeton, N.J.: Princeton University Press, 1971), esp. the discussion of "The Symbolism of the Center," pp. 12–17.

11

Communal Ritual Practices

WORSHIP AND THE INNER SELF

It is difficult to determine accurately another individual's psychological state of mind during worship. This is a subject for psychological studies, but short of that, some general observations can be made about the matter. Recall from Chapter 5 that as *shakir*, a Muslim is "one who is thankful" to God for the goodness of life and the hope of reward in the Hereafter.[1] The Qur'an and the Sunna of the Prophet engender this response. The proper forms of this response in ritual and worship can be described in terms of what Muslims *appear* to be doing. Each Muslim believes, however, that one's own private attitudes or intentions are known only to oneself and to God. Therefore, before prayer, pilgrimage, and other times of worship, each Muslim privately declares the intention to worship. The private declaration of intention, known as the *niya*, forms a part of the act of worship itself. Thus worship is both an individual and a corporate act.

During worship, the inner self is felt to stand in the presence of God. Although in common parlance the term "ritual" often connotes a meaningless repetition of acts, this value judgment would be difficult to maintain in any serious study of religions. Like other religious people, Muslims vary among themselves in the intensity of their devotion. The performance of worship may seem empty or meaningless to any observer who does not look beyond what is immediately apparent. Thus the student of religions must seek to grasp the world view and the nature of the personal commitment within which religious performances take on their culturally determined values and meanings.

The religious duties, or *'ibadat*, are often referred to as the "Five Pillars of Islam." These were described in Chapter 1: witnessing (shahada); canonical prayer (salat); alms (zakat); fasting (sawm); and pilgrimage to Mecca (hajj). Sometimes a sixth is added: striving in the path of God (jihad). In this chapter we will look more closely at the annual festivals associated with these religious duties, as well as certain others marked in the Muslim calendar. In the following chapter, we will look more closely at the pilgrimage rites of hajj, ziyara and ta'ziya. First, however, it is necessary to look once again at concepts pertaining to worship and ritual in religious studies. The framework for our discussion of Islam in this chapter is the Hijra calendar.

SACRED SPACE AND TIME

Sacred Space

A non-Muslim would not be allowed to enter the vicinity of Mecca, and certainly not to approach the sacred Ka'ba. Western visitors to Islamic cities are often only cautiously admitted to mosques, and women in attire regarded by Muslims as immodest are frequently turned away. Why? From the Islamic point of view, such intrusions into these places is forbidden by the system of religious jurisprudence known as the Shari'a, and perhaps by a deeply felt sense of taboo. Even a Muslim involved in a serious ritual pollution (najasa), as described in the preceding chapter, would not defile a mosque by entering it under these conditions. The comparative study of religions sheds some light on this phenomenon. Insofar as religious traditions create attitudes and conceptions of reality that organize one's sense of sacred and profane geography in definite patterns and structures, some places are given more value than others. Mircea Eliade calls these *sacred spaces*, which he defines as follows:

> For religious man, space is not homogeneous; he experiences interruptions, breaks in it; some parts of space are qualitatively different from others. "Draw not nigh hither," says the Lord to Moses; "put off thy shoes from thy feet, for the place whereon thou standest is holy ground" [Exodus 3:5]. There is, then, a sacred space, and hence a strong, significant space; there are other spaces that are not sacred and so are without structure or consistency, amorphous.[2]

Consecrated spaces, such as altars within churches, temples and shrines, are examples of sacred spaces. Each tradition defines sacred spaces and establishes rules for their consecration. Without rules for the preparatory conditions, these spaces or the persons entering them would be defiled. The Hebrew Bible (Old Testament), for example, speaks about the sacred character of the Yahwist Sanctuary, the rituals appropriate to it, and the rules that govern its sanctity. Like the dietary laws discussed in the previous chapter, rules regarding the sanctity of places of worship appear in long passages in the Bible.

The Islamic Shari'a also lays down rules governing appointed places of worship. Strictly speaking, however, the distinction between "sacred" and "profane" (worldly, secular) when applied to the masjid (mosque) is not recognized by Muslims. The mosque is the place where Muslims prefer to perform the ritual of salat, the canonical prayer. One may pray only after performing wudu' or ghusl, the prescribed ablution for removing a transient effect or a more serious contamination, which we discussed in the previous chapter. For that matter, the prayer may be performed anywhere. Whether in a formal masjid, a private home, a place of business, or the mall at State University, the place of prayer is structurally oriented by the qibla, the direction of Mecca. Nothing else is necessary to perform salat.

The notion of the "sacred" as defined by Eliade applies more nearly to the territory around Mecca during the pilgrimage. The shrines in and near Mecca are surrounded by boundaries called the *miqat*. Within those boundaries is the territory called the *haram*, which is especially sacred during the last two and a half months of the Hijra calendar. Before Muslim pilgrims reach the haram, they declare to themselves and God the niya, "intention," to make the Greater or Lesser pilgrimage. One thereby becomes *muhrim*, a "consecrated" pilgrim. When one becomes muhrim, a ghusl is performed and special attire called *ihram* is donned. Within the haram, special activities derived from the Prophet's Sunna are followed by pilgrims (but not by other Muslims who may happen to be there).

Many Muslims also make visits to shrines or tombs of saints, although such visits are not considered obligatory "Acts of Worship," as described in Chapter 1. From crude huts to elaborate mosques and mausoleums, these shrines constitute sacred spaces possessing a special spiritual power or blessing, called *baraka*, from the saint whom each shrine commemorates. Pilgrims visit shrines to receive the baraka of the saints they esteem.

Time and the Sacred

The act of worship and the rituals it entails are characterized by specially marked-out patterns of time. We used this term earlier to describe the special moment in the sacred history of Islam when the Qur'an was revealed to the Prophet Muhammad. Following Eliade, we said that a sacred time is a "time out of time." It is a time when believers experience an interruption of the sacred into the profane: that is, the ordinary experience of time.[3] The night

Figure 11.1 Traditional Muslim women at Sayyida Zaynab shrine, Cairo, to receive the entombed saint's *baraka* (blessing). (Photo by the author.)

Muhammad is said to have received the divine message is celebrated on the 27th of Ramadan, which is regarded as an especially propitious anniversary. Ramadan is also the month of the Fast, and as well a month in which the unseen evil forces of Iblis and the Satans are said to be diminished by the original sacred event of revelation. Other times are also highly valued. For example, the canonical prayer is performed within designated periods of time each day, announced by the call of the muezzin. These are significant moments that punctuate each day. The first part of the last month of the year, Dhu al-Hijja, the last portion of the seventy-day period of the annual pilgrimage, is important not only for pilgrims, but also for those who remain at home. In addition, for the Shi'a especially, the tenth of the first month, Muharram, is the anniversary of the martyrdom of the fallen Husayn.

The conditions that govern the places and times of Islamic worship are found in the Shari'a. A Muslim's life is regulated by patterns established in the Hijra calendar. It will be useful at this point to describe briefly the annual, monthly, weekly, and daily patterns followed in the Islamic world.

In Table 11-1, the months of the Hijra calendar are presented with their Islamic names. We learned earlier that Hijra years have about 354 days consisting of twelve lunar months of twenty-nine or thirty days, reckoned by the sighting of the new moon. Until the time of the Prophet, the Arab shrine

TABLE 11-1   HIJRA CALENDAR

Month	Major Celebrations Common to Sunni and Shi'ite Islam
1 Muharran	New Year: Ashura (10th)
2 Safar	
3 Rabi' al-Awwai	Prophet's Birthday (12th)
4 Rabi' al-Thani	
5 Jumada al-Ula	
6 Jumada al Akhira	
7 Rajab	Muhammad's Ascension (27th)
8 Sha'ban	
9 Ramadan	Month of Fast; Night of Power (27th)
10 Shawwal	Breaking the Fast (1st); Pilgrimage Season
11 Dhu al-Qa'da	Pilgrimage Season
12 Dhu al-Hijja	Hajj (8th-13th); Festival of Sacrifice (10th)

known as the Ka'ba in Mecca was also governed by a lunar year, but in pagan times (Jahiliyya) an additional month was added every three years to adjust the otherwise shorter year to the full annual cycle of seasons. The Qur'an had forbidden the addition of this month, perhaps because it interrupted the sacred months set aside for the Arabs to make the pilgrimage to Mecca.

The shortened lunar year had the effect of making Islamic festivals occur eleven days earlier each year in relation to the more widely used solar calendar. This had two important results. First, like other religious traditions, such as Judaism and Christianity, Islam had its own distinctive schedule of holy days and festivals. Second, since the lunar calendar does not conform to the annual seasons, Islamic festivals and holy days are not identified with specific seasons of the year, such as the agricultural times of planting and harvest.[4] Thus, in each thirty three year cycle, rituals such as the pilgrimage and the Ramadan Fast will be observed in all seasons.

Islamic months are cycles in seven-day weeks. The first five days are known as "First Day," "Second Day," "Third Day," and so on. Jum'a, "Day of the Congregation," is the day of common gathering for the noon prayer, corresponding to Friday in the Western calendar. In Islamic cities and villages, shops and offices close at that time.

The five daily prayers also form a pattern that structures each day. Chanted by the muezzin, nowadays over loudspeakers, the summons to prayer is anticipated by a culturally conditioned sense of timing. The first prayer period begins with the muezzin's call to prayer at dawn. Muslims may perform this prayer later in the morning, in their homes, because the

---

TABLE 11–2   DAYS OF THE WEEK

Arabic Name	Corresponding English Name
Yawm al-Ahad (First Day)	Sunday
Yawm al-Ithnayn (Second Day)	Monday
Yawm al-Thalatha (Third Day)	Tuesday
Yawm al-Arba (Fourth Day)	Wednesday
Yawm al-Khamis (Fifth Day)	Thursday
Yawm al-Jum'a (Day of Congregation)	Friday
Yawm al-Sabt (Day of Sabbath*)	Saturday

* "Sabbath" is the literal meaning of *sabt*, although it does not carry that connotation when used in this context.

---

time of the prayer extends until the next prayer period is announced by the muezzin. The second prayer period begins at noon. Many Muslims perform the noon prayer in their schools or place of business, if not in a masjid. Sometimes the noon repast, followed by a rest from daily activities, separates this prayer from the third, which begins later in the afternoon. Many businesses, shops, and offices stay open until the fourth prayer is called at sunset. Religious instruction and guidance are offered by imams in mosques in many parts of the Islamic world before or after the sunset salat. At this hour many will return home for the evening meal with their families. The final prayer of the day is called about two hours after sunset. Muslims in many parts of the world schedule the evening dinner and social intercourse with family and friends after that hour.

TABLE 11–3   TIMES OF PRAYER

Arabic Name	Period of Time*
Salat al-Fajr (The Dawn Prayer)	From dawn to sunrise
Salat al-Zuhr	From noon to early afternoon
Salat al-Asr	From end of afternoon prayer to sunset
Salat al-Maghrib	From after sunset to end of P.M. twilight
Salat al-Isha	From after P.M. twilight to before A.M. twilight

* The call to prayer is given at the beginning of the period and the prayer said and performed at some time before the next call to prayer is given.

ISLAMIC FESTIVALS AND HOLIDAYS

During many of the twelve months of the Hijra year, Islamic festivals, called *'id* in the singular (pronounced "eed"), are observed. Some festivals are universally observed throughout Islam. Others derive from local traditions, not from the Qur'an and the Sunna. For example, the annual Hindu pilgrimage in Sri Lanka centers on the shrine of a Hindu deity. One scholar reports that "temples, priests, and pilgrims of both Hinduism and Buddhism are found at the site; Muslims and Christians also attend the annual festivities. The atmosphere is one of tolerance and ecumenism."[5] Clifford Geertz has compared two local Muslim saints, one in North Africa and the other in Indonesia, describing both the common Islamic and the distinctively local legends and ceremonials that surround these figures.[6] Although the local colorations that are infused with Islamic worship and ritual are not without significance, we will confine ourselves here to the more universally observed Islamic elements.

Muharram

The first day of Muharram, the first month of the Muslim calendar, marks the beginning of the new year in Islam. It is the anniversary of the Prophet's Hijra from Mecca to Medina. The tenth of Muharram originally began a fast that lasted for twenty-four hours. Called *'ashura'*, meaning "tenth," this holy day at the beginning of the Prophet's mission corresponded with Yom Kippur, the Day of Atonement in Judaism. Muslim authorities have also traced the significance of this 'id to pre-Islamic origins. The Prophet had felt betrayed by the Jews in Medina. (This is reminiscent of Jesus' conflict with the Pharisees and the Hebrew Prophets' conflict with the priests of Ba'al.) A quranic revelation prescribed that the period of fasting should be the month of Ramadan rather than 'ashura. 'Ashura has remained a voluntary day of fasting. According to the Sunna of the Prophet, it is recommended but not obligatory to fast on that day.[7]

Shi'i Muslims attach quite a different significance to the tenth of Muharram. It is the traditional anniversary of the martyrdom of Husayn, son of 'Ali. The ritual and drama of this day for Shi'i Muslims is extremely important. We have given a brief description of this Passion drama in Chapter 1, and we will analyze its meaning in more detail later in this chapter.

Birthday of the Prophet: Mawlid al-Nabi

Muhammad's birthday is celebrated on the twelfth day of the third month, Rabi' al-Awwal. During the first two centuries of Islam, this festival was not observed. For one thing, the exact date of Muhammad's birth was not known; nor was there much demand to know it at first. By the ninth century,

Figure 11.2 Mawlid al-Nabi (Birthday of the Prophet) celebrations on 12 'Rabi al-Awwal in Cairo. (Photo by the author.)

a set body of traditions about the Sunna of the Prophet had become standardized. One precedent in the Prophet's life that emerged was that many important events had occurred on Mondays, *yawm al-ithnayn*. His Hijra to Medina and his death were thought by many to have occurred on that day of the week. Tradition also formed in favor of Monday, the twelfth day of Rabi' al-Awwal, as the anniversary of Muhammad's birth. Even though this anniversary does not necessarily fall on a Monday, many Muslims have regarded Mondays as particularly auspicious days of voluntary fasting.

The twelfth of Rabi' al-Awwal has become a major religious festival for Muslims in many parts of the Islamic world. Not only the Prophet, but other holy men are remembered with religious celebrations on the anniversaries of their birth or death. In addition, Shi'i Muslims also celebrate the birthday anniversaries that tradition has assigned to 'Ali and members of his family. The Sufis elaborately honor their saints in the same fashion. Most Muslims observe the 'id of Mawlid al-Nabi. Some Sunni Muslims (particularly in Saudi Arabia) have refrained because the celebration, in their view, is an "innovation" (*bid'a*). That is, it was not mentioned by the Prophet or his closest companions. More alarming for some is that this holiday has tended to deify the Prophet at the expense of his humanity.[8]

An anthropologist who lived for some time in a small village near Cairo has written an interesting description of the celebration of the Mawlid al-Nabi among the villagers.[9] They begin their actual preparations for the celebration as much as four days prior to the twelfth of Rabi' al-Awwal. Homes are decorated, and in many yards tents are set up to provide shelter from the sun for the large number of friends and family that will gather. In the evenings, over loudspeakers, trained reciters from the village chant verses from the Qur'an and a specially prepared text about the life of the Prophet.

Mawlid al-Nabi is a legal holiday throughout Egypt. On that day, homes and the tents are filled with friends and relatives, and the mood is one of festivity. In the village of Kafr el-Elow, merchants arrive in wagons to sell varieties of candy, including some shaped as knights on horses for boys and doll brides for girls, Egyptian symbols for Muhammad's birthday.[10]

Festival of Breaking Off the Fast ('id al-fitr)

This religious holiday, also called the Minor Festival or Lesser Bayram, occurs on the first day of the month of Shawwal, immediately after the Ramadan fast.[11] The day stands in sharp contrast to the preceding thirty days of fasting and self-denial. It begins in the morning with a visit, mostly by the menfolk, to the mosque for morning prayer. This is followed, according to the Sunna of the Prophet, by a visit to cemeteries. These more solemn religious expressions then change into a happy festival in the homes of heads of families. It is an occasion for dressing up in one's best clothing.

The thematic shift from death to life, from deceased relatives to living children, is expressed in several ways. Gifts and money are given to children and to the homes of newly married daughters. More significant is the joyous return for all to a normal life without the symbolic denial of vital processes of life-giving activities—eating and sexual intercourse. In many places this festival lasts for three days, and in many lands it is also a national holiday. Islamic law requires that *zakat al-fitr* (sometimes called *sadaqat al fitr*), "alms of breaking off the fast," be given to the poor. This would seem to heighten one meaning of the fast, namely, focusing one's attention on the poor (who often go hungry) by making their plight easier. This meaning is suggested by the fact that in the time of the Prophet, and for some time thereafter, payment of zakat al-fitr was in the form of food, as the following hadith indicates:

> Narrated Ibn 'Umar: Allah's Apostle, prayers and peace be upon him, enjoined the payment of one *sa'* [approximately 6 pounds] of barley as Zakat al-Fitr on every Muslim slave or free, male or female, young or old, and he ordered that it be paid before the people went out to offer the 'Id prayer.[12]

Giving this special zakat, in addition to the general religious duty of zakat, which will be discussed later, is a personal response in ritual form to having experienced hunger and denial, and an aid to the needy to help them share in the festivities.

Festival of the Sacrifice ('id al-'adha).

This religious festival, also called the Major Festival or Greater Bayram, is celebrated on the tenth of Dhu al-Hijja, the last month of the Muslim calendar. Although Muslims observe this holiday in their hometowns all around the world, its most sacred observance is in Mina, a small village four miles East of Mecca. There hundreds of thousands of Muslims (about two million per year in the early 1990s) observe the sacrifice as part of the pilgrimage to Mecca and to other sacred sites nearby. The Sunna of the Prophet requires heads of families who are able to do so to purchase a sheep for the sacrifice. The meat of the slaughtered animal must be shared with the poor; common practice has been to give one-third to the poor, one-third to neighbors and friends, and one-third to oneself and family. Like 'id al-fitr, 'id al-'adha lasts three days. For pilgrims camped at Mina near Mecca, the day marks a return to normal life. These days are spent in conviviality with other pilgrims from around the world.

Muslims not making the pilgrimage celebrate the Festival of the Sacrifice in their hometowns and villages. In the Egyptian village of Kafr el-Elow, the festival is celebrated in much the same fashion as the breaking off of the fast. It begins on the first day with morning prayers in the local mosque followed by visits to the graves of deceased family. Then sheep are sacrificed. Sweets and great quantities of food are prepared for family and guests. Again, one's best clothes are worn, and the general mood is one of happiness and hospitality.

It is important to note in closing that the same two ingredients—the Qur'an and the Sunna on the one side, and local variations of custom in places such as Africa, Arabia, Tajikastan, Pakistan, and Indonesia on the other—determine the general ethos and local color of Muslim festivals. Baptist Christians in Des Moines, Iowa, celebrating Christmas with Coptic Christians in Upper Egypt might be surprised at some of the differences in the experience of this important Christian festival, including the date on which it is observed in each place. So, too, Islamic festivals derive something of their ethos, their social patterns and customary performance, from local culture: North American, Arabian, Malaysian, South African, etc. With this "unity and variety" theme in mind, we now turn to the experience of pilgrimage and religious theater in Islam.

NOTES

1. An antonym of *shakir* is *kafir*, which is usually translated "unbeliever" or "infidel," but has the connotation of "ingrate."

2. Mircea Eliade, *The Sacred and the Profane: The Nature of Religion*, trans. Willard R. Trask (New York: Harcourt, Brace & World, Inc., 1959), p. 20, and generally Chapter 1, "Sacred Space and Making the World Sacred," pp. 20–65.

3. See Eliade, *The Sacred and the Profane*, "Sacred Time and Myths," pp. 68–113.
4 On the Islamic calendar see Marshall G.S. Hodgson, *The Venture of Islam*, 3 volumes (Chicago: University of Chicago Press, 1974), vol. 1, pp. 20–22.
5. Brian Pfaffenberger, "The Kataragamma Pilgrimage: Hindu, Buddhist Interaction and Its Significance in Sri Lanka's Polythenic Social System," *Journal of Asian Studies*, 38, no. 2, (1979), 253.
6. Clifford Geertz, *Islam Observed* (New Haven, Conn.: Yale University Press, 1968).
7. See *Encyclopaedia of Islam*, 2nd ed., s.v., "'Ashura'" and "Muharram."
8. Information on the history of this festival is summarized in the article "Mawlid" in *Encyclopaedia of Islam*, 2nd ed.
9. Hani Fakhouri, *Kafr el-Elow: An Egyptian Village in Transition* (New York: Holt, Rinehart & Winston, 1972). pp. 85–86. A broader, more historical treatment of the festival in Islam is found in Gustav E. von Grunebaum, *Muhammaden Festivals* (London and New York: Abelard-Schuman, 1958).
10. See Fakhouri, *Kafr el-Elow*, p. 86. I am indebted to Dr. Muhammad Abdul-Rauf, former director of the Islamic Center in Washington, D.C., for this and many other details about these celebrations.
11. See *Encyclopaedia of Islam*, 2nd ed., s.v., "'Id al-Fitr."
12. Al-Bukhari, *The Translation of the Meanings of Sahih al-Bukhari: Arabic-English*, ed. Muhammad Muhsin Khan (Chicago: Kazi Publications, Inc., 1977), 2:339 (Book XXV [Sadaqat al-Fitr], No. 579).

12

Religious Renewal Through Pilgrimage and Drama

VISITING SACRED PLACES

Pilgrimage—the "On the Road" experience of persons in search of what is felt to be missing in everyday religion and life—is found in most religious traditions in one form or another. Pilgrimage is usually to a particular place, and often in the company of fellow travelers. Pilgrimages are great occasions that bring human society, or selected wayfarers from a given community, together in a state of brotherhood: what anthropologist Victor Turner labeled *communitas*.

The most general term for pilgrimage in Islam—sojourning to sacred places—is *ziyara*, literally "visiting." Ziyara is usually a visit made to the tombs of saints, who in life had been teachers and spiritual guides, known as shaykhs, walis, and pirs. In many parts of the Islamic world the shrines of these saints are close by, making visits affordable and repeatable for ordinary people. The spiritual powers of these saints did not diminish with death, but in fact increased. The term for the power experienced in the close vicinity of a saint's tomb, baraka, literally means "blessing." It is mostly the tombs of Sufi masters that have attracted visitors, year after year—in many cases for hundreds of years—to receive baraka, along with petitions and supplications for intercession with God.

FIGURE 12.1 Preparing bread during visit (ziyara) to saint's shrine in Pakistan. (Photo by the author.)

Tombs of saints have been erected in most places where Islam has spread. Visiting saints' tombs has been extensive in traditional Islam, and remains so today in much of the Islamic world. Nonetheless, ziyara, though widely practiced, is not a religious duty in Islam. Indeed, some Sunni Muslims, particularly those who associate with the Hanbali madh-hab in Islamic law (mostly in the Arabian peninsula) and who have been influenced by the late medieval reformer Ibn Taymiya, have frowned upon popular practices such as ziyara, which are not enjoined by the Qur'an and the Sunna. Popular religion is shaped by local custom, 'ada. Local variations on putting the words of the Sunna of the Prophet into practice are influenced by 'ada. In Egypt, one can speak of the 'ada of Nubians in upper Egypt, the 'ada of Sa'idis in the middle Nile Valley, and the 'ada of the Delta region. The hajj to Mecca itself was once 'ada—that is, customary practice for pre-Islamic Arabs, who had many such pilgrimage sites in Arabia. With the rise of Islam, popular practice was reified, redefined in terms of monotheistic symbols: in short, "Islamized."

Historians of religion have asked: What is the relationship between the Sunna and 'ada? The anthropologist Robert Redfield, to whom we will refer again in the next chapter, employed the concepts of great and little traditions, that is, the great urban traditions of clergy, monumental architecture, literary texts, and legal, interpretive schools, in contrast to religion among the nonliterate, rural, and pastoral masses, who mix the religion of the elites with local practices, such as visiting the mausolea of Sufi saints in search of miracles and blessings. Sometimes this dichotomy is generalized as the difference between official religion and popular religion. "Orthodox" versus "heterodox" religion is another way this distinction is often made. Islamic practice that includes visits to the tombs of local saints has sometimes come under sharp attack by the ulama, the religious leaders trained in the texts and interpretations preserved by the great tradition. In other words, little traditions of popular, local religious practice are often seen as contaminations of the main tradition, to use the idiom of tahara from Chapter 10.

Peter Brown, a historian of late antiquity, has argued that popular religion and "little traditions" should be studied on their own terms.

> The model of "popular religion" that is usually presented by scholars of late antiquity has the disadvantage that it assumes that "popular religion" can be understood only from the viewpoint of the elite. "Popular religion" is presented as in some ways a diminution, a misconception or a contamination of "*un*-popular religion." Whether it is presented, bluntly, as "popular superstition" or categorized as "lower forms of belief," it is assumed that "popular religion" exhibits modes of thinking and worshipping that are best intelligible in terms of a failure to be something else.[1]

Brown argues that the rise of the cult of the saints in Latin Christianity of the Mediterranean world was not so much a corruption of Christian belief and practice in the early church as it was a response to social changes of late antiquity. In Brown's words, ". . .the cult of the saints involved imaginative changes that seem, at least, congruent to changing patterns of human relations in late-Roman society at large."[2] In other words, so-called heterodox religious practices, such as visits to saints' tombs (whether in medieval Christianity or in medieval Islam) can be seen as the evolution of orthodox religion (Sunni and Shi'i Islam), not the devolution of a great tradition into a corrupt little tradition.

The main topic of this chapter is the great annual universal Muslim pilgrimage to Mecca, the hajj. As Victor Turner has pointed out, ". . .pilgrimage is very much more than its theology. It is a field of social relations and cultural contents of the most diverse types, formal and informal, orthodox and heterodox, dogmatic and mythical, often juxtaposed rather than fused, interrelated, or systematized."[3] The "theology" of the hajj is found in how it is interpreted in the Shari'a. In this chapter, the social experience of the hajj, as an ingathering of the many ethnic groups of Muslims that make up the world of Islam, will also be emphasized.

Related to the spiritual experience of pilgrimage is the narration and drama of great religious moments in the sacred history of Islam. The final section of this chapter describes the Passion of Husayn, known as the *ta'ziya*, celebrated in poems, storytelling, and drama since the tragic murder of Husayn, which triggered the second great fitna in the first century of Islam.

We will see that the fitna, the experience of social conflict dramatized in the ta'ziya, illumines the category of pathos, which was discussed in Chapter 3.

PILGRIMAGE TO MECCA

Each year during the last month of the Islamic calendar, Dhu al-Hijja, over one million Muslims make the pilgrimage called the hajj to Mecca. It is the fifth Pillar of Islam, and both the Qur'an and the Sunna of the Prophet offer information and guidance to Muslims who decide to make this journey. Many of the Prophet's sayings and many pages in the books of Islamic law describe and regulate one's participation in the hajj. Although it is an obligatory religious duty, practical considerations exist. Only those who can afford the journey and who are physically able to endure its hardships are required to make the hajj.

Until recently, Muslims from such faraway places as Spain and India had to begin months in advance, often as much as a year, in order to reach Mecca at the appointed time. Muslims from these and other lands would join regular processions of pilgrims along well-traveled routes leading to Mecca from Syria, Iraq, Egypt, and South Arabia. Those who wrote about their adventures and experiences along the way became important sources of information about Islamic lands and local customs in the Middle Ages.

Nowadays the city of Jidda on the western coast of Saudi Arabia, about fifty miles west of Mecca, is the main port of entry. By chartered plane and ship, pilgrims arrive in great throngs at Jidda in the tenth month, Shawwal. From this swelling port of entry they proceed to Mecca. At some point before reaching the haram, the sacred territory surrounding the Ka'ba, usually even before arriving in Jidda, they consecrate themselves for the sacred ritual. Buses and cars have replaced the camel as the chief means of transportation to Mecca. Nonetheless, pilgrims on foot or astride camels and donkeys are still to be seen on the road to Mecca during the season of the hajj.

The person who makes the hajj is called a Hajji (Hajjiya if female). Both before departing and after returning, a Hajji is a celebrated person in his or her hometown. Many who cannot afford the sacred journey experience it vicariously through those who can. Those who are physically unable to make the journey may send a substitute, whose performance of the hajj rites meets the duty of the ill person to perform this Pillar of Islamic practice. Poems and songs about the hajj are sung with neighbors and friends. This is the ceremony of leavetaking from one's family and friends that enlivens homes and neighborhoods across the world of Islam in the weeks before departure. Hajjis in rural Egypt often paint special symbols on their homes, depicting their experiences. Wealthier Muslims may offer to finance the trip for those who are less fortunate. Throughout the Islamic world, newspapers, radio, and television stations cover the many aspects of this mass ritual.

FIGURE 12.2 Muslim pilgrims line up at the airport in Senegal-Dakar to make travel arrangements for the holy pilgrimage to Mecca. (Photo by Eugene Gordon.)

Although only a fraction of the Muslim population makes the hajj in any given year, the entire world of Islam participates in this important religious festival, the Fifth Pillar of Islam. This worldwide sharing of the hajj experience has been enhanced by the televising of the major events.

The Pilgrimage Experience

In the following pages we shall follow the footsteps of Muslims making the hajj. Their responses to the symbols and rituals involved have been conditioned by their Islamic environment since childhood. Through the encounter between the hajj experience and the scholarly study of religious symbols and rituals, we hope to illuminate both an internal and an external view of the fifth Pillar of Islam.[4]

As the plane first lands at Jidda on the western coast of Saudi Arabia, one is caught in a bundle of emotions.[5] First, there are immigration checkpoints, clogged with thousands of people of all races. Language and communication appear to be a problem. Confusion seems to prevail at first. Even with family and friends, one feels like a small drop in a vast ocean of people. Yet this is not a "lonely crowd." Despite differences of color, language, and socioecononic status, all have come to participate in the special Islamic brother-hood that is experienced in this rite. All are dressed alike; all share identical beliefs; and despite language barriers, all can speak common words of greeting. During the events of the next few days, the acquaintance of many people is made along the way. By the end of the hajj a common feeling of brotherhood among pilgrims from many countries will be established.

The difficulties of negotiating one's way during the hajj are considerable. Therefore, over the centuries Muslims from afar have often employed agents to handle local arrangements for them and to guide them on their journey. More recently, organizations have formed to handle arrangements for entire groups.

Pilgrims normally exchange their street clothes for the sacred white ihram garb before arriving in Jidda. For men it consists of two white pieces of cloth, each about the size of a large towel, one draped over the shoulder and knotted on the opposite side, the other fastened around the waist. Most women wear full-length white dresses and a white head covering. By donning the attire of ihram, a Muslim enters a consecrated state (*ihram*); he or she becomes *muhrim*. Hair and fingernails may not be cut, colognes and perfumes may not be worn, and sexual activities are to be suspended. Bathing is also discontinued during the state of ihram, except to remove a major pollution (*najas*), such as menstruation for women and nocturnal emission for men.

The trip from Jidda to Mecca is one of mounting excitement and anticipation. As pilgrims pass through the boundaries that mark the haram, shouts

FIGURE 12.3 Folk art depicting the hajj on a home in rural Egypt. (Photo by the author.)

of *labbayka* pierce the air. It is the *talbiya*, the traditional exclamation of Muslim pilgrims, and it means, roughly, "Here I am, O Lord." Loudly and frequently announcing one's presence in God's sanctuary, the haram, is an old practice, at least as old as Islam, as the following hadith indicates: "Narrated Nafi': The Prophet (prayers and peace be upon him) recited Talbiya when he had mounted his Mount and was ready to set out [in a direction facing the qibla]."[6]

Crossing the border into the haram, the state of consecration becomes complete. No shedding of blood or fomenting any kind of strife is permitted. Animals may not be hunted, and even plant life must be left undisturbed. Just as there is bodily cessation of bathing and cutting of hair and nails, the land within the haram is itself consecrated for those in the state of ihram. Fasting, on the other hand, is not required. The student of religion will recognize in ihram the larger realm of tahara, the state of ritual purity.

A great welling of emotion comes when the pilgrims enter the city of Mecca. They invariably head straight to the Great Mosque: within its giant courtyard stands the Ka'ba. Several times each day of their lives in their hometowns, Muslim pilgrims have oriented themselves toward the Ka'ba during the canonical prayer. All of a sudden it looms very large and real, a cubical stone edifice covered by a black cloth embroidered in gold calligraphy. It would be difficult to grasp or describe all the possible feelings Muslims might have at this moment. The famous nineteenth-century British traveler and adventurer, Sir Richard Burton, once posed as a Muslim in order to make the hajj. His impressions of his first glimpse of the Ka'ba are worth quoting.

> There at last it lay, the bourn of my long and weary Pilgrimage, realising the plans and hopes of many and many a year. The mirage medium of Fancy invested the huge catafalque and its gloomy pall with peculiar charms. There were no giant fragments of hoar[y] antiquity as in Egypt, no remains of graceful and harmonious beauty as in Greece and Italy, no barbarous gorgeousness as in the buildings of India; yet the view was strange, unique—and how few have looked upon the celebrated shrine!. . . It was as if the poetical legends of the Arabs spoke the truth, and that the waving wings of angels, not the sweet breeze of morning, were agitating and swelling the black covering of the shrine.[7]

The 'Umra or Lesser Pilgrimage

By declaring a niya (prayer of intention), a Muslim may choose to perform the Lesser Pilgrimage, the 'umra, prior to the main performance of the hajj or Greater Pilgrimage. Some pilgrims will perform the Lesser Pilgrimage later, or even at another time of the year. After the first few moments of awe, one may join hundreds of other Muslims circumambulating the Ka'ba.

The 'umra is highlighted by seven such counterclockwise circuits. This circling is known as the *tawaf*. The Ka'ba, which stands in the center of this

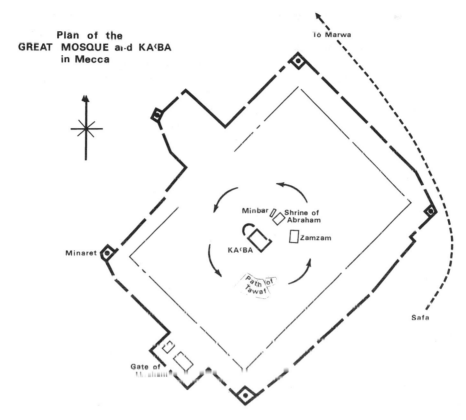

FIGURE 12.4 Plan of the Ka'ba and the Great Mosque. (Based on an illustration by David Stodola.)

activity, is so situated that each of its four corners points in one of the four cardinal points of the compass (see Figure 12.4).

Set in the east corner of the Ka'ba is a black stone rimmed by a silver casing. The first tawaf around the Ka'ba begins on the side of the courtyard of the Great Mosque nearest the stone. An attempt to actually touch it—the desire of every pilgrim—may be blocked by the press of the crowd. Many get close enough to actually kiss the stone. This custom recalls a hadith based on the practice of the second caliph:

> Narrated Zaid bin Aslam that his father said, "I saw 'Umar bin al-Khattab kissing the Black Stone and he then said (to it) 'Had I not seen Allah's Apostle (prayers and peace be upon him) kissing you (stone), I would not have kissed you.'"[8]

Aerial views of the tawaf show just how massive yet homogeneous the ritual process is nowadays. Thousands of Muslims dressed in the common ihram attire move in a common gesture around the House of God, the sacred geographical center of Islam.

The Ka'ba is not the only sacred monument within the Great Mosque of Mecca. Out from the northeast wall of the Ka'ba is the Place of Ibrahim (Abraham), a smaller, more ornate shrine that commemorates the ancient Patriarch's founding of the first house of worship. Closer to the black stone is the well of Zamzam. Tradition has it that while Hagar searched frantically for water, her infant Isma'il (Ishmael) kicked the ground and water miraculously sprang forth.

All pilgrim visitors to the shrine seek a draught of the sacred refreshment that continues to flow in the well of Zamzam. Adjacent to the Place of Ibrahim is a decorated pulpit or *minbar* that looks out over the central grounds from atop a flight of stairs. On Fridays prior to the hajj, pilgrims gather to hear a sermon delivered by a leading imam. The purpose of the sermon is to prepare pilgrims for the spiritual journey ahead.

After the tawaf, Muslims making the Lesser Pilgrimage head for the eastern gate of the courtyard of the Great Mosque and pass into a long covered corridor that connects two points known as Safa and Marwa (see Figure 12.4). Each pilgrim runs or walks rapidly the distance of a few blocks from one point to the other, seven trips in all. The traditional meaning of this act is a symbolic remembrance of the plight of Hagar, who ran in desperation between these two points in search of water and help against the harsh conditions of the barren desert. Following the "running" between Safa and Marwa, pilgrims have a lock of hair cut, removing themselves from the state of ihram. The duties of the 'umra have been fulfilled.

The Hajj or Greater Pilgrimage

Day of Watering (Yawm al-Tarwiya).   On the eighth day of Dhu al-Hijja, great masses of Muslims set out from Mecca with the niya (intention) of making the Greater Pilgrimage (unless this was already declared before reaching Jidda). The day is also known as "Going out to Mina," a small town four miles to the east of Mecca. It is reported that during his Farewell Pilgrimage just before he died, Muhammad spent his first night in Mina. The name "Day of Watering" has puzzled Muslim historians. Some have concluded that it was originally a day for watering camels in preparation for the days ahead. It remains a day of spiritual and physical preparation for the rigors of the hajj. Thousands of tents are tightly arranged along the valley floor at Mina to accommodate the increasing number of pilgrims each year. Many pilgrims, however, move on to Arafat to be at the next day's station ahead of the rush.

Day at Arafat (Yawm Arafat).   On the ninth day of Dhu al-Hijja, pilgrims begin to gather at the easternmost distant station of the hajj, the Plain of Arafat. As they swarm onto the plain, they pass between two markers that designate the boundary of the haram; Arafat lies just outside it. At noon, both the midday and afternoon prayers are performed together. The afternoon is then spent standing at the foot of a small rocky hill called the Mount of Mercy. From a position on the hill during his Farewell Pilgrimage, Muhammad had delivered a sermon to his followers gathered on the plain. This event has been commemorated since the early days of Islam with a sermon delivered by a respected imam. The homily repeats the Prophet's farewell call for peace and harmony among his followers. (This is a theme, as we shall see, that is common to pilgrims in the world religions.) Many Muslims will spend the entire afternoon standing beneath or even on the hill; the more pious hope to locate themselves near where Muhammad had stood. Those unable to take the long hours of heat, especially in years when Dhu al-Hijja occurs during the summer, retire after a while to tents erected on the plain for that purpose. They too will spend the afternoon in prayer and quiet reflection.

At sunset a signal is given for the "Hurrying to Muzdalifa," a small town back on the road to Mecca. As camp in the Plain of Arafat is broken, shouts of labbayka pierce the air. The mood of somber reflection disappears with the sun; excitement and anticipation rouse the crowd into frantic activity. Reports from Muslim travelers in the Middle Ages confirm the impressions of Sir Richard Burton.

> The Pilgrims. . . rushed down the hill [of Arafat] with a "Labbayk" sounding like a blast, and took the road to Muna [Mina]. Then I saw the scene which has given this part of the ceremonies the name of the "Hurry from Arafat." Every man urged his beast with might and main: it was sunset; the plain bristled with tent-pegs, litters were crushed, pedestrians were trampled, camels were overthrown. . .briefly, it was chaotic confusion.[9]

Like many religious ceremonials, the hajj has quick changes of tempo. The entire experience stands in sharp contrast to everyday life. Following this description we will evaluate some of these contrasts. With so many people presently making the hajj journey, some logistic control over the Hurry to Muzdalifa has been exerted by the Saudi Arabian authorities, the caretakers of the two holy places, Mecca and Medina. Many pilgrims nowadays ride in buses from site to site, but the sense of excitement and anticipation runs high nonetheless.

Arriving in Muzdalifa after dark, pilgrims recite the sunset and late evening prayers together. This is a relaxation that applies during any journey in order to provide for keeping the prayer without interrupting necessary activities. That evening a lighted mosque on a nearby hill draws one's attention. Around the camp in Muzdalifa, pilgrims may be seen gathering numerous small stones that will be ritually tossed at symbolic representations of Satan on the following days.

Festival of the Sacrifice ('id al-adha). Before daybreak on the morning of the tenth of Dhu al-Hijja, a signal again rouses the encamped pilgrims to

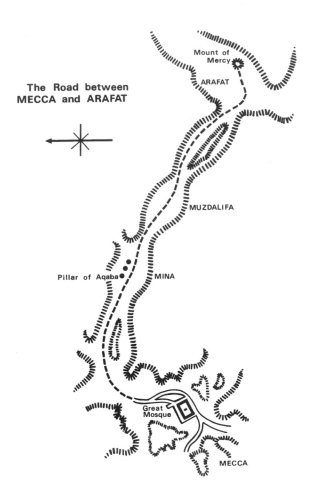

The Road between MECCA and ARAFAT

Mount of Mercy

ARAFAT

MUZDALIFA

Pillar of Aqaba • MINA

Great Mosque

MECCA

FIGURE 12.5 Plan of the hajj stations. (Based on an illustration by David Stodola.)

break camp and move on. Arriving in Mina, they carry the stones gathered the previous evening to a stone pillar called 'Aqaba. Seven stones are thrown by each pilgrim at this symbol of Satan. Islamic sacred history, recorded in the Qur'an and elaborated in tradition, relates the story that God had called upon Ibrahim to sacrifice his son Isma'il. Satan repeatedly sought to tempt Ibrahim into ignoring the command, and each time Ibrahim resisted temptation, remaining steadfast in his intention to carry out God's costly command. At the last minute God spared Ibrahim this painful duty.

The stoning of 'Aqaba is a ritual repulsion of the Tempter, Satan. After tossing the stones, pilgrims move to the edge of the plain around Mina and begin the sacrifice. Sheep and other animals are purchased and slaughtered on the open plain. We have described this festival as a ritual that takes place throughout the Islamic world, not just at Mina. The sacrifice signifies

Ibrahim's willingness to sacrifice what was most precious to him, his son. The sacrificer symbolically affirms he is willing to give up, for the sake of God, that which is dearest to him. It is a sacred gesture of thanksgiving and measure of charity. Like the parallel story of the (near) sacrifice of Isaac in the Bible, the substitution of a ram at the last minute symbolizes God's pleasure at Ibrahim's willingness to carry out the sacrifice. Following the sacrifice, male pilgrims form in line to have their hair cut. In privacy, women will cut a lock of hair, again as a symbolic gesture. Many men will have their heads shaven—a sign of being a Hajji. Others may choose to have only a "trim," which, as a ritual gesture, is considered efficacious. Then pilgrims doff the ihram garb and thereby deconsecrate themselves to the extent allowed while still within the haram around Mecca. Normal street clothes can now be worn. Bathing and grooming then follows as all Muslims return to normal life. Only sexual activity (including kissing and entering into a marriage contract) is forbidden until the "post Arafat" tawaf is performed at the Great Mosque. While the pilgrims have been on the hajj, the Ka'ba has received a new *kiswa,* or black shroud, beautifully embroidered in calligraphy enunciating quranic verses appropriate to the hajj. Those who have not yet made the Lesser Pilgrimage may do so at this time.

Days of Social Gathering (Ayyam al-Tashriq). The eleventh through the thirteenth days of Dhu al Hijja provide a happy, convivial climax to the hajj. Pilgrims remain encamped at Mina, where they enjoy a period of deepening friendships gained along the way. Muslims from around the world have gotten to know each other during the entire pilgrimage. Even if two hajj acquaintances do not speak a common language, usually someone nearby can interpret for them. Arabic, the liturgical language of the hajj ritual, is the language heard most often. All Muslims learn to exchange religious greetings in Arabic. On each of the three days pilgrims return to 'Aqaba and the two other stone pillars in the center of Mina to toss seven stones at each, ritually repulsing Satan. On the third and final day of social gathering, many Muslims return to Mecca to make a final tawaf around the Ka'ba in the Great Mosque. Afterwards many purchase a few mementos to bring back to friends. Then buses are boarded for the trip to Jidda, and back home.

Many Muslims take this opportunity to make another pilgrimage. Nearby Medina is the second holy city of Islam (Jerusalem is the third). The Prophet's mosque and tomb are visited by thousands of pilgrims each year, particularly at this time. Muslims visit Medina to offer salutations to the Prophet and to seek forgiveness of their sins at the mosque and house from which he directed the establishment of the Islamic umma during the last ten years of his mission. Muslims believe Muhammad brought the Guidance to humankind, and their reverence and thankfulness are especially keen on this second pilgrimage to Medina.

Interpreting the Pilgrimage Experience

Throughout the centuries, many travelers have made the hajj and described their experiences. Interesting as these reports are to readers who are otherwise unfamiliar with this phenomenon, understanding the pilgrimage experience offers the student of religion a considerable challenge. One point to be considered is that the hajj was an important ritual in pagan Arabia long before the rise of Islam. As a young man, Muhammad is said to have made the hajj while the rite still bore its pre-Islamic meanings. The Muslims from Mecca who emigrated with Muhammad to Medina were denied access to this important ritual until the sixth year after the Hijra. The Prophet himself became a "Muslim" pilgrim in 632, and his performance that year significantly changed certain aspects and much of the meaning of the ancient ritual. The following hadith, narrated on the authority of Abu Huraira, indicates that many of the rules had to change during the transition from the pagan to the Islamic form of the hajj:

> In the year prior to the last Hajj of the Prophet (prayers and peace be upon him) when Allah's Apostle (prayers and peace be upon him) made Abu Bakr leader of the pilgrims, the latter (Abu Bakr) sent me [Abu Huraira] in the company of a group of people to make a public announcement (proclaiming): "no pagan is allowed to perform Hajj after this year, and no naked person is allowed to perform Tawaf of the Ka'ba."[10]

Both references are to pre-Islamic practice, the period Muslims refer to as Jahiliyya.

The sacred history of Ibrahim's journey to Mecca with Hagar and Isma'il is the Islamic understanding of the origin of the Meccan shrine. The story of Ibrahim's difficult duty to sacrifice his son became the Islamic sacred history of the Festival of the Sacrifice in Mina known as 'id al-adha, the celebration of which was described in the preceding chapter. The Plain of Arafat, which lay just beyond the boundaries of the haram, was originally the scene of an annual fair held during the pilgrimage season. Muhammad's Farewell Pilgrimage brought his own person directly into the meaning of the several sacred days precisely in the middle of the journey at the extreme geographic outpost beyond the ancient sacred boundaries. The Islamic understanding of the hajj took its classic form with reference to the Sunna of the Prophet. It was the work of the legal theorists of the orthodox Shari'a law schools that clarified the duties and options incumbent upon all Hajjis. Tradition, both popular and formal, gave the ancient practice continued life with new meanings. The fine points of duties and options, such as how long one should stand at Arafat, were established by consensus in the law schools of the Shari'a.

The social, cultural, and economic effects of the hajj in medieval Islam, writes historian Bernard Lewis, are of immense importance.

Every year, great numbers of Muslims, from all parts of the Islamic world, from many races and from different social strata, left their homes and travelled, often over vast distances, to take part in a common act of worship. . . . The needs of the pilgrimage—the commands of the faith reinforcing the requirements of government and commerce—help to maintain an adequate network of communications between the far-flung Muslim lands; the experience of the pilgrimage gives rise to a rich literature of travel, bringing information about distant places, and a heightened awareness of belonging to a larger whole. This awareness is reinforced by participation in the common ritual and ceremonies of the pilgrimage in Mecca and Medina, and the communion with fellow-Muslims of other lands and peoples. . . . The pilgrimage was not the only factor making for cultural unity and social mobility in the Islamic world [during the Middle Ages] but it was certainly an important one, perhaps the most important.[11]

The religious significance of the pilgrimages performed in a variety of the religions of humankind has been studied by anthropologists and historians of religions. The writings of Arnold van Gennep and Victor Turner, in particular, have offered vital new insights. Earlier theories about rites of passage in tribal societies showed that a cross-cultural pattern can be discerned in the rites of all peoples, as, for example, in initiation ceremonials. A major shift takes place between the structured society in which one lives his or her everyday life, and the sense of brotherhood or community that is created by the ceremonial. In the society of one's village or city, vertical relations based on social class and economic status are clearly defined. These are dissolved when one enters the community that has been created by ceremonial rites. Society is a secular or "profane" phenomenon; community is sacred. This was the theory proposed by the anthropologist van Gennep.

Victor Turner took the argument further by proposing that pilgrimages performed in the major living religious traditions of the world are manifestations of the same patterns of movement from secular to sacred and back to secular life that is characteristic of many rites of passage. The term used by social scientists for the religious experience of a sacred community is an anglicized Latin word, *liminality*. Turner defines liminality as follows:

The attributes of liminality or of liminal personae ("threshold people") are necessarily ambiguous, since this condition and these persons elude or slip through the network of classifications that normally locate states and positions in cultural space. Liminal entities are neither here nor there; they are betwixt and between the positions assigned and arrayed by law, custom, convention, and ceremonial. As such, their ambiguous and indeterminate attributes are expressed by a rich variety of symbols in the many societies that ritualize social and cultural transitions. Thus, liminality is frequently likened to death, to being in the womb, to invisibility, to darkness, to bisexuality, to the wilderness, and to an eclipse of the sun or moon.

Liminal entities. . .may be represented as possessing nothing. They may be disguised as monsters, wear only a strip of clothing, or even go naked, to demon-

strate that as liminal beings they have no status, property, insignia, secular clothing indicating rank or role, position in a kinship system—in short, nothing that
may distinguish them from their fellow neophytes or initiands (i.e.,
pilgrims)."[12]

Turner's illuminating analysis provides some valuable insights into the hajj
experience. The pilgrimage to Mecca is a liminal experience. The Shari'a
carefully lays out the structure of relationships and obligations that ought to
prevail in Islamic society. The respective roles of men and women, the
proper forms of government, even the everyday performance of prayer and
other religious duties belong to the domain of "society" in social scientific
terms. But within this highly structured mode of living, pressures build up;
sin and human failure alienate one from fellow human beings. One then
becomes a pilgrim, setting out on a sacred journey to a sacred space within
which the binding structures and obligations of society are altered or dissolved. Equality with other human beings is felt as never before, and spiritual renewal is keenly experienced. It is a rich adventure. Pilgrims cross
social and political boundaries in order to reach a sacred center. At the sacred
center (the Ka'ba in Islam), brotherhood is achieved in a way that is not fea-
sible back in one's normal social setting.

During the state of ihram or "consecration," Muslims suspend or reverse
the usual patterns of both sacred and secular life back at home. As we have
seen, the pilgrim alters the normal times of prayer at Arafat. Cutting the hair
and nails is suspended. Street clothes, the symbol of one's status in society, are
exchanged for a common garb, the ihram. Sexual activity, the force that per-
petuates society, is temporarily ceased. The liminal experience of brotherhood
relieves the burden of society, and one's responsibilities within it are lifted. A
true community of believers is experienced. Then this process of inversion
ends, and the pilgrim returns to his or her normal social context. It is a process
of renewal that each Muslim must decide whether, and when, to undertake in
his or her own personal quest for salvation. Hajj is a duty incumbent on all
Muslims once in their lifetime—one that many do not fulfill for want of funds,
freedom from obligations back home, health, spiritual dedication, etc.

THE MUHARRAM PASSION

The pathos of the death of righteous youth at the hands of unjust leaders is a
common theme in world literature. In Shi'i Islam, the dramatic reenactment of
the unjust murders of Husayn, son of 'Ali, and his family is known as *ta'ziya*.

The Ta'ziya of Qasim

Qasim, son of Hasan, is betrothed to his cousin, Fatima. The marriage had
been the wish of Imam Hasan before his death. Qasim also feels compelled

to join his family's fight against the troops of the Umayyads, led by Caliph Yazid. This conflict has already taken the life of his cousin, 'Ali Akbar. In this particular performance of the Iranian ta'ziya theater, Qasim himself must face a violent end. All of these events form separate episodes of the main tragedy of Shi'i salvation history, the violent death of Imam Husayn at the hands of the troops of Yazid, who was caliph and commander of the Umayyad troops.

In the ta'ziya of Qasim, Imam Husayn is reluctant to let his nephew march off to war. "How can I send him? He is the living memory of my brother (Hasan), an unwed boy in the flower of his youth who has not yet tasted the pleasures of life."[13] As the family tearfully discusses whether or not Qasim should join the battle, a riderless horse appears. Piercing wails rise up from the grief-stricken family. It is the mount belonging to the martyred 'Ali Akbar, son of Husayn and cousin of Qasim. Qasim's desire to seek revenge is now overwhelming. He will go to war. But first he must wed the beautiful Fatima, daughter of Husayn and Sister of 'Ali Akbar.

Thus in the midst of grief for the dead, a traditional Islamic wedding ceremonial is prepared. Qasim will wear the bridegroom costume of his fallen cousin, 'Ali Akbar. Imam Husayn, the living family patriarch, sends sweets to his enemies. This symbolic gesture is based on the custom that the family hosts the nuptial celebrations with entertainment and food for the larger community. After the wedding, when they are finally alone, Qasim tells Fatima that he must leave immediately for war. Theirs is to be an unrequited love. Time and events will not allow them to consummate the marriage. Against Fatima's protests, Qasim offers the consolation that perhaps their union will become beautifully complete in Heaven.

In the battle that is next staged, Qasim fights bravely, but he is soon stricken from his mount, ironically by the enemy to whom the ceremonial sweets had been sent announcing his marriage. Qasim begs for a reprieve to see his bride and fulfill his love for her before the death blow is struck. As Qasim is cradled in the arms of the mourning patriarch, Imam Husayn, his plea is ignored. The enemy delivers the fatal blow. As he breathes his last breaths, Qasim refuses to let Husayn return his mutilated body to Fatima. When Qasim expires on the field of battle, Husayn returns to the family encampment to deliver the tragic news.[14]

The Ta'ziya in History War and marriage, passion and unrequited love, gestures of friendship and cruelties of revenge, heaven and earth—these and other conflicting themes emerge as actors and audience participate together in the Shi'i rituals of sacred history. As a stage performance, the ta'ziya is a recent form of a classic mode of Shi'i piety. Karbala, Iraq, was the historic scene of the martyrdom of Husayn on the tenth of Muharram in 680. This was the seed event that inspired the many episodes of the ta'ziya performance. Until the nineteenth century, the main form of piety was the pilgrimages (*ziyarat*) to the shrines of the Shi'i martyrs, especially to the site at

FIGURE 12.6   Ta'ziya of the *Martyrdom of Iman Husayn*, Shiraz, Iran. (Photo courtesy of Peter Chelkowski.)

Karbala. In addition, in Persian cities and villages, scripts of the scenes of their martyrdom were read before emotion-filled audiences. In time, special performance halls were erected. A stage constructed especially for ta'ziya performances is called a *takiya*; it marks out a sacred space, and the events that are performed within its boundaries become moments of sacred time. Peter Chelkowski says of the ta'ziya performance:

> The word ta'ziyeh literally means expressions of sympathy, mourning and consolation. As a dramatic form it has its origins in the Muharram processions commemorating [Husayn's] martyrdom and throughout its evolution the representation of the siege and carnage at Kerbela has remained the centerpoint. Ta'ziyeh has never lost its religious implications. Because early Shi'i tes viewed [Husayn's] death as a sacred redemptive act, the performance of the Muharram ceremonies was believed to be an aid to salvation; later they also believed that participation, both by actors and spectators, in the Ta'ziyeh dramas would gain them [Husayn"s] intercession on the day of the Last Judgment.[15]

Pathos in Sacred Time and Space

Personal salvation is a theme common to monotheistic religious traditions. It is a major theme of the ta'ziya's dramatized ritual. The sufferings of the

Prophet's cousin and son-in-law, 'Ali, and of 'Ali's family, are paradigmatic experiences for the Shi'i minority. The many unfolding episodes involving tragedy, heroism, and loyalty to Ali's branch of the Prophet's family provide Shi'i Muslims a distinct identity within the Islamic umma. The historic conflict with governmental oppression is dramatized in the ritual experience of sacred space and time. It is a form of religious pathos that distinguishes Shi'i from Sunni Muslims.

Sacred Space. The Islamic proscription against the artistic representation of living beings, discussed in Chapter 9, is not observed in the ta'ziya performance. Many paintings of this scene have been made. On the stage and throughout the space occupied by takiya theaters, players boldly represent the main personalities of Shi'i salvation history. A takiya theater constitutes a sacred space, and Shi'i pilgrimage to the takiya is a liminal experience.

The design of the takiya indicates the sacral character of the many dramas performed by audience and actors alike. Chelkowski's description is illuminating.

> The design of the *takiyeh* preserved and enhanced the dramatic interplay between actors and spectators which was characteristic of the traditional Muharram rites. The main action took place on a stark, curtainless raised platform in the center of the building. Surrounding it was a narrow circular band of space used by the performers for sub-plots and to indicate journeys, passage of time, and change of scene. At the periphery of this space, extending into the audience-filled pit, small secondary stages were often erected. Scenes of special significance were acted upon them and sometimes players from these auxiliary stages would engage in dialogue or action with those on the central stage.[16]

A takiya may be enclosed by an outer wall, itself a prop used to dramatic effect. Action courses along aisles leading from gateways through the walls to the central stage. Messengers, riders, soldiers, and even directors and managers of the performance busily traverse these passageways. The drama is seldom confined to a single action. The siege of 'Ali's family is symbolized by the very arrangement of the takiya space, with the audience surrounding the central stage, and actors pushing toward it, often through the crowd.

Sacred Time. Scholarly studies of the ta'ziya performance indicate an aspect of sacred time. Ta'ziya performers are not actors in the usual sense of the word in Western theatrical traditions. The players *represent* scenes and personalities from Shi'i sacred history that are well known to the audience. Costumes and props are more symbolic than actual reproductions of authentic clothing and items from the days of Husayn and Caliph Yazid. For example, sunglasses may be worn to indicate the player is an enemy. Green worn by a player designates him as a good member of Husayn's party; red identifies the evil members of Yazid's party. A white shroud worn by the player who represents, say, Qasim, signifies that he will be martyred gladly. Even the very form in which the lines are uttered differentiates good from evil players: good characters chant their lines in the pleasing mode of poetry whereas evil characters shout their lines with unpleasant gruffness. Thus the entire performance—and there are literally hundreds of different ta'ziya scenarios—is a curious combination of symbolic representations, both traditional and modern. Players do not act their parts; through symbolic and formalized speech, emotions, and attire, they represent moments in sacred history. Although there is no element of suspense comparable to that in Western drama, audience involvement in the staged events is vicarious and deeply emotional. The unavoidable result of the ta'ziya, Husayn's murder, is well known to everyone present. His martyrdom becomes their salvation. Their collective and individual sufferings in history are resolved in the ta'ziya experience even as the historic conflict of Shi'i sm will be ultimately resolved in the sacred time of Judgment.

In Chapter 3 we spoke of the pathos of religion, the experience of tragic conflict that cannot be resolved here and now, which the Shi'i celebration of the Passion of Husayn epitomizes and dramatizes for the entire community to relive and experience. Only in Paradise will such tragic injustices be reversed for the righteous. In the following chapters, we move from the pathos of sacred beginnings and eschatology to the ethos of religion and society in everyday life.

NOTES

1. Peter Brown, *The Cult of the Saints: Its Rise and Function in Latin Christianity* (Chicago: University of Chicago Press, 1981), p. 19.
2. Brown, *Cult of the Saints*, p. 21.
3. Victor Turner and Edith Turner, *Image and Pilgrimage in Christian Culture: Anthropological Perspectives* (New York: Columbia University Press, 1978), p. 106.
4. The account of the hajj that follows has been gathered from many sources, several of which will be noted in the next few pages. Conversations with Muslim friends who have made the hajj have inspired the medium of personal observation injected into the narrative description.
5. A moving personal account by a black American Muslim making the hajj was given by Malcolm X in *Autobiography of Malcolm X* (New York: Grove Press, Inc., 1966), pp. 318–42.
6. Al-Bukhari, *The Translation of Meanings of Sahih al-Bukhari*, trans. Muhammad Muhsin Khan (Chicago: Kazi Publication Inc., 1977), 2:362 (Book XXXIV, Chapter 27, no. 624).
7. Richard F. Burton, *Personal Narrative of a Pilgrimage to Al-Madinah and Meccah*, 2 volumes, ed. Isabel Burton, (London: G. Bell & Sons, Ltd., 1898), 2:160–61.
8. Bukhari, *Translation*, 2:396 (Book XXXIV, Chapter 59, no. 679).
9. Burton, *Pilgrimage*, 2:199.
10. Bukhari, 2:401–402 (Book XXXIV, Chapter 66, no. 689).

11. Bernard Lewis on the social aspects of the hajj in the article "Hadjdj," *Encyclopaedia of Islam*, 2nd ed.
12. Reprinted from Victor Turner, *The Ritual Process: Structure and Anti-Structure* (Ithaca, N.Y.: Cornell University Press, 1969), p. 95. Copyright (c) 1969 by Victor W. Turner. Used by permission of the publisher, Cornell University Press.
13. Line from the Ta'ziya of Qasim cited by Sadeq Humayuni, "An Analysis of the Ta'ziyeh of Qasem," in *Ta'ziyeh: Ritual and Drama in Iran*, ed. Peter Chelkowski (New York: New York University Press. 1979), p. 13. Copyright (c) 1979 by New York University.
14. A fuller account and analysis of this scene is given by Humayuni, "Ta'ziyeh of Qasim," pp. 2–23.
15. Peter Chelkowski. "Ta'ziyeh: Indigenous Avant-Garde Theatre of Iran," in *Ta'ziyeh: Ritual and Drama in Iran*, p. 2. Copyright (c) 1979 by New York University.
16. Chelkowski. "Ta'ziyeh," p. 5. Copyright (c) by New York University.

13

Community
and Society
in Islam

ISLAMIC SOCIAL STRUCTURES

The Western traveler to the Islamic world is immediately struck by obvious cultural differences. In the study of religion, these distinctive cultural characteristics are usually referred to as the ethos of a society. In the Middle East, for example, clothing is different, especially clothing worn by villagers and the urban poor and working classes. Men wear ankle-length beltless robes called *jalabiyas*. It is a practical garb for almost all kinds of work and activity. Many men also wear cloth turbans or brimless caps and hats. Women, too, wear clothing that covers their arms, legs, and hair. For the peasant woman, this often consists of a print dress over which a black outergarment is worn. The veil, still worn by many women, derives from ancient tradition, not from the Qur'an itself.

Apart from traditional attire, social relations also appear to be differently ordered in an Islamic ethos. In the Middle East, where Islam has had the most direct effect upon society, several characteristics are readily noticed. Couples, whether married or not, are not usually seen together in public. On the other hand, men are often seen in the company of other men in public—at coffee houses, on the streets, or at places of work. Women, too, keep each other company while they perform household chores, but the Western visitor to villages and traditional neighborhoods in Islamic cities is not likely to see women in public as much. Signs of affection between the sexes are seldom noticed, but within groups of men (or women), friendship and affection are more openly displayed. Occasionally these patterns of social relations are punctuated by arguments and loud shouting that seldom go beyond the level of verbal exchange.

Sexual relations between men and women outside marriage are strictly forbidden. Even within marriage, sex is a very private matter. On the other hand, in households where extended families live under one roof, intimacies between parents must necessarily occur in a crowded social space. In extended families, the eldest male is usually the patriarch of the household, although sons are expected to relieve their fathers of the burden of providing for so many people as soon as possible. The wife of the male head of the house usually rules the domestic affairs of the family. Family-run businesses predominate in the marketplace.

Given this kind of social structure, it would be improper to ask a Muslim male, "How's your wife?" It is more appropriate to pay respects by inquiring, "How is your family?" The answer will invariably be *al-hamdu li-llah*, "praise be to God (they are well)." This matter of courtesy is still just as appropriate among the urban middle and upper classes, where the traditional social patterns are changing under the impact of modernization.

On the streets of towns and cities, the Western visitor is quickly engulfed in a fascinating apparent confusion of activity. There is much clamoring and noise, especially in the marketplace, called the *suq* (Arabic) or *bazaar* (Persian). As one walks through these crowded mazes of booths and shops, the direct relation of craftsman, product, and customer is quite impressive. Jewelry-making and metalworking are done right before your eyes. The noises of hammering and grinding compete with the cries of vendors and merchants in a cacophony of sounds. Less desirable commercial activities, such as the slaughtering of animals and tanning, are usually at some distance from grocers, booksellers, craftsmen, and merchants of sundry items. In more traditional suqs, shops specializing in one kind of product are often clumped together, making the comparison of prices and quality much easier on the feet. Food shops usually specialize in particular kinds of consumables, making grocery shopping a complicated art. One shop may specialize in fruits and vegetables. Another may be filled with sacks of grains, rice, and pastas. Individual portions must be weighed under the watchful eyes of both seller and buyer. Price tags are seldom seen; prices are established in the ritual of bargaining—a process that requires seller and buyer to come to mutual agreement about value for each exchange. If the purchase is an involved one, or if a close friend or visitor to the neighborhood is discerned, tea or Turkish coffee will be offered to balance the contest of bargaining with the pleasantries of hospitality.

FIGURE 13.1   Iranian peasant woman in traditional attire. (Courtesy of the United Nations.)

International trade in the Middle East was known even in the time of the ancient Babylonians and Egyptians. In the time of the Prophet, goods from Byzantium and India passed through Arabia in caravans contracted by the merchants of Mecca. However, small businesses in local markets have been run by families which, by and large, have produced their own goods. This has been the traditional form of commercial activity in Islamic society for centuries. Thus the bazaar is a social experience at the heart of Islamic society. Masjids (mosques) and madrasas (religious schools) form a part of the social ecology of religion and life within the bazaar. It is a social space enmeshed with the normative requirements of the Qur'an and the Sunna.

In the larger cities, supermarkets and department stores compete with the more traditional economy of the neighborhood bazaar. The social effects are noticeable. Western clothing is worn by men and women working for corporations, larger businesses, and the government. Young men and women are leaving traditional family means of support to look for new opportunities in the modernized sectors of cities. In particular, many men leave their families for months and even years at a time to earn better wages and get paid in hard currency in Europe or the petroleum-producing countries of the Gulf. The result has been that traditional social and religious values have been challenged by the forces of modernization. The ulama in particular and traditional Muslims in general have sought ways to counter the eroding effects of modernization upon Islamic life.

How is Islamic society structured and organized? What types of social organization are found within the Islamic world? What sorts of problems and aspirations do members of Islamic society attempt to meet through their patterns of behavior? The answers to these questions are as complex as the variety of discrete cultures encompassed within Islam, from North Africa to Southeast Asia. The process of modernization and change must also be factored into the discussion. We now turn to some general observations about the study of Islamic society. This will be followed by descriptions of select social groups and settings within the Islamic world.

RELIGION AND SOCIETY

Definitions of religion often specify beliefs and rituals as essential elements. Religion, however, is also structured by social relations. Families, schools, occupations, and governments are products of human society; and society itself—along with history, art, beliefs, and rituals—is created by human beings. We have seen that ideally the Shari'a governs the totality of human life. In addition to religious duties, social, economic, and political responsibilities fall within its scope. Beyond the sacred precincts of shrines such as the ones at Mecca and Medina, the home, bazaar, and bureau are institutions that assume distinctive forms in Islamic society. Social behavior, then,

FIGURE 13.2 Religious college (madrasa) of Madari-i-Shah at Isfahan, Iran. (Courtesy of the United Nations.)

FIGURE 13.3 Mosque and market-place share adjacent social space. (Photo by the author.)

belongs to the study of Islam. Islamic society is the achievement of Muslims who, throughout history, have responded to the precepts of the Shari'a, under local climatic, geographic, and political conditions, thus producing distinctive forms of behavior.

The Dialectic of Humans and Society

The dialectic of human beings producing society and society shaping human beings is discussed by the sociologist of religion, Peter L. Berger.[1] In the tradition of German sociologist Max Weber, Berger believes that religion is a corporate, social phenomenon. The Friday congregational prayer and commerce are social activities. The masjid and bazaar are social spaces. The study of how individuals actually perform in these settings is different from but related to the study of what the Shari'a stipulates they *ought* to do. Beyond these questions are others relating to stages of life, attitudes toward the opposite sex, and types of social groupings.

The title of Berger's work, *The Sacred Canopy*, which recalls notions of cosmology, also indicates his point that reality as seen within in a religious tradition is itself a social product. Middle Eastern (and other) traditions have viewed the cosmos in three levels of reality corresponding to Heaven, Earth, and the underworld. As we found in Chapter 3, supernatural forces are thought to operate within and upon the natural ones. In some traditions there is no clear distinction between the natural and the supernatural. Religious expressions of the interconnections between divine forces, revealed laws, myths, and rituals are the data with which students of religions must reconstruct the reality that was or is experienced within a given tradition. These data are found to be closely associated with patterns of behavior at home, in the marketplace, and in other social and political institutions.

The process of becoming a social being is related to the process of learning the native language of one's culture. It begins in infancy and develops through each stage of life. Our native language is learned from and within the society into which we are born, and through language we interact with society. With additional languages such as gestures, art, music, and rituals, we creatively express our individual participation through the idioms we use to communicate with others.

Like other traditions, Islam presents a world view that is learned from society and that forms a basis for being in society. Shared beliefs and myths make possible common attitudes toward good and evil, individual and collective goals, and other shared concerns. The hajj, salat, zakat and other rituals are shared idioms that mediate between the ideals of belief and the realities of life. Languages and religions alike respond to historical changes—not rapidly, but change there is. Elizabethan English and contemporary American English are modes of expression appropriate to much different historical and social circumstances, despite the obvious fact that they are both dialects of the same language. Islam has adapted to many historical changes. From conquering and incorporating many ethnic and religious groups in the seventh century, to being conquered by Turkish, Persian, and Mongol warlords in the Middle Ages, to experiencing the impact of Westernization and modernization in the nineteenth and twentieth centuries, Islam has persisted as a social reality. It has done so within a structure suggested by the Qur'an and the Sunna, and perpetuated by individuals and social groups that have interpreted and constructed "Islamic" world views to each new situation, more, or less, successfully.

Great Tradition and Little Tradition

Western study of Islam began in a serious way in the mid-nineteenth century. Much of that study has concentrated on the texts of Islamic history and religions, and very little has been devoted to the study of the lives of Muslim peoples. The strong literary tradition in Islam since the eighth century drew European and American scholarly interest to the important initial task of locating and learning to read, translate, and interpret the texts and documents of religion and history. This type of scholarly activity is not yet complete. More and more manuscripts—some quite old—in Arabic and other Islamic languages are being discovered in ancient mosques and libraries. In addition to the textual studies of historians and humanists, anthropologists and sociologists are beginning to show increased interest in the social orga-

nization of Islamic tribes, villages, and cities. Political scientists and econo-
mists are also interested in Islamic social phenomena. Often the published
writings of these social scientists read much differently than the older historical studies. For one thing, social scientists pay less attention to official statements about religion and more attention to its actual practice. The official
teachings of the more distinguished personalities and writers of the ulama
and the intelligentsia are often found to differ from the expression of religion
at the popular level. For example, historians have usually explained Islamic
religion by consulting theological manuals. Social scientists often ignore
these and describe instead their observations of rituals and practices in the
everyday life of a Muslim village.

Robert Redfield, an anthropologist, has offered a solution to this diversity
of scholarship (which admittedly can be very confusing to the newcomer to
Islamic studies). As we saw in the last chapter, Redfield makes a distinction
between great and little traditions. He describes the humanist-historian as
one whose "studies are *textual*: he studies not only written texts but art and
architecture as part of his textual corpus. Ours [social scientists], are *contextual*. We relate some element of the great tradition—sacred book, story-ele-
ment, ceremony or supernatural being—to the life of the ordinary people, in
the *context* of daily life as in the village we see it happen."[2] The *great tradition*
is reflected in the more readily accessible literary products of theologians,
judges, and lawyers of the Islamic academies of learning. The *little tradition*
exists in the tribes, villages, and groups within cities where, in the process of
social organization, people must attempt to apply the Qur'an and the Sunna
to everyday life, in varying contexts and under diverse circumstances. Religion in these more local contexts is often called "popular religion."

In the next chapter, rituals of person and gender will be the focus of study.
In Chapter 15, we will take a closer look at different social contexts in
Islam—the medieval Islamic city, a village in Egypt, the urban bazaar in Iran,
and a Sufi cloister in North Africa. Each of these contexts stands in strong,
but quite different, relation to the great tradition of normative Islamic teaching. In the remainder of this chapter, the concern is with more general concepts in Islamic societies.

ELEMENTS OF SOCIAL STRUCTURE IN ISLAM

Umma and Caliphate

Umma. The model for all subsequent societies in Islam was the one that
formed around the figure of the Prophet in Medina after the Hijra from
Mecca in 622. In the Qur'an, "umma" appears frequently in reference to ethnic and religious groups (or nations) that are part of the divine plan of salvation. The people of Abraham, Lot, Noah, Moses, and Jesus were termed

ummas. An umma is usually identified as a nation to which God has sent a messenger or prophet. The Qur'an states that past ummas rejected their messengers, for which they suffered divine acts of retribution. Muhammad's first appearance as a Messenger/Warner in Mecca also met with rejection, by all but a very few close followers. The sacred history of past ummas was preached as a warning. In Medina, however, an umma was formed which was more receptive to the Prophet. The Medinan umma included Jews and other non-Muslims, and although not all members of the Islamic umma were loyal to the Prophet, the concept of inclusiveness within the community of Islam was to have far-reaching consequences for the subsequent development of Islamic society.

During the reign of the first four caliphs, from 632 to 661, the Arabian conquests of Middle Eastern lands resulted in a religious empire that sought to implement the notion of the Quranic umma on a much grander scale than the Medinan community. The Abode of Islam was now much more than Arabia, Arabs, and even Islam. It was a multiethnic empire comprising several religious traditions. For six centuries the empire was ruled by caliphs.

Caliphate. The term "caliph" (*khalifa*, successor, vice-regent) designates the rulers who assumed Muhammad's function as head of the umma, but not his function as Messenger of Allah. Also called "Commanders of the Faithful," the caliphs became, as a result of the Conquests, imperial rulers over vast territories and diverse peoples. This political order lasted until the thirteenth century, when Mongol warlords destroyed the caliphate and themselves assumed political rule over much of the Islamic world. Many of the Mongol conquerors converted to Islam. When the last caliph, al-Musta'sim, was put to death by the Mongol commander Hugalu in 1258, it was a great catastrophe for Islamdom. For all practical purposes the caliphate had been destroyed. The loss of the caliphate was perhaps not unlike the destruction of the Jerusalem Temple for Jews—the loss of an institution, and more importantly a symbol, that would always be remembered and missed and celebrated in the tradition. Two relatives of Musta'sim escaped to Egypt, where they were enthroned in succession as caliph, but with virtually no authority, even in Egypt. The Ottoman Turkish sultans also claimed the title of caliph, for which they sought recognition from the rest of the Muslim world. The caliphate was finally abolished in Turkey when the Ottoman sultanate was abolished and Turkey became an independent republic. Some Islamist revivalist movements have called for the dissolution of Western-style national governments and the restoration of the caliphate.

For more than thirteen centuries of history, the basic concept of Islamic society has been the Prophet's umma. In the Middle Ages, the umma contained numerous ethnic and religious groups—social groups with individual social characteristics. In matters of religion and civil affairs, each group or minority was allowed to maintain its own traditionally conceived order. The Islamic city, as we have seen, preserved this arrangement by forming separate quarters for each religious group and ethnic minority. Rabbis, bishops, and other leaders replaced some of the roles of the ulama within non-Muslim groups. In modern times and without the caliphate, the Islamic umma may find itself to be the predominant religious group, as it is in Egypt, or a minority group among many others, as it is in India. In all settings throughout history, the umma has attempted to heed the Quranic warning of what had happened to past ummas that rejected God and His Messengers. The Qur'an and the Sunna of the Prophet are the central symbols and sources of guidance for the Islamic umma. Local historical and political circumstances have determined the specific forms the umma has taken as expressions of human society.

Ulama. By now "ulama" is a familiar term in the vocabulary of our study of Islam. A few observations about this class of religious leaders within Islamic society should be reiterated at this point. First, the term is a plural of the Arabic *'alim,* which means "one who is knowledgeable (that is, about the Shari'a)." Thus the ulama are the custodians of traditional learning about the Qur'an, the Sunna of the Prophet, and the legal theory and application of sacred law to all aspects of life. The ulama serve in the functional occupations of trained Qur'an reciters, teachers in madrasas and schools, imams (prayer leaders) and khatibs (preachers) of local mosques, and professors of sacred law and theology on university faculties.

Second, in Sunni Islam, the class of scholars known as the ulama is but loosely organized in an institutional sense. Its members are implicitly recognized by Muslims to be the purveyors of guidance to each community by virtue of their training and learning. Their authority is effective to the extent that they are able to reach a consensus among themselves and to articulate relevantly the idiom of consensus of past tradition to the exigencies of present circumstances. In Shi'i Islam, the ulama carry on the special interpretation of the Shari'a derived from 'Ali, the fourth caliph and cousin of the prophet, and from the imams who succeeded 'Ali as spiritual leaders of the Shi'i community. Today, the highest-ranking members of the Twelver Shi'i ulama, known as *ayatollahs,* lead the Shi'i community in the temporary absence of the twelfth imam, who went into occultation in the ninth century. The supreme living spiritual leader of Twelver Shi'a is known as the *marja'i-taqlid.* The Shi'i ulama serve the same basic functional occupations as in Sunni Islam, but with a greater degree of hierarchical authority. The requirement of consensus is implicitly there, but the theoretical basis of their interpretations of the Qur'an and the Sunna is also channeled through the received teaching of the twelve imams about the Qur'an and the Sunna.

Third, let us recall from Chapter 1 that the ulama perform no sacral functions. This is the reason behind the often stated observation that in Islam there is no priesthood and thus no institution comparable to the church. The ulama perform duties as a body of learned ones of Islam; no ordination, sacral office, or priestly function is involved. Virtually any Muslim can perform most of the duties of the ulama, such as leading the Friday congregational prayer.

Popular resentment against the leadership of the ulama in various historical periods, particularly in Sunni Islam, has differed from lay anti-clericalism in the history of Christianity. The main function of the ulama has been to remain in touch with the pulse of Islamic society in order to guide it in its real concerns, and to maintain lines of communication and understanding between central political authorities and the people. In periods when members of the ulama have become excessively preoccupied with scholastic dogmatism, popular religious sentiment has openly defied their leadership. Often in those periods, the popular alternative to the leadership of the ulama has been the spiritual appeal of Sufi masters, centered in convents and the shrines of famous saints.

Waqf. Without a church or corporate religious entity to effect religiously inspired humanitarianism, how has the religious establishment in Islam been able to provide tangible benefits to Islamic society? The answer lies in legal provisions in the Shari'a for the establishment of pious foundations. The term for such foundations is *waqf.* Tradition teaches that when the Prophet once sought to purchase land on which to build a mosque, he was refused; instead the tribal leaders who owned the land gave it to him "for the sake of God." Precedent for religious endowments has been traced to such early incidents recorded in the Sunna of the Prophet and his Companions. Another form of waqf is the income from a piece of land or property that is specifically assigned by its owner to religious (mosques, madrasas) or charitable (hospitals, orphanages) institutions. During the course of Islamic history, more and more land has been given or committed to waqf endowments. The growth of endowment lands has reduced available taxable lands.

Waqf endowments, then, have provided the ulama with the means to run religious and charitable institutions within Islamic society, as well as the power that results from having control of such activities. In traditional Islam, waqf endowments established madrasas for each of the law madhhabs (schools). The Seljuq period, which began in 1055 and lasted until the fall of the caliphate in 1258, was a period in which the establishment of waqfs for charitable, particularly religious and educational, institutions was particularly active. The waqf institutions known as madrasas, which were established in the eleventh and twelfth centuries, stabilized the four Sunni legal madhhabs and provided the ulama with a more or less standardized education, a system of certification, and recognized position in society.

However, with the rise of national states within the Islamic world, government ministries of education, welfare, health, and culture have assumed the state's interests and responsibilities in these areas. In addition, modern states have instituted civil and criminal courts and legal systems that have functioned independently of the Shari'a courts of the ulama. The effect of parallel sacred and secular systems within Islamic society is more pronounced in cities, especially political capitals, than in villages and nomadic regions. The general observation that Islam does not separate the domains of church and state must be qualified when one is speaking about these trends of Islamic society in modern times.

An interesting result of the earlier development of parallel functions by the ulama and the national governments has been the resurgent vital appeal of Islamic and Muslim leadership. Popular movements in both predominantly Sunni and predominantly Shi'i countries have sought to bring the authority of the Shari'a more directly into the structure of modern society and into national constitutions and governmental processes, as we have repeatedly seen in this study. This has led to various kinds of conflict in public and political arenas, where Islamists have challenged secular, Western-oriented leadership. For this reason, it has become all the more important to appreciate the cultural heritage to which more and more Muslims are turning to articulate their identity within the world of nations. Beneath the more salient manifestations of confrontation and political unrest is an identifiable process of boundary formation and maintenance meant to reestablish personal and group identity in a world that is interpreted as increasingly alien to religion.

CONTEXTS OF ISLAMIC SOCIETY

To illustrate the point that religion can be studied as a form of social behavior, the following pages focus on different specific social contexts in the Islamic world. In each case, specific examples drawn from the textual studies of Islamicists and the contextual field work of social scientists will serve as fixed points from which to make some general remarks.

The Islamic City

In the discussion in Chapter 4 on the building of the city of Baghdad, several general characteristics of Islamic towns and cities were given briefly. Baghdad is usually considered a good example of a truly Islamic city because it was deliberately planned and developed with Islamic principles in mind. Many other cities that were conquered or built by the Muslims sooner or later exhibited similar characteristics. In an important essay entitled "Structure of the Muslim Town," Gustav E. von Grunebaum made the following observation: "To the Muslim, a town was a settlement in which his religious duties and his ideals could be completely fulfilled."[3] The validity of this remark is not difficult to see. Although such religious duties of Islam as the canonical prayer can be fulfilled anywhere, even in the desert (by performing tayammum wudu' with sand instead of water), the important Friday congregational prayer requires a masjid, which is to say, a city. Moreover,

FIGURE 13.4 Cathedral mosque courtyard, Baghdad. (Courtesy of the United Nations.)

throughout the ages the city has attracted rural and pastoral nomadic elements in search of spiritual, intellectual, and economic opportunities. By naturally forming in quarters and neighborhoods of ethnic and sectarian groups, the cities preserved the social ideals of Middle Eastern peoples.

The Cathedral Mosque. Like Baghdad, most Islamic cities and towns had an identifiable orientation with certain fixed points. At the center stood the jami', the cathedral mosque. If the city was the seat of the caliph, a provincial governor, or other high appointed official, state buildings were in the near vicinity of the cathedral mosque. Also at the center was a *hamam*, a public fountain, which provided a place of social gathering as well as a place for worshippers to perform ritual ablutions before their prayers. Thus the central crossroads of the two main thoroughfares of the city was a hub that combined social, religious, and political activities.

The cathedral mosque served several other important functions. Politically it was the main public platform for governmental communications to the people. From the pulpit (minbar) of the mosque, the caliph's name was mentioned each Friday during the sermon of the congregational prayer. Often the ruling official of the city would deliver the sermon at these weekly gatherings of the general population, and the message could be just as appropriately political as religious in nature.

The cathedral mosque also served as an intellectual center for the town and neighboring villages. Before the rise of separate schools and universities in the eleventh century, teachers of the religious sciences, who were usually members of the ulama, attracted circles of students in the courtyards and hallways of the mosque. Their pupils might come from the surrounding city or nearby villages. If the teacher was particularly famous, students from distant lands would find their way to his lectures. Such lectures were carefully dictated and copied. If the circle of students was particularly large, more advanced students, or "assistants," would stand midway and relay each phrase to the back of the audience. A professor's signature in a student's notebook was the traditional form of credential that marked a scholar's preparation to gather his own students.

The major schools of Shari'a law in Sunni and Shi'i Islam sat in the cathedral mosque, or in a madrasa attached to it, where professors deliberated on points of interpretation within their schools. Scholars and judges delivered opinions and judgments on specific cases brought before them. For this reason, other functionaries were required in the service of the mosque, such as notaries and witnesses. The chief judge within each principality, called a qadi, was a political appointee of the governor of the province. The professors of law who deliberated on more theoretical issues and the lawyers who dealt with specific cases were members of the ulama. They were independent of the political seat of power, although in Sunni Islam the ulama has tended to support the government in most matters. This has been less true in Shi'i Islam.

The Marketplace. The Qur'an is replete with allusions to commercial concepts. Mecca and Medina had thriving markets in the time of the Prophet. Islam teaches that a man should provide for his family, and it encourages worldly success and prosperity while cautioning just and fair practices in commerce. Thus a second fixed point of the Muslim city was, as we have already seen, the suq or bazaar. The suq had an officially appointed functionary, known as the *muhtasib*, who was in charge of maintaining order and fair practice in the market. It was his business to resolve matters of violations, quarrels, and thievery.

We have already established some sense of the physical arrangement of the suq within the city. Closest to the cathedral mosque in the center of town were the booths selling materials necessary to the religious, educational, and professional activities of the mosque. Books, candles, paper, ink, and the like could be purchased from the nearest merchants. Next came the textile district, where booths were gathered under a large roof to protect the goods from bad weather. Beyond the textile quarter were craftsmen who fashioned pots, wooden objects, and jewelry right in their shops. Then came the sellers of foodstuffs. At the far end of the suq were located the least desirable enterprises: potters, tanners, and dyers.

The Quarter. The makeup of the residential sections within each city and town has exhibited strong separatist tendencies. Tribal, ethnic, and sectarian groups preserve cultural affinities brought to the city from village and nomadic environments. During the Middle Ages, the Arabs who moved to

FIGURE 13.5 Baladi women and vendor in village market (suq). (Photo by the author.)

towns and cities settled in districts composed of tribal groups. Dialects and familiar lines of clan leadership no doubt provided part of the rationale for maintaining separate quarters. Jews, Christians, and other non-Muslim groups also held to their separate quarters, as did the Shi'a and other specific religious minorities within Islam.

In modern times this pattern has begun to dissolve, but very slowly. Surrounding villages rather than tribes feed into counterpart quarters or neighborhoods in nearby cities. Young men, with or without their families, move to the city bringing a trade or skill (or looking for a new one) from the local village. Under such circumstances, immigrants to towns and cities are naturally attracted to the districts where relatives from their hometown have settled. Finding jobs and places to live is thereby made simpler. Local village politics and gossip form natural topics of social intercourse for neighborhood gatherings. A fair amount of commuting between village and urban neighborhoods continues, and portions of wages earned in the city are sent back home, where economic opportunities are less promising.

Modernity, and particularly European colonialism, have induced obvious architectural changes in Islamic cities. The traditional older Islamic cities, called *madinas*, preserved traditional architecture. As European colonial powers established themselves, modern urban construction was established

FIGURE 13.6 The Islamic city combines traditional and modern scenes. (Photo by Eugene Gordon.)

adjacent to, or surrounding the madina. The madinas preserved the traditional suq, madrasas, jami's, and other aspects of the ethos of premodern Islamic society. The Westernized suburbs are where supermarkets, government offices, schools, and modern universities are usually located. This dichotomy of space, style, culture, and ethos has sometimes heightened social conflicts.

Ulama, the Unifying Factor. The foregoing description of Muslim cities as collections of separate social entities raises interesting questions. In what sense, if any, was the Muslim city a unified social phenomenon? Was it a geographical implosion of scattered social groups that, once gathered under a common urban administration, failed to achieve anything greater than the sum of its parts? Had the Prophet's replacement of tribal loyalties with a higher loyalty to the religion of Islam failed after all?

An Islamic historian who has studied the Muslim city in great depth, Ira M. Lapidus, has argued that Islam *was* able to transcend persisting social and political boundaries within the cities—at least those boundaries that traditionally existed between Muslim groups. The ulama formed the religious intellectual elite. Local concerns and views within quarters were transcended by the more universal ideals of Islam. Islam provided a common idiom of expression outside indigenous quarters. The ulama could write and speak in the highly valued classical Arabic (as opposed to village or tribal dialects). The Qur'an and the Sunna of the Prophet were sources of guidance in everyday matters that were shared by all Muslims. The ulama articulated a world view that cut across persisting social divisions.[4]

Several aspects of community and society in Islam have been introduced or reviewed in this chapter. The next chapter looks at another dimension of Islamic social ethos, the rituals of person, gender, and social conflict.

NOTES

1. Peter L. Berger, *The Sacred Canopy: Elements of a Sociological Theory of Religion* (New York: Anchor Books, 1969).
2. Robert Redfield, "The Social Organization of Tradition," *The Far Eastern Quarterly* 15 (1955), 17. (Italics added.)
3. Gustav E. von Grunebaum, *Islam: Essays on the Nature and Growth of a Cultural Tradition* (Totowa, N.J.: Barnes & Noble Books, 1961), p. 142.
4. See Ira M. Lapidus, "Muslim Cities and Islamic Societies," in *Middle Eastern Cities*, ed. Ira M. Lapidus (Berkeley: University of California Press, 1969), pp. 47–79.

14

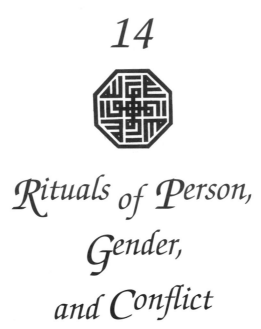

$Rituals$ of $Person,$ $Gender,$ and $Conflict$

ELEMENTS OF IDENTITY

In Chapter 5, the metaphor of boundaries was introduced as a model for understanding religious communities. Concepts of self and Other are defined by cultural boundaries. Ethnicity is one such boundary, religion another. Both remain extremely powerful contexts of personal and group identity in the modern world.

We have already seen that within Islamicate society, Muslims, Christians, Jews, and other communities are separated by confessional and ritual boundaries that must be negotiated. Within Islam, madhhab (legal rite) is another boundary, distinguishing the social identity of a Hanbali community, say, from a Shafi'i community in terms of the differences between them in their interpretations of Shari'a. Concepts of children and family pertain to very basic notions of self. One's family provides the most elemental and earliest reference of identity; this continues throughout life, especially in social systems that stress kinship and extended families, as in much of the world of Islam. The boundary of gender is one of the most pronounced in most civilizations.

Identity in family, religion, and gender is structured in most civilizations by social rituals called "rites of passage." The purpose of this chapter is to

216

describe patterns of identity formation in Islamic societies through rites of passage and gender relationships.

RITES OF PASSAGE

Muslim villagers as well as Muslims in urban environments are governed in ritual and worship by religious duties, as interpreted by the madhhab to which they adhere. In Chapters 11 and 12, the distinctively Islamic occasions of worship were discussed at length. Special sets of occasions in the lives of individual Muslims which have both social and religious significance are life events identified by anthropologists as *rites of passage*. These ritualized occasions are found in most cultures. However, each culture understands and experiences these transitional moments according to its own myths, rituals, and laws. For Muslims, major religious events in life include birth, circumcision, memorization of the Qur'an, pilgrimage, marriage, and death.

Scripture memorization and pilgrimage are not rites of passage in the usual sense. Memorizing the Qur'an, usually in one's teens, brings social recognition in one's community and the respectful title of "*hafiz*" (memorizer). To make the hajj to Mecca and earn the title of Hajji is another rite that earns social status; it is a duty for all Muslims, but in reality, only a few are able to fulfill it.

In addition to their obvious religious overtones, these events are also important social rites for the family, the larger clan of relatives, and the entire village (or urban neighborhood). The social group as a whole helps individuals and their families to celebrate these important passages from one stage of life to the next. Thus in the study of rites of passage, the Qur'an and the Sunna may blend with folk and popular religion. The following descriptions are of villages in Egypt, but the situation is not much different in urban environments. Some of the specific details vary from one region or ethnic group to the next, but overall the pattern is much the same in traditional Islamic social groups.

Birth

The birth of a child is a very happy occasion for the entire village. Throughout pregnancy, the mother is to be protected by her family from any activity that might endanger a healthy delivery. At the end of the first week after birth, a ceremony called *usbu'* (week) or *aqiqa* is held for the naming of the child, particularly for the first son. In one sense, sons are preferred to daughters, because sons will one day relieve their fathers from the burden of family support. Yet daughters are a great help to their mothers around the house. Traditional families harbor fears that their daughters might bring them shame through sexual indiscretions. However, fathers love their daughters, too, and it is believed that girls will be more compassionate when their parents are older.[1]

Circumcision

Male Circumcision. One of the terms for male circumcision is *tahara*, which, as noted in Chapter 10, means ritual purity. This semantic point reminds us again that ritual practice, including rites of passage, has to do with purity and removing conditions of pollution. The normal term for male circumcision, however, is *khitan*.

Muslim male children are circumcised between the ages of three and seven. In the province of Aswan, Egypt, the event calls for a village celebration. At the invitation of the parents, the men and women of the village gather on the eve of the event to dine and celebrate with the family. The boy to be circumcised, with his playmates, issues another invitation the following day by running through the village. At the family home the people of the village gather once again. This day may also be celebrated with a meal, followed by prayers, Qur'an recitations, and readings from the story of the Prophet's birthday (Mawlid al-Nabi). The actual circumcision is performed in this case by the village barber. When weather permits, the men gather outside, where the operation is to take place, and the women inside. In one region it is the custom for the young boy to wear a girl's headcloth around his neck. First his head is shaved a little at a time as each gift brought to the father from relatives and well-wishers is announced. Then the girl's headcloth is removed and a special white shirt is put on, on top of which a green covering garment is worn. During the operation (for which Egyptian barbers nowadays are trained by the Ministry of Health and supplied surgical instruments), the boy is encouraged to be brave and to ignore the pain. Following the operation, the entire gathering of men, women, and children heads toward the village mosque for prayers. Then sweets are distributed. A week or so later the newly circumcised boy again goes through the village with his friends, asking for gifts of food. These are brought home to his mother, who prepares a sumptuous meal for his friends. The entire ceremony marks the bringing of a child out into village society. Circumcision brings honor and gifts to the father and the entire family. The boundary of gender, which is ambivalent in childhood, is made clear with the rite of khitan. Also it symbolically, if not physically, prepares the boy for marriage.[2]

Female Circumcision. A form of female circumcision called clitoridectomy (*khafd*) is performed in some parts of the Muslim world, most extensively in the Nile Valley. In its most extreme form, infibulation, the genitalia are mutilated. Although it is not considered Sunna or recommended in Islamic jurisprudence, khafd is apparently an old practice, as indicated by the following hadith, which is widely attested: "If the two circumcised parts [male and female] are in contact [a bath (ghusl) is necessary."[3] We saw in Chapter 10 that the ground for this ritual requirement of ghusl is that a man and woman become *junub*, ritually impure, following sexual intercourse. The point here, however, is that female circumcision seems to be alluded to in a hadith attributed to the Prophet Muhammad. Nonetheless, in much of the Islamic world khafd was not, and is not, practiced. The preponderance of fatwas issued by Muslim jurists among the ulama have been against clitoridectomy. Moreover, in modern times, several governments have declared clitoridectomy and infibulation to be illegal—for example, Egypt in 1959. The continuing practice of khafd in a few parts of the Muslim world, although diminishing, is testimony to persistence of local custom, 'ada, despite the institutional judgment of the great tradition.[4]

Marriage

'Alqama, a companion of the Prophet, was the source of the following hadith on wedlock (*nikah*):

> While I was with 'Abdullah ['Alqama reports], 'Uthman [later, third caliph] met him at Mina and said, "O Abu 'Abdur-Rahman! I have something to say to you." So both of them went aside and 'Uthman said, "O Abu 'Abdur-Rahman! Shall we marry you to a virgin who will make you remember your past days?" When 'Abdullah [realized] he was not in need of that, he beckoned me (to join him) saying, O 'Alqama!" Then I heard him saying (in reply to 'Uthman), "As for [what you said], the Prophet, prayers and peace be upon him, once said to us, 'O young people! Whoever among you is able to marry, should marry, and whoever is not able to marry, is recommended to fast, as fasting diminishes his sexual power.'"[5]

This narrative tells us several things about sexuality and marriage in the world view of hadith literature. First, marriage is enjoined on all Muslims if they are able; marriage is the norm in Islamic society. Second, sexual intercourse is confined to marriage and thus bounded by rules of Shari'a and 'ada, religion and local custom. Third, sexuality is recognized as a power that diminishes with age, though one may attempt to revive it, as 'Uthman's humorous remark to Abu 'Abdur-Rahman indicates. Fourth, if this power of sexuality tempts one to cross the marriage boundary to commit adultery or fornication (*zina*), one should resort to fasting, in order to diminish the power of sexuality.

In traditional Arabic society, marriage (*nikah*) is usually within the clan, often between paternal first cousins. It is assumed that marriages will take place inside this pattern; if a marriage is outside this pattern, special arrangements and mediation are required. Once a match has been arranged, an engagement ceremony is held at the home of the prospective bride. The groom's family sends gifts prior to arrival at the home of the bride's parents for the celebration. At the home of the bride, after an exchange of greetings (and more recently, of rings), the groom or his father advances a portion of the marriage payment (*mahr*) to the bride, although in actual practice the payment is sometimes taken by the bride's father. The rest of the marriage payment is held until such time as the marriage may end in the death of the husband, or in divorce. The mahr payment serves both to discourage easy divorce and to assist the bride's father if he should have to resume her care. The amount of the marriage payment is negotiated on the basis of the social status of the families. Such payments are warranted in the Shari'a.

Next, a day is set for the signing of the marriage contract. On the appointed day the couple and their families again gather at the home of the bride. The opening chapter (Fatiha) of the Qur'an is recited by all assembled. The recitation of the Fatiha is the essence of the nuptial ceremony. Now the couple is legally married, although it is customary for the couple to wait until after yet another ceremony to consummate the marriage. A few days before the final ceremony, in much the same fashion as with the circumcision rite, the groom and his friends (usually mostly cousins) go through the village inviting guests. On the eve of the wedding, the bride and groom entertain friends at their respective homes.

As in the rituals of circumcision and pilgrimage, the nuptial rite of passage calls for ceremonial grooming. On the day of the wedding in the home of a friend or cousin of the groom, the village barber cuts the groom's hair and bathes him. At her own home, the bride is also bathed and beautified by female family members and friends. Once prepared, the groom leads a procession of his friends through the village to his parents' home, where guests are gathering along with musicians and perhaps a Qur'an reciter.

At the groom's home often a pavilion tent is set up to accommodate the many guests. Again gifts are brought, and the barber receives and records the names of donors. Later the bride and her family arrive, and the bride is seated in a conspicuous place for all to see. Sweets, soft drinks, and food are served. Water pipes may be smoked by the men. The celebration lasts into the evening, at which time the groom finally retires to his wife's room, which she now takes in the house of the groom's father. As we have come to expect, entry (*dukhla*) into the marriage house is with the right foot first. In traditional Middle Eastern Islamic society, particularly in rural areas, the chaste honor of the bride is celebrated, and tested, by a rite also known as dukhla, entry in the sexual sense. Wedding guests await the public presentation of a bloodstained cloth to prove the virginity and honor of the bride. Various stratagems may be employed to produce the awaited sign. The public display of the cloth is a form of 'ada, popular custom, that is slowly going out of practice.

More generally speaking, the ritual of marriage, like other rites of passage, establishes bonds and relationships between and within village families. Thus it provides occasions for social cohesion throughout the village.[6]

Death

The death of a Muslim is also an occasion to express family and clan solidarity. Juan Campo has described the overall rites surrounding death in Egypt as consisting of a funeral cycle (*janaza*) and a mourning cycle (*hidad*).[7] The janaza is further formed by four stages. As death approaches, the "ascent of the soul" stage includes, if possible, an attempt on the part of the dying person to perform ritual ablution (wudu'). Immediate family or nearest of kin recite Qur'an verses and the shahada, the First Pillar testimonial that there is no God but Allah and that Muhammad is His messenger. When death comes, friends, neighbors, and distant relatives must be notified.

In the second stage, a ritual lustration (ghusl), is performed, normally by a professional body washer. The purified corpse is dressed in a shroud and kept in the home with its head tilted to the right—a cultural reflex on the right/left ritual symbolism discussed earlier. Again, the shahada and the Qur'an are recited. The third and fourth stages, procession (janaza) and burial (*dafna*), are to be performed within twenty-four hours if possible. The body of the decedent is taken first by male bearers to a mosque, where it is placed in front of the participants, wrapped in a shroud, facing the qibla, that is, the mihrab wall of the mosque. Prayers and Qur'an recitation, often by a trained reciter, mark the ceremony at the mosque.

The procession bearing the decedent then resumes on to the cemetery for interment. At the grave the body is placed on its right side facing Mecca, again recalling the cosmological ritual orientations of hajj and salat. In Islamic eschatology, two angels, Munkar and Nakir, will interrogate the decedent at the grave on that evening. Accordingly, an aspect of dafna, the burial ritual, is instruction to the decedent by a shaykh on how to answer Munkar and Nakir. The Qur'an is also recited. In another ritual reflex, on the Pillar of alms-giving (zakat), the family distributes gifts to the poor, who gather for that purpose at the grave.

The hidad cycle of mourning also has discernible stages. The ritual observance of mourning among Sunni Muslims in Egypt, as described by Campo,[8] is greatest during the first three days, when the family home of the decedent is open to friends and neighbors who wish to express their condolences. Refreshments are served. Men and women observe the Islamic rules of modesty by gathering in separate parts of the house. The Qur'an is recited, in some cases by a professional reciter in a special, colorful tent set up in the yard. The family expresses its bereavement at the end of the first several weeks. Mourning is again expressed ritually on the fortieth day, when family, friends and neighbors gather again at the home of the decedent, to hear the Qur'an recited, visit the graveside, and give money and gifts to the poor.

Wealthier families may set up a special tent in the yard or in the neighborhood for the occasion. On the first anniversary of the death, the hidad cycle
ends with an observance that repeats the fortieth-day observance.

Rites of Passage and Blood Sacrifice

At the funeral ceremonial and other rites of passage, it is not uncommon for
villagers and some urban dwellers who can afford it to sacrifice an animal,
usually a lamb. Ammar reports that in the district of Aswan in Egypt it is
common for the "flowing of blood" ritual to take place at such ceremonies as
the naming of the child, the honoring of a youth who has memorized the
Qur'an, and the honoring of a Hajji's return from the pilgrimage.[9] The sacred
history of Ibrahim's duty to sacrifice his son Isma'il (in which at the last
minute a Heaven-sent ram was sacrificed instead) gives meaning derived
from sacred history to several important stages of a Muslim's life. It seems to
be appropriate to celebrate the blood sacrifice on those occasions when one
has acquired something new. It is a thanksgiving offering that is deeply
rooted in the sacred history that Islam shares with other Middle Eastern religious traditions.

GENDER

The cultural boundaries discussed in the introduction to this chapter—ethnicity, religion, sect, family, and gender—are interrelated categories. We discuss them separately here only for the purposes of analysis. Among the most
legislated boundaries in traditions such as Judaism and Islam is that of gender, to which we now turn.

Muslim Family Law

The role of women in Islamic societies has been the subject of much writing and discussion in recent years. There are at least two important reasons for this. In the West, feminists and postmodern critics have
heightened academic and public attention to gender issues, including the
unequal status and treatment of women in virtually every society around
the world. Islam has received a great deal of attention in this regard. On
the other side, in much of the Islamic world, colonial rule restricted the
scope of the traditional Shari'a courts to the religious duties ('ibadat) and
to what is usually called "Muslim family law." Muslim family law focuses
on personal property and relations: mainly inheritance, marriage, and
divorce. Thus, colonialism and nationalism have restricted much of the

FIGURE 14.1   Mother in traditional attire, with child, Morocco. (Photo by Eugene Gordon.)

social influence of the traditional ulama to matters that pertain to family and women. European colonial governments often assumed jurisdiction over political, criminal, and other more public aspects of law. Newly independent governments, therefore, assumed legal jurisdiction over many matters formerly handled by the ulama and the Shari'a system of jurisprudence. Muslim reformers have sought to bring virtually all political, economic, criminal and other matters of the secular courts back under the umbrage of the Shari'a.

The importance of gender issues and of the role of women in Islamic societies, however, is not simply a result of modern feminist movements and the impact of European colonialism. One of the largest suras of the Qur'an, the fourth sura, is titled "Women" (*surat al-nisa'*). Passages that discuss women, marriage, divorce, inheritance, children, and tahara regulations are found in this sura and throughout the Qur'an. As we have already seen, ritual purity (tahara) largely concerns matters pertaining to sexual relations, menstruation, and other aspects of gender. The topically arranged canonical hadith collections of al-Bukhari and others have large sections on gender issues. Many of these hadiths pertaining to family and gender matters were transmitted by the Prophet's wives who survived him, especially Aisha. Similarly, fiqh books—the manuals that summarize the interpretations of the Sunni and Shi'i madhhabs on each point within the scope of the Shari'a—have large sections on women and gender issues.

The Boundaries of Marriageable Women

Marriage as a rite of passage in Islamic societies was discussed above. In the sura on "Women" (Qur'an 4), verses 19 to 24 mention those women a Muslim male is ineligible to marry. This passage and topic is discussed at greater length in the hadith and fiqh literature: for example, in al-Bukhari's collection of hadith.[10] Included among the women a Muslim male is ineligible to marry are: female blood relatives, such as mothers, sisters, and daughters, as well as female nonblood relatives, such as foster-mothers and sisters, step-mothers, and stepdaughters; in general, women who belong to one's household. The converse of this category is what verse 24 states: "Lawful for you are all other [women], whom you may seek with your wealth in virtue, not in depravity." The Qur'an also stipulates that a Muslim man may marry up to four wives so long as he is able provide for them equally. This includes non-Muslim women (in quranic context, Christian and Jewish women, primarily). On the other side, Muslim women may have only one spouse at a time, and he must be Muslim.

The Sura on Women contains a passage that Western critics of gender relations in Islam, especially feminists, have written about extensively (Qur'an 4:34):

> Men are in charge of women, because God has made the former to excel over the latter, and because [men] spend of their property [for women]. Thus, virtuous women are those who are obedient, who guard in secret what God has guarded. As for those from whom you fear rebellion, admonish them and remand [them] to separate beds and beat [them]. Then, if they obey you, seek not a way against them. Truly, God is exalted, great!

Many non-Muslims have interpreted this and other verses (for example, 2:228) to mean that women are unequal to men in Islamic societies. Muslim interpreters, including many Muslim women, have argued to the contrary that these passages show that men and women have different, not unequal, responsibilities. Men are responsible to earn a living and provide for their families; women bear children and run the household.

Gender Differentiation

The Qur'an, the Sunna and the Shari'a clearly distinguish between men and women in important areas of personal and family law. For example, in verse 282 of the Sura of the Cow (Qur'an 2), it is mentioned that two males are required to witness the signing of a commercial contract. If two men are not available, then one man and two women should act as witnesses. In another example, divorce (*talaq*) is permitted in Islam, but it is much easier for men than for women. Women and men both may initiate divorce proceedings in the Shari'a court. However, only men may also obtain a divorce by declaring the talaq formula ("I divorce you"), in which the bond is dissolved after a three-month waiting period to determine whether or not there has been a pregnancy. Women in Islam may inherit property from their parents. In the time of the Prophet, this was an improvement over the pre-Islamic practice in Arabia, according to which women could not inherit property. We read in verses 11-12 of the Sura on Women (Qur'an 4): "God charges you concerning (the provisions for) your children: to the male the equivalent of two females." The passage is in fact much longer and involved, stipulating the portion to be inherited if other relatives are eligible to inherit. A Muslim colleague of the author prepared a will before a qadi (Muslim judge) stipulating that his children, male and female, were to inherit equally. This stipulation that one's children should inherit equally is apparently being done more frequently nowadays.

On what ground would a Muslim, such as the author's friend just mentioned, challenge traditionalist interpretations of the passages from the Sura on Women (Qur'an 4), cited above? The answer is: on Islamic grounds. As we have noted in this book, the Shari'a is a process aimed at negotiating an authoritative, usable interpretation of a particular matter that may be in conflict between two parties. Should one's daughter inherit as much as one's son, or only one-half as much? The first cultural impulse of Muslims is to ask: What do the Qur'an and the Sunna say? Then one must ask: What does that mean? One may go to a mufti and seek a fatwa, a legal opinion on the matter. Less traditionally, one may think the matter through on quranic and rational grounds, or seek the guidance of Muslim teachers who have done so. On the particular matter of female inheritance, one modern Muslim thinker, Fazlur Rahman, has interpreted Qur'an 2:282, on the ruling that two female witness equal one male witness, as follows.

> The reason for having two female witnesses instead of one male is that women would be more "forgetful" than men, since women in those days were normally not used to dealing with credit. According to the traditionalist understanding, the law that two female witnesses equal one male is eternal and a social change that enabled a woman to get used to financial transactions would be "un-Islamic." The modernist, on the other hand, would say that since the testimony of a woman being considered of less value than that of a man was dependent on her weaker power of memory concerning financial matters, when women became conversant with such matters—with which there is not only nothing wrong but which is for the betterment of society—their evidence can equal that of men.[11]

Not every Muslim would interpret Qur'an 2:282 as Fazlur Rahman did. Nonetheless, his answer was based on trying to determine why the law of witnesses was enunciated as it was in the quranic context, and whether the intent of that law could be preserved by counting women equal to men when in fact they were.

FIGURE 14.2 Muslim girls learning to recite the Qu'ran at a religious school in Egypt. (Photo by the author.)

Gender and Modesty

The physical and cultural boundaries in traditional Islamic societies that separate women from men, and a man's wife and female family members from other men, can be seen in clothing (veiling), as well as in the architecture and arrangements of houses, which we have discussed in previous chapters. Islamic codes of female modesty are drawn from such passages as the Sura of the Light (Qur'an 24:31):

> And tell believing women to lower their gazes and be modest, and to display of their adornment only that which is apparent, and to draw their veils over their bosoms, and not to reveal their adornment except to their own husbands or fathers or husbands' fathers. . .or male attendants who lack vigor, or children who have not known women's nakedness. And let them not stamp their feet so as to reveal what they hide of their adornment.

Wearing the veil has not been universal among Muslim women throughout history, nor has it in the past or present been worn by all women. The veil, called *hijab* or *chador,* may cover the head and most of the face save the eyes, or it may be much less extensive, covering the hair only as a bandanna would; displaying the hair, in particular, is seen as a severe form of immodesty and male provocation. So, too, is wearing clothing that leaves arms, legs, or parts of the torso bare. With respect to social class, women among the elite classes have been more likely to wear the veil in public than peasant and servant women. What constitutes a veil has much to do with local custom ('ada) and social class.

The notion of seclusion or privacy, that is, the inviolability of space designated for women, is known in Arabic by the terms *harim* (English, "harem") and *khalwa*. In other words, the home replicates the gender divisions of the masjid, where the place for women to pray is separate from that of men, usually behind a screen to the rear or side of where the men pray. Not just women, but small children observe the boundaries of the harim.[12] Modern apartment living and Muslim women seeking employment in modern corporations and government offices have forced some of the gender codes to be relaxed, or to be observed in creative new ways. In France since the late 1980s, female Muslim schoolchildren have adopted the hijab headcovering against the objections of school authorities. At issue, among other things, is the matter of Muslim identity in an environment in which it is otherwise being lost among modern, secular, non-Muslim social codes.

The issues of veiling, gender separation, and the role of women in society are matters that are much discussed in the Islamic world, and have been for nearly a century. Male Muslim reformers at the beginning of the twentieth century argued that Muslim countries would remain backward and subject to undue colonial influence until Muslims became better educated, including Muslim women. Education was seen as a prerequisite for emancipation. The secular governments that ruled Islamic states after independence at mid-century have sought to educate women as well as men and to hire more women in jobs in the public sector.

Revivalist Islamic movements (sometimes labeled "fundamentalism") have resisted these attempts to modernize and Westernize the traditional Islamic social ethos by calling for a return to the traditional boundaries of hijab, khalwa, and harim. For example, Islamic groups in Egypt have intervened in crowded public places, such as bus stations and in large lecture halls at universities, to insure that women unattended by appropriate males have their own space in which to stand or sit and not be bothered by men. Women who dress immodestly by Islamist standards are admonished to be more modest when going out in public. A more general Islamic impetus for this male intervention is that it is a collective duty of Muslims to insure social order and stability—something that Islamists believe is threatened by unaccompanied women moving about in public spaces. Islamist intervention is seen by some as a gratuitous imposition of traditional male values on women, by others as a welcome restoration of traditional values that preserve the dignity of women. Again, the argument is an Islamic one. To be sure, Western feminists, academics, and pundits have had much to say about the treatment of women in Islamic societies. Nonetheless, non-Muslims will not understand Islamic societies until they develop interpretive strategies for understanding the symbolic and ritual grounds for the "culture wars" going on over gender in Islamic societies.

Rituals of Social Conflict

A scene takes place on a crowded street in Cairo. Two cars have slightly bumped into each other as the drivers tried to avoid hitting dozens of pedestrians crossing the street in front of and around them. Immediately doors swing open, and the drivers (who may know each other slightly) advance toward each other angrily, hurling insults and threats, and shaking their fists. Soon a crowd gathers around both drivers and their cars, including other passengers from cars that have stopped, patrons of nearby coffee shops and other establishments, other passerbys, and an occasional onlooking policeman. Men and women, Muslims and Christian Copts, children and dogs converge on a scene that quickly becomes what Turner might have recognized as a liminal social space without gender and most other cultural boundaries. As the shouting and confusion seem to escalate, the observer will realize he or she is witness to what one scholar has called the "folk ballet of violence." In Egyptian Arabic it is called a *dowshah*.[13]

The dowshah is also referred to as a "ritual pantomime." It is the pantomime aspect that interests us here as much as the ritual dimension. Andrea B. Rugh, an anthropologist who has lived in Cairo, describes several stages to the dowshah. First is the *provocation*, an incident or festering problem that brings two parties into open conflict, each one thinking that he or she is completely in the right and the other one totally in the wrong. Next comes a *letting off steam* phase. This is the stage of the ritual in which insults are hurled and verbal threats are made, perhaps accompanied by physical gestures such as the shaking of fists or other, more rude, gestures. The crowd for its part encourages the combatants verbally to let the anger out of their systems. The third is the *mediation* stage, when someone from the crowd, usually an older person, a shaykh-like figure, steps in between the two combatants, beginning a negotiation process that allows each combatant to voice his or her complaint freely. With Sulayman- (Solomon-) like skills, the mediator usually tries to get both sides to make concessions to achieve a workable resolution to the conflict. The determination of absolute right and wrong is not the function of the mediator, nor is it possible in many such cases. The crowd at this stage switches from goading on the combatants to working with the mediator to bring about peace. The final stage, that of *reconciliation*, may be signaled by a handshake or even an embrace between the two combatants. Following reconciliation, the crowd may disperse slowly, as combatants and onlookers alike linger on to rehash the event.[14]

The dowshah, it should be clear by now, is not only a ritual, it is an impromptu social event of some significance. Occasionally, the conflict breaks out into physical violence, but most of the time the combat is verbal and gestural, and combatants are willingly restrained by bystanders from actually swinging their fists. In most cases, the cause of the conflict is a problem of some standing between two persons in the community who know each other. Feuds between family members within the same household, on the other side, though also frequent, generally do not become public events. Commenting on the dowshah, Rugh points out the following:

> There are a number of ways that the *dowshah* differs from conflicts in other cultural traditions, to mention the most obvious: the phasing and the timing that prolongs the tension-release period; the significant role of the mediator and the eagerness of even complete strangers to play this role; the meeting in the middle, each giving up part of what he wanted; and the readiness to make generous concessions at the end. The audience generally reacts sympathetically, regarding anger as an 'outside affliction' rather than a 'lack of control,' and its members are willing to work out a resolution with the combatants. Community harmony is usually restored through this process until the next *dowshah* erupts.[15]

Contemporary interest has grown in recent decades in what social scientists refer to as "conflict resolution"—a discipline that sees war and violence as acute social problems that must be resolved. What is interesting about the dowshah and other similar social "ritual pantomimes" is that they appear to be indigenous cultural patters of conflict resolution that operate in local contexts. That rituals like the dowshah should occur in Islamic societies is perhaps not accidental. We recall that the Prophet Muhammad was invited to Yathrib (Medina) to negotiate peace among conflicting tribal factions. Maintaining public order, which can be fragile in most societies, is a duty prescribed in the Shari'a that falls upon the community, not just individuals.

Recalling Religious Disputation

In the discussion of Islamic religious thought in earlier chapters, it was pointed out that Sunni Islamic civilization has attained orthodox consensus according to a model of leadership that does not rely on infallible central authorities or councils of higher clergy. The social implications of madhhab—the conflicting, partisan schools of interpretation that arose in kalam, fiqh, and other religious disciplines—are that conflict is normal in Islamicate society. Conflict of view (*ikhtilaf*) is a necessary aspect of *consensus*, an important ingredient of the discipline of fiqh. As we saw earlier, religious disputations (*munazarat*) among spokesmen for Muslim madhhabs and between Muslim and non-Muslim communities often became noisy and loud, as in the case of the Egyptian dowshah. Nonetheless, rules of engagement, written and unwritten, existed and were generally followed. The munazarat among medieval scholars, like the dowshah in contemporary Egypt, was an indigenous, cultural form of conflict resolution. Further study of these ritual phenomena in Islamic and other religious societies is warranted.

The role of religion in society is marked by boundaries that must be negotiated through ritual and legal means, as we have seen. In the next chapter we will consider the Muslim ethos in select contexts of Islamic societies.

NOTES

1. See Hamed Ammar, *Growing Up in an Egyptian Village* (New York: Octagon Books, 1966). pp. 91–95.
2. Ammar, *Egyptian Village*, pp. 116–24. See also Hani Fakhouri, *Kafr el-Elow: A Egyptian Village in Transition* (New York: Holt, Rinehart and Winston, 1972), pp. 86–87.
3. Al-Bukhari, *The Translation of the Meanings of Sahih al-Bukhari: Arabic-English*, trans. Muhammad Muhsin Khan (Chicago: Kazi Publications Inc., 1976), 1:174 (Book V, Chapter 29). The translation offered here is more literal than that of M. M. Khan's translation, which is more a paraphrase to indicate the sense of the hadith. Khan's rendering: "If male and female organs come into close contact (bath becomes compulsory)."
4. Fakhouri, *Kafr el-Elow*, (pp. 86–87) discusses clitoridectomy in the pages cited in the preceding notes. For additional bibliography, see Dale F. Eickelman, *The Middle East: An Anthropological Approach*, 2nd ed. (Englewood Cliffs, N.J.: Prentice Hall, 1989), p. 193 and Note 34.
5. Al-Bukhari, *Translation*, 7:3 (Book LXII [Nikah], Chapter 2, no. 3).
6. Fakouri, *Kafr el-Elow*, pp. 63–70; Ammar, *Growing Up in an Egyptian Village*, pp. 193–201; see M. Berger, *Arab World*, pp. 106–109. For an excellent discussion of marriage and other rites of passage in Egypt, see Juan Eduardo Campo, *The Other Sides of Paradise: Explorations into the Religious Meanings of Domestic Space in Islam* (Columbia, S.C.: University of South Carolina Press, 1991). The information on the *dukhla* ceremony is found on pp. 110–12.
7. See Campo, *Paradise*, pp. 115–16, on which the following account of the funeral and mourning cycles are based.
8. Campo, *Paradise*, p. 116.
9. Ammar, *Growing Up in an Egyptian Village*, pp. 91–92.
10. Al-Bukhari, *Translation*, 7:28–30 (Book LXII [Wedlock], Chapter 25, and following chapters).
11. Fazlur Rahman, *Major Themes of the Qur'an* (Minneapolis: Bibliotheca Islamica, 1989), pp. 48–49.
12. For a description of domestic space from a male child's point of view, see the semi-fictional historical novel by Roy Mottahedeh, *The Mantle of the Prophet: Religion and Politics in Iran* (New York: Pantheon Books, 1885), pp. 26–28.
13. Andrea B. Rugh, citing Desmond Stewart, in her Foreword to Nayra Atiya, *Khul-Khaal: Five Egyptian Women Tell Their Stories* (Cairo: American University in Cairo Press, 1984), p. xvi.
14. Rugh, "Foreword," pp. xvi–xvii.
15. Rugh, "Foreword," p. xvii.

15

Islamic Ethos

in

Select Contexts

PEASANT SOCIETIES

Islamic societies around the world are still predominantly rural, peasant societies. Rapidly growing urban complexes, such as Cairo and Lahore, are expanding in part due to large numbers of people leaving the countryside to find work and other opportunities in the city. Thus, even large cities in the Islamic world, despite their modern ways, preserve much of the traditional ethos of rural Islam in some neighborhoods. Social scientists have referred to this as the "ruralification" of cities like Cairo. It does seem clear that, in order to understand traditional Islamic societies, it is important to consider peasant culture. In this chapter, we will also look more closely at the social and religious ethos of the bazaar in Iran and the Sufi tariqas in Egypt, both of which form discrete communities within larger communities of Muslims.

AN EGYPTIAN VILLAGE

Today, as in the past, the majority of Muslims dwell in village settlements, living mainly by agriculture. Less accessible to the Western media than the city, and less romantic to be pictured in novels and movies than the world of the Bedouin, the Muslim village has remained nearly eclipsed from outside view. Even specialists on Islam have preferred to focus upon the more visible intellectual and cultural achievements of Islamic urban civilization. Lacking cathedral mosques and other aspects of high culture, villages do not normally produce literary texts and other cultural products in high demand by distant scholars. Village life has been available for analysis only to those willing to go to the villages themselves. Thus we must turn for information to the fieldwork of anthropologists and sociologists.

The late President Gamal Abd al-Nasser of Egypt once startled the press, both at home and abroad, by remarking that the media gave "too much space to sensational trivialities." Nasser, as one social scientist has told it, "pointed to a village near Alexandria, Kafr el Batikh, as the place where the 'true' Egypt might be found."[1] Nasser knew what people in the West and even many among the sophisticated urban population of Cairo did not, namely, that cities in the Middle East draw their population largely from the countryside. Traditional cultural patterns are transformed more rapidly in cities, under the constant urban trend toward modernization. It is in the village, then, that we must seek to discover ways of life that have survived for centuries. The movable Bedouin camp has resisted the winds of change more successfully than the village, but the village has been more hospitable to such Islamic institutions as the masjid and the leadership of the ulama than Bedouin life could or would sustain.[2]

Kafr el-Elow

Located eighteen miles south of Cairo and five miles southwest of Helwan, Kafr el-Elow covers a land area of about four square kilometers along the east side of the Nile River. In 1960 its population was 6,087.[3] The village is actually comprised of four distinct settlements which, for cultural and administrative reasons, are considered a single entity. A single masjid provides the religious focal point for all four settlements, and all four are governed by a single 'umda, or mayor. The subdivision of the village into settlements reflects a common feature of peasant populations in the Arab world. Villages, like cities, have been formed by Bedouins and other migrants in search of new opportunities. Family, tribal, and former geographic roots are maintained in the social structure of village life.

Historical knowledge and cultural expression are kept alive chiefly through oral tradition and popular folk religion in Islamic (and all) peasant societies. The traditional role of the ulama as educators and spiritual leaders of Islamic society ties local societies into the universals of Islamic culture. Tradition has it that six families founded Kafr el-Elow in the mid-eighteenth century. Notable ancestry is traced to these families and to the settlements from which they originated. The main occupation for two hundred years has

FIGURE 15.1 Village near Luxor, Egypt. (Photo by the author.)

been agriculture. The *fellahīn* (plural of *fellah*, peasant) constitute the vast majority of the population of Egypt and of many other Islamic countries. The image of the ageless character of traditional peasant ways of life in Kafr el-Elow is heightened by the ancient pyramids of Giza, which dominate the distant landscape.

Like other villages in the Islamic world, Kafr el-Elow has not been unresponsive to the changes going on in the modern world. Village workers commute to nearby Cairo and Helwan, and, in turn, schoolteachers, health officials, and other professionals bring something of the modern world into Kafr el-Elow. Radio broadcasts from Cairo are received in the village, and the growing literacy rate, which is due to modern mandatory curricula, makes newspapers another source of knowledge. Thus regional Arab-world politics and international events are now subjects of local conversations. A century ago, peasant world views were limited to the immediate concerns of the villagers. Studies have shown that the gap between the levels of political sophistication in cities such as Cairo and villages such as Kafr el-Elow is not so great as one might suspect.[4]

Villages do not have clearly defined social classes. The most obvious distinction has been between those who own the land and those who work the land. Land reform, in Egypt and elsewhere, has altered somewhat the abuses of absentee landlordism and the terrible gap between the rich and the poor, offering greater stability to tenant farming, ownership of small

FIGURE 15.2 Local notables and children in village near Luxor, Egypt. (Photo by the author.)

parcels of land, and other relationships between fellahin and the land. But life remains extremely simple in the village. Social distinctions are made on the basis of degrees of piety and levels of education as much as wealth. Most villages are headed by a mayor, 'umda, who is advised by a council of elders. These leaders usually serve without pay, although they receive certain privileges and enjoy a certain prestige within their communities. A small police force is maintained, but crime is not a major problem in village societies.[5] Services in education, health, and other areas of public works connected with the national government bring trained personnel from the cities into the villages. Jurisdiction in these matters belongs to the national, not the local, government.

As modernization increases in the Islamic world, traditional values are maintained in villages more than cities. For example, hospitality is still regarded a solemn duty, and the ability to honor guests lavishly is a mark of one's status within the community. A village mayor is often chosen from among those who have the means to entertain political and other kinds of guests. Respect for age and the elderly is another noticeable social value. Social and moral qualities are extolled and inculcated through quranic verses and folk proverbs that are often quoted in everyday discourse.

Houses in Kafr el-Elow are made of unbaked mud bricks. This has been true of peasant homes in Egypt since the time of the pharaohs, and only recently have a few buildings of modern construction begun to appear outside the cities. In the traditional house, a single door leads into the square or rectangular edifice and out into a small courtyard. The courtyard is the scene of many household activities of a practical nature. Cooking is done there during the warmer months, and washing may also be done there, or in nearby canals that flow through the village. An outdoor privy usually stands enclosed in one corner of the yard.

Most villagers are too poor to own much furniture and household orna-ments. Various rooms in the enclosed structure around the courtyard are the dwelling quarters of the many members of the extended family who share the house. Next to the main entrance, most houses have guest rooms, to which male visitors are ushered and entertained by heads of the house. On such occasions, the women of the house disappear from sight until the guests are seated and the door is closed.[6]

Food and diet vary considerably throughout the Islamic world, but Kafr el-Elow is typical of Egypt. The main item in every villager's diet is flat bread (known as pita or pocket bread in the West), usually called *khubs* or *'aysh* (the latter literally means "life"). It is made of wheat or corn flour and baked in small, flat loaves. Twice each week women prepare the dough in their own homes; then groups of several women gather in the home of one woman who has agreed to play hostess that day. While the bread is baking, children play together and the women socialize, gossip, and joke with one another. It is an important and regular social ritual of village life. Of course, under the impact of modernization, the preparation of the dough for baking is being done more and more by commercial bakers.

Villagers' diets may include some meat—usually beef, lamb, or, more fre-quently, chicken—but in small quantities. As noted in Chapter 1, the eating of pork is forbidden by the Qur'an. A large portion of the diet consists of vegetables and fruits, especially melons and cucumbers. The main spices are garlic and peppers. A plentiful source of protein is the fava bean, known as *ful* (pronounced "fool") in Egypt. *Ta'miya* is a dish made with fava beans ground together with parsley and spices, then deep-fried in small patties. It is found all over Egypt and much of the Middle East. The visitor to Cairo will find ta'miya vendors along the streets and vendors of many other favorite dishes as well. A sandwich made of ta'miya placed in flatbread with chopped vegetables, known as *falafel*, is now an international delicatessen item; peasants in Egypt have been eating it for centuries. This very ancient traditional dish is similar to vegetarian burgers, now being developed as a meat substitute for cholesterol-conscious Americans. A type of meatless chili called *ful mudamas* is prepared by boiling and mashing the fava beans and simmering them in spices. Coffee is not often served in villages because it is too expensive. Guests and friends usually socialize over a dark, thickly brewed tea that is heavily sweetened with sugar.[7]

THE IRANIAN BAZAAR

In Sunni Islam, the village exemplified Redfield's notion of the little tradi-tion. The village stands at some geographical and intellectual distance from the great tradition of law and theology that is dominated by the leaders of the ulama in the cathedral mosques and universities of the cities. In Shi'i Islam, the urban bazaar is the chief social context within which the ulama wield their most effective influence. The bazaar is more than the mercantile district of each town and city; it is a socioreligious community with its own internal structure. The normative guidance of the Qur'an, the Sunna, and the teachings of the imams prevail over national and local political directives. Even in modern times the bazaar communities of Iran have remained the chief Shi'i expressions of Islam as a total way of life. At the same time the national trend toward modernization in Iran has made the bazaar an interesting case study of the dynamic conflict between the norms of traditional religion and the pressures for social change.

The Role of the Shi'i Ulama

The Shi'i ulama are in many ways similar to the ulama in Sunni Islam. In both branches, the ulama derive their authority from social recognition of their compentence and knowledge of the Qur'an, the Sunna, and the application of the Shari'a to all aspects of life. The Twelver Shi'i ulama, in addition, represent the teachings of the twelve imams. Like the Sunni ulama, Shi'i religious leaders serve as teachers, Shari'a lawyers, and mosque functionaries. But whereas the Sunni ulama have traditionally supported the government (whether caliph or modern secular state), Shi'i religious leaders have often led the Shi'i community in opposition to governments felt to be oppressive toward Shi'i Islam. The Shi'i ulama in Iran are organized in a more definite hierarchy. Representing the twelfth (hidden) imam are several Grand Ayatollahs, whose honorific title means "sign of God." Beneath them are other ayatollahs. Another class of distinguished religious leaders bears the title *Hojjat al-Islam*, which means "argument" or "proof of Islam." Throughout the many towns, villages, and urban neighborhoods in which there are Shi'i communities, local religious leaders are called *mullas*. They have usually received their training from one of the renowned ayatollahs or hojjas, but their occupation as a teacher or mosque functionary in a local neighborhood places them in constant contact with the everyday lives and needs of the people.

The Merchant

Gustav Thaiss has studied the bazaar communities in Tehran, Iran. In his words,

> A Persian bazaar, from one point of view, can be considered just a marketplace where goods of all types and sizes can be bought and sold. In reality, however, it is much more than this. It is a total social phenomenon, a social and cultural world nearly complete in itself. The bazaar is a multi-faceted entity comprising

religious, commercial, political, and broadly social elements. Such diversity governs its complexity and importance, since it is able to adapt to various situations by emphasizing one or several of its many facets at any particular time. Thus, it is far from being just a marketplace.[8]

The chief occupation of the *bazaari* (one who lives physically and culturally within the bazaar community) is that of merchant. Since the time of the Prophet, marketplaces have been important social spaces within the Islamic world. While the bazaar community has directed much criticism at and pressed for reforms by governments, the military, and other sectors of Islamic society, it has been hospitable to the normative religious values and teachings of the Qur'an and the Sunna. Mosques and schools form a more natural part of the social ecology of the bazaar than they do in modernized parts of the city. Commercial exchange requires a degree of literacy, and thus the religious and the practical curricula of commerce have been taught to bazaari children by the ulama. Also, the traditional attire of Persian Muslims, including the veil for women, is more likely to be seen in the bazaar than elsewhere in the city.

Kinship ties have remained strong in bazaar communities, even in modern times. Traditional marriages between paternal first cousins are still assumed, although, as in Sunni villages, there are provisions for other arrangements through the negotiations of the families involved. The practice of Islam is facilitated by the strong influence the ulama have within the bazaar. If there is anything like the tension between great tradition and little tradition described above, it would be in the bazaaris' popular celebrations of the Tenth of Muharram ceremonies commemorating the martyrdom of Husayn. The great tradition, represented by the educated ulama, has frowned upon the excessive emotionalism the bazaaris often exhibit in the ta'ziya dramas. At times, however, the ulama have also capitalized upon this annual display of intense unity within the little tradition in order to foment opposition to unpopular governmental policies.

THE SUFI ORDER

Cities, villages, and marketplaces are environments conducive to the Islamic way of life. Into these social environments, which themselves are typical of most civilizations, the Qur'an and the Sunna are woven to produce distinctively Islamic cultural patterns. The term *society* refers to such structured collectives as tribes, towns, cities, and neighborhoods. Society is structured by layers of social strata, ethnic and sectarian boundaries, and other demarcations that serve to organize and regulate human behavior. Brotherhoods and religious orders comprise social contexts of a different type than those described earlier in this chapter. The term *community* is more appropriately applied to these religious orders. In Islam, the concept of umma, defined as the community of believers living by the teachings of the Qur'an and the Sunna, has been an ideal that has stood in tension with the realities of everyday life. Community is created annually by Hajjis on the road to Mecca. But the pilgrims' common state of consecration (ihram) is temporary; each Hajji must return to his or her hometown, where society is more structured, less egalitarian. Therefore, like other religious traditions, Islam has witnessed the departure of some individuals and groups who were dissatisfied with society. Many wandered from town to village, wanting no earthly home for themselves. Others formed brotherhoods or communities on faraway frontier outposts or in compounds built within or near towns and cities. They were Sufis. The social significance of Sufi orders also derives from the Qur'an and the Sunna, but the impetus for Sufis has been to live in *community*, not society.

The institution of the Sufi order, *tariqa*, is a combined spiritual and social response to several developments in Islamic history. First, from the earliest days of conquest and empire, many Muslims felt that the acquisition of wealth and worldly gain had destroyed the possibility of one's living according to the Qur'an and the Sunna. These Muslims preferred a life of asceticism, that is, a life of poverty for the sake of God. Second, the formal structure of Islam, as defined and implemented by the ulama, has seemed to some Muslims a much too static environment within which to experience religion. Especially among simpler folk, religious needs for a more personal *experience* of the divine have been felt. Thus many Muslims have chosen to live in a community under the spiritual guidance of a respected shaykh or holy man, a saint who in the eyes of his followers displays signs of nearness to God.[9] Third, as Islam expanded into such regions as Africa and India, where other religious traditions were quite alien to the Qur'an and the Sunna, the exclusivist claims of Sunni and Shi'i Islam, requiring absolute conversion, have set Islam over and against other traditions. The more universalistic, inclusive, and encompassing qualities of Sufism have proved to be more successful in bringing non-Muslims and the uneducated into contact with the literary demands of the Qur'an and the Sunna.[10]

The Sufis' search for union (tawhid) with God through living in community set apart from society has created certain tensions with the more orthodox ulama establishment. For one thing, the Sufis have developed their own interpretations of the Qur'an and the Sunna, and as a result charges of heresy have often been leveled against them by the ulama, especially, as we saw in Chapter 5, during the late Middle Ages. Another problem has been the broad, popular appeal that many Sufi saints and shaykhs have enjoyed, often at the expense of popular respect for the ulama. Still another problem, again of interpretation, can be found in Sufi forms of worship. Music, dancing, poetry, and even prayers—either forbidden or carefully regulated in interpretations of the Qur'an and the Sunna by the ulama—are used to exploit emotions in the communal and private rituals of mystical Islam. Although in more recent times Sufi orders have become more like voluntary associations, and thus less like separate institutions apart from Islamic society, Sufism remains an important area of study for the student who wishes to grasp the variety of expressions within Islamic culture.

The Tariqa

The Arabic term *tariqa* can mean both "path" and "method." In Sufism a tariqa is both a way of life and a set of religious practices that focus on God through distinct interpretations of the Qur'an and the Sunna. Like the Shi'a, who derive their special teachings from the traditional lore of the twelve imams, Sufis preserve the sacred biographies of revered saints, whose near-miraculous lives form models of behavior for the Sufi tariqa.

By the eleventh century, tariqa acquired a social significance as well. It designated a common life (community) of several disciples living under the spiritual supervision of the shaykh. Thus the social concept of umma became for Sufis the tariqa, and the functions of the ulama were performed by the saint or shaykh. From the eleventh century until the present day hundreds of tariqas have formed, in most lands where Islam has spread. Most of these tariqas belong to one of a dozen main lines that trace their spiritual heritage back to famous saints in the Middle Ages. Each saint in turn possessed a spiritual heritage which was traced to the Prophet Muhammad, and thus to God. This tree-like structure with a single source and a diffusion of branches forms the background of the world view and sacred history that characterize mystical Islam.[11]

The impact of the religious and social notions of tariqa upon Islam has been considerable, with effects felt beyond Sufi organizations themselves. In a geographic sense, the numerous shrines and mausolea of Sufi saints that dot the landscape in many Muslim countries have become focal points of local pilgrimages. The shrines, through the baraka or blessings of their founding saints, attract the commonfolk of nearby villages. Although the commonfolk making pilgrimages to Sufi shrines do not normally strike out on the Sufi path as a constant way of life, the shrines encourage social gatherings that have the significance of creating a temporary experience of community for people in local regions. Observers report that Christian, Hindu, and other religious peoples also visit the shrines of Sufi saints. Thus Sufism, more than Shi'i and Sunni Islam, has an ecumenical spirit about it that has avoided interfaith polemics while at the same time attracting conversions to Islam.

The Sufi tariqas have also played important social and educational roles in local villages and within neighborhoods of cities. Ammar reports that in the village of Silwa, Egypt, the Nakshabandi Sufi order is present to the extent that a shaykh of that tariqa maintains a headquarters in a room adjacent to the village mosque. Young men gather for the evening prayers, led by the Nakshabandi shaykh. The disciples thus live with their families and work or perhaps attend the village school during the day. At night in a room of the mosque, young disciples stand around the shaykh to perform the Sufi form of prayer known as the *dhikr*. Dhikr means "remembrance," and for Sufis, who stress the Islamic belief that the world causes one to forget God, prayer consists of repeating the name of God hundreds, perhaps thousands of times. As the chanting proceeds, the circle of young men begins to sway back and forth, the tempo increasing as the shaykh, standing in the center, claps his hands or himself dances. This part of the dhikr is punctuated every quarter of an hour or so by cessation of dancing and chanting while the shaykh recites a religious poem attributed to a saint from the sacred history of the tariqa.[12]

In villages like Silwa, the youths who are sent to Sufi schools and dhikr ceremonies are known as young men of "the Path" (tariqa). They are often from families that cannot afford the expense of sending their children to schools in the cities, or from families who wish their children to have a more religious education than can be had in the state-run village schools. Combining education by oral tradition (in the poems and teachings of the shaykh) with the social solidarity experienced in the dhikr, the tariqa performs important social and religious functions in Islamic society, especially among the poorer, less educated village people.

The village is not the entire extent or only social place occupied by Sufism, today or in the past. The mystical dimension of Islam has been felt and experienced at all levels of Islamic society. Sufi shaykhs and intellectuals have also ranked among the higher echelons of the ulama. The study of Islam is not complete without a consideration of Sufism, and Sufism cannot be understood apart from the cultural and religious context of Islam.[13]

Many topics about Islamic religion have been covered in the preceding chapters. After reading this book, the next stage for students of Islam in the history of religions is to study Islamic religious texts themselves as well as more advanced scholarly studies. Comparative studies of Islam and other religions must ultimately be based on greater familiarity with the texts and social data of Islamic civilization. Some guidance in choosing such texts and studies is given in the bibliography. It remains only to conclude our introductory study of Islam in the next and final chapter.

NOTES

1. Monroe Berger, *The Arab World Today* (Garden City, N.Y.: Anchor Books, 1962), p. 75, referring to *New York Times*, June 4, 1961, p. 4.
2. For a discussion of the differences among the pastoral nomadic communities, villages, and cities in the Arab world, see M. Berger, *Arab World*, pp. 42–97. On Iran, these same three types of societies are discussed by Brian Spooner, "Religion and Society Today: An Anthropological Perspective," in *Iran Faces the Seventies*, ed. Ehsan Yar-Shater (New York: Praeger Publishers, Inc., 1971), pp. 166–88.

3. Hani Fakhouri, *Kafr el-Elow: A Egyptian Village in Transition* (New York: Holt, Rinehart and Winston, 1972), p. 13. Fakhouri's useful descriptive study of the village has been a source of the following remarks on Muslim villages.
4. M. Berger, *Arab World*, pp. 68–69.
5. M. Berger, *Arab World*, pp. 61–62.
6. Fakhouri, *Kafr el-Elow*, pp. 17–18.
7. Fakhouri discusses food, clothing, education, economy, and several other aspects of the culture of Kafr el-Elow.
8. Gustav Thaiss, "The Bazaar as a Case Study of Religion and Social Change" in *Iran Faces the Seventies*, ed. Ehsan Yar-Shater (New York: Praeger Publishers, Inc., 1971). p. 193.
9. The term for "saint" is *wali*, which has the connotation of "friend of God."
10. On the process of conversion to Islam in South Asia and the role of Sufis in that process, see Richard M. Eaton, *The Rise of Islam and the Bengal Frontier, 1204-1760* (Berkeley: University of California Press, 1993), especially Part 5, "Mass Conversion to Islam: Theories and Protagonists," pp. 113–34.
11. A useful historical survey of the Sufi orders in Islam is J. Spencer Trimingham, *The Sufi Orders in Islam* (New York: Oxford University Press, 1971). Among other things, Trimingham discusses the main tariqa lines, how the orders were organized socially, and the rituals and forms of worship followed by different orders.
12. Ammar, *Egyptian Village*, p. 187.
13. Two works in particular are recommended to those who wish to learn more about Sufism. Annemarie Schimmel, *The Mystical Dimension of Islam* (Chapel Hill: University of North Carolina Press, 1975), brings together a massive amount of material by Muslim and non-Muslim scholars who have studied Sufism in depth, and the author's own insights are extremely valuable. Martin Lings, *A Sufi Saint of the Twentieth Century* (Berkeley and Los Angeles: University of California Press, 1973) is a sensitive biographical study of a North African saint, Shaykh Ahmad al-Alawi, and of his social and religious impact on his disciples and the people of the surrounding area.

PART V   STUDYING ISLAM

16

Whither the Study of Islam?

"ENDINGS"

Texts on living religions must end with a semicolon, not a period. World religions in general have experienced a revival of interest and influence in today's world. "Ending" the story of Islam, in any sense of the word, would be inappropriate and premature. The question is: Where to go from here? Throughout the twentieth century the chief interest of Western scholars in the future of Islam has been in religious movements for modernism and reform. The Oxford and Harvard scholar H. A. R. Gibb edited a volume in 1932 titled *Whither Islam?* which raised these questions. Readers of the present book will recognize that interest in Islamic revival and reform movements (the term "fundamentalism" is often used) in the Abode of Islam still runs high and determines the chief interest that American politicians and the media have in Islam. A book that introduces readers to the study of Islamic religion must "end" differently, however. The question this final chapter seeks to answer is: How should one go about the continued study of Islam?

242

FIGURE 16.1   Sunset, Cairo. (Photo by the author.)

PAST STUDY OF ISLAM IN THE WEST

In further reading about Islam, one will not get far before encountering the term "Orientalism." It has become a negative term in many circles. What is Orientalism? Much of the scholarship done on Islamic texts, history, and religion in the late nineteenth and the first half of the twentieth century was done by European specialists in the philology of Middle Eastern languages. When the Orientalists began their work in the nineteenth century, Europe (and America) knew very little about Islam beyond what the Cluniac translation movement, led by Peter the Venerable in France, had produced in the twelfth century (see Chapter 2). Not many texts in Arabic and other Middle Eastern languages had been edited and published. Much that had been translated and written about Islam was in Latin, not in modern European languages. Therefore, at Oxford, Paris, Leiden, and other European universities, research was begun by scholars whose first task was to locate, edit, translate, and explain Islamic texts.

The problem was that studying Islam in those days required knowledge of so many languages, and the patient reading of so many handwritten manuscripts, that few people, even scholars, knew much about Islam. Orientalism became a field of study for specialists in Arabic manuscripts and texts, not a more general field of study. There was another problem. Another group of people in the West who came to know something about Islam was composed of Christian missionaries from European and North American churches (as opposed to Orthodox and other Middle Eastern churches). Much of the early ethnographic work on actual Muslim communities was done by Christian missionaries.

It is easy to understand why Muslims would come to resent the intrusion of European and North American Christian missionaries into their societies, as well as the biases that Muslims could find in missionary writings about Islam. What about the Orientalists? Surely the recovery, editing, and study of Islamic texts was beneficial to Muslims themselves and thus above criticism. That, however, was not the case. For one thing, many Orientalists looked upon manuscripts of ancient Arabic texts as their own and European property; manuscripts by the thousands were taken from Middle Eastern repositories, where they were often kept in poor condition, and shipped to libraries in such places as Oxford, Paris, Leiden, Berlin, and the Vatican, where they were identified, catalogued, and made available to European scholars. More recently, governments of Muslim countries have established their own system of recovering and preserving textual archives.

A more serious criticism of Orientalism was related to the period of European colonialism. From the late nineteenth and early twentieth centuries until the mid-twentieth century, European powers had colonized Muslim lands in North Africa, the Middle East, and Southeast Asia. Scholarship on Islamic religion, history, and texts thrived in this period, during which European colonial governments controlled Muslim lands. The paradigm example of this was the landing of Napoleon in 1798 in Egypt, with an army of soldiers and political functionaries, including scholars whose task was to study and analyze the ancient and modern languages, religions, cultures, and societies of the Egyptian people. Thereafter, an important aspect of European colonial rule in Muslim lands was Orientalist scholarship.

In 1978, a book titled *Orientalism* by Edward W. Said was published, in which the author, a professor of English Literature at Columbia University who was born to Christian Palestinian parents in the Middle East, severely criticized the Western study of Islam. Arguing with the French philosopher Michel Foucault that "knowledge is power," Said claimed that Orientalists, in the service of European colonial governments, created a "discourse" about Islam that sought to control it. In a now famous passage, Said characterized Orientalist scholarship as follows:

> The Orientalist surveys the Orient from above, with the aim of getting hold of the whole sprawling panorama before him—culture, religion, mind, history, society. To do this he must see every detail through the device of a set of reductive categories (the Semites, the Muslim mind, the Orient, and so forth). Since these categories are primarily schematic and efficient ones, and since it is more or less assumed that no Oriental can know himself the way an Orientalist can, any vision of the Orient ultimately comes to rely for its coherence and force on the person, institution, or discourse whose property it is.[1]

Orientalists, their books, and the very way they wrote and spoke about Islam was, in Said's view, a "discourse" meant to control the subject matter, namely, Muslims and Islam.

Said's provocative thesis resonated among Western scholars who were critical of the history and results of Western domination of so-called Third World nations. Muslims also found in Said's argument an echo of their own, sometimes mixed, feelings about Western scholars who studied them and their religion. Readers of the present volume who are interested in this topic—the politics of the study of Islam—are recommended to read *Orientalism* as well as the very heated response the book drew from Orientalists themselves. For assessments of Islamic studies in the West from different perspectives, *Europe and the Mystique of Islam* by Maxime Rodinson and *Islam in European Thought* by Albert Hourani are both recommended. This and other works cited in this chapter are found in the bibliography.

GOING TO THE SOURCES

One positive result of Orientalist scholarship is that now the average reader can find many basic Islamic texts in English translation. The quality of the translations is uneven, as one might expect. For an overview of Islamic texts, or parts of texts, that are available in English translation (as of 1980), one should consult Margaret Anderson, *Arabic Materials in Translation: A Bibliography of Works from the Pre-Islamic Period to 1977*. I shall mention here only a few of the religious texts that are basic to understanding the fundamentals of Islamic world views.

Students who wish to read the Qur'an will find several translations, some with interfacing Arabic text. *The Meaning of the Glorious Qur'an* by Marmaduke Pickthall, a British convert to Islam, is a fairly accurate, literal rendering of the text. *The Koran Interpreted* by A. J. Arberry captures more of the poetic cadences of the original Arabic, but unfortunately the numbering of verses is according to the older European edition of the Arabic text, not the Egyptian edition that is now used by Muslims and by most Western scholars. Studying the text of the Qur'an, and particularly finding passages on different topics and themes, is now enhanced by the publication of *A Concordance of the Qur'an* by Hanna E. Kassis. It is a comprehensive volume with indices both in English and by Arabic root in transliteration.

Study of some hadith collections is much less advanced. Nonetheless a translation of the famous collection by al-Bukhari, with interfacing Arabic text, has been made by Muhammad Muhsin Khan, *The Translation of the Meanings of Sahih al-Bukhari* in nine volumes. The table of contents in Volume 1 for all nine volumes will help the reader locate themes and topics. The standard classical biography of the Prophet was translated by Alfred Guillaume, *The Life of Muhammad: A Translation of Ishaq's Sirat Rasul Allah*. The famous "History of Prophets and Kings" by Muhammad ibn Jarir al-Tabari (d. 923), a universal history of Islam from the Creation to the time of the author, is now coming out as *The History of al-Tabari (Ta'rikh al-rusul wa'l-muluk)*, edited by Ehsan Yar-Shater. These sources in translation, and the many others one can locate through bibliographies such as Anderson, *Arabic Materials in Translation* (cited above), will allow students of religion to work directly with Islamic texts.

For secondary literature about the study of Islamic religious topics, a brief bibliography is given at the end of this work. In addition, students in religious studies will want to consult some of the indexes available in most university libraries. *Religion Index One: Periodicals* is published annually, arranged by topic, and includes an author/editor index. The companion index for multi-authored volumes is *Religion Index Two: Multi-Author Works.* Students will find works on other religions as well as comparative studies of Islam and other religions with respect to particular topics in these bibliographical indexes. For Islamic studies specifically, one should consult the group of works titled *Index Islamicus.*

Allahu akbar, the Islamic declaration of divine majesty that has summoned the faithful to prayer for more than thirteen centuries, opened the pages of this book. We now come to the final pages, again with reference to the unifying theme of the people and faith we have studied: God is the Greatest! Of course, the history of Islam is far from over. As Wilfred Cantwell Smith wrote at the end of the thirteenth Islamic century, "a Muslim might presumably look forward to . . . another thirteen centuries still to come."[2] Whatever the future may be for Islam, it will draw from past structures and symbols essential to its tradition, and as in the past, it will confront the forces of history, and there will be change. As long as there is history, religious traditions will change. Islam changed during the period of the Rashidun caliphs from a local cult in Arabia to a world religion. Forms of leadership and government have changed in every major period since the beginning. The ethnic and linguistic composition of the Islamic world has changed. The bulk of the population of the world of Islam lies far to the east of Arabia and the central lands of the once great caliphate; yet, the twentieth-century strategic position of much of the Middle East with respect to oil and international politics will continue to bring about changes for Muslim peoples in that region. So, too, in Central Asia, Southeast Asia, Africa, Europe, and North America, Muslim societies and communities are changing. In the future as well as in the present and the past, "God is the Greatest" expresses an underlying foundation upon which the edifice of Islam is built and presumably will continue to stand. Within the structure the religious kaleidoscope of images expressed in myth, ritual, symbol, art, social groupings, and historic events blend together to form variegated but changing patterns that join at one point: *Allahu akbar!*

An underlying thesis of this book has been that we cannot discern the meaning of the present, much less guess about the future, without learning about the past. We have tried to confront the problem of learning how to interpret and explain the process of symbolization and of arriving at meanings in the Islamic world. There can never be a final word on this subject. Muslims repeat a symbol from the Qur'an that perhaps is most apt as we close this book: *Allahu a'lam ahkam*—God is the most knowing, the most wise!

NOTES

1. Edward W. Said, *Orientalism* (New York: Random House, 1978) p. 239.
2. From Wilfred Cantwell Smith, *Islam in Modern History* (Princeton, N.J.: Princeton University Press, 1977), p. 11.

GLOSSARY

This Glossary includes many terms that may be unfamiliar to newcomers to the academic study of religion and of Islam. Additional names of ideas, concepts, and persons can be found in the book by consulting the Index. Each item in the Glossary presents the term as it is spelled in the book followed by a set of parentheses that give alternate spellings. Alternate spellings of the same word (for example, Qur'an, Qoran, Koran) are an indication of linguistic conventions adopted by scholars writing in different European languages. Thus, Qur'an, Quran, and Koran are not misspellings so much as differences in transliteration from the Arabic language and alphabet to Western languages using the Roman alphabet.

In parentheses following each main entry below, the common transliteration of Arabic words employed in most English language journals is given in italics with diacritical marks. In some cases there is no difference in spelling, for example, shirk and *shirk*. The diacritical marks include overbar lengtheners of vowels, underdot intensifiers of some consonants, in addition to the raised backward and forward commas (',`), the 'ayn and hamza respectively, which have been retained in the text in the spelling of such words as Shari'a and Qur'an. If the term is transliterated differently in the *Encyclopaedia of Islam* (first or second editions or the *Shorter Encyclopaedia of Islam*), that spelling is given in Roman type in parentheses.

Abode of Islam Known in Arabic as *dār al-islām*, a the concept in Islamic law for land under Muslim rule and thus in observance of the Shari'a.
Abode of War In Arabic *dār al-ḥarb*, the Islamic term for land that is not under Muslim rule or under treaty with Muslim rulers.
Adab Knowledge and learning in poetry and literature, particularly of an urbane, witty, and secular nature. Hence Adab came to be distinguished from religious knowledge on the one hand and scientific knowledge on the other. Today Adab means the study of literature.
Alid A term for members of Shi'i sects that trace their spiritual paths to the family of 'Ali, the Prophet's cousin and son-in-law.
Ash'ariyya *(Ash'arite)* The orthodox Sunni school of theology (Kalam) named after Abu l-Hasan al-Ash'ari (d. 935).
Ashura *('āshūrā')* The tenth of the first month of the Islamic calendar, Muharram. Originally an important day of fasting and subsequently a Shi'i sacred anniversary commemorating the martyrdom of the third imam Husayn in 680.
Aya *(āya)* A verse of the Qur'an. Aya has another, related meaning of "sign," "miracle," or "mark." Thus the honorific title of *Ayatollah* means "mark of Allah" and designates a higher member of the Shi'i ulama.

248

Ayatollah (*Āyatullāh*) See *Aya*.

Baraka (*baraka*) A spiritual blessing derived from the power of holiness associated with a Sufi saint, the saint's tomb, or other auspicious manifestation of God's power.
Bazaar (*bāzār*) Marketplace (see *Suq*).
Bedouin (Badw) A pastoral nomad of Arabian blood and/or linguistic and cultural stock found chiefly in Syria, Arabia, and North Africa.
Bid‘a Innovation in Islamic doctrine and practice. Bid‘a is considered by Traditionalists especially to be a punishable deviation from the straight path of faith and practice.

Caliph (*khalīfa*) The "successor" or "viceregent" of the Prophet who was elected (appointed or otherwise designated) to head the Muslim state. The office of caliph or *caliphate* was subsumed under three periods, the latter two of which were dynastic: the Rashidun (632–661); The Umayyads (661–750); and the Abbasids (750–1258). The caliph was also known as "imam" (leader) and "Commander of the Faithful."
Cosmology The structural system (and its analysis) of total reality, the cosmos, including divine and spiritual beings, and their interactions and communications.

Dhikr "Remembrance" (with the mind) or "mentioning" (with the tongue) Allah or the many names of Allah. Dhikr is a Sufi term for spiritual exercises that focus the consciousness upon God.
Dhimmi (*dhimmī, dhimma*) A tolerated religious people of the Book (that is, primarily Jews and Christians) living within lands under Islamic rule. Under the Shari‘a, dhimmis are granted the right of retaining their non-Muslim religious status in exchange for payment of a poll tax (*jizya*) and meeting certain other obligations to the Muslim body politic.

Eschatology The beliefs surrounding the "eschaton," the final hour or Day of Judgment, especially in monotheistic religions.
Ethos The social manifestation of religious values and beliefs, manifested in codes of public behavior, rituals, and other symbolic acts.

Fiqh (Fikh) The science of Islamic jurisprudence based on the four roots: Qur'an, hadith, consensus, and analogical reasoning.

Fitna (fitna) Sectarian strife that disrupts the social order. The first of several fitnas in Islam was occasioned by the assassination of Caliph ‘Uthman (reg. 644–656).
Fuqaha (*fuqahā’*, sing. *faqīh*) A member of the ulama who specializes in the study of fiqh.

Ghusl A ritual bath of the entire body to remove a major pollution resulting from sexual activity and contact with corpses, blood, and other serious pollutants.

Hadath (hadath) A minor ritual pollution caused by such things as going to the toilet, touching genitals, sleeping, and passing wind. Hadath is removed prior to such ritual activities as prayer and reciting the Qu'ran by performing the ablution known as wudu'.

Hadith (*ḥadīth*) A tradition or saying traced back to the Prophet though a chain of trusted human transmitters. The orthodox collections of hadith comprise the literary code of the Prophet's Sunna, or customary practice.

Hajj (*ḥajj, Ḥadjdj*) Pilgrimage to Mecca, the Fifth Pillar of Islam. It is a duty for every Muslim to make the hajj once in his or her lifetime if physically, mentally, and financially able to do so. Women must make the journey under the protection of male members of their families.

Halal (*ḥalāl*) The attribute of being permissible under Islamic law. Eating properly slain and blessed cattle is halal according to the Shari'a. The contrary attribute of halal is haram (*ḥarām*).

Hanafi (Hanafite) The Sunni madhhab that traces its interpretation of Islamic law (fiqh) to Abu Hanifa (d. 767). The Hanafi madhhab is especially strong today in Egypt and Turkey.

Hanbali (Hanbalite) The Sunni madhhab that traces its interpretation of Islamic law (fiqh) to Ahmad ibn Hanbal (d. 855). The Hanbali madhhab is found today primarily in the Gulf Arab states.

Haram (*ḥaram* [pronounced ha'-ram]) The sacred space or territory associated with the cities of Mecca, Medina, and Jerusalem. The Shari'a prohibits certain activities within the haram and enjoins others (see *Muhrim*).

Haram (*ḥarām* [pronounced ha-raam']) The attribute of being forbidden under Islamic law. Such acts as stealing or eating pork are haram, according to the Shari'a. The contrary attribute of haram is halal (*ḥalāl*).

Hijra (Latin *Hegira*; Hidjra) The migration of the Prophet and his followers from Mecca to Yathrib (henceforth called Medina) in 622 C.E. (= A.H. 1).

Ibadat (*'ibādāt*) The ordinances of Muslim worship and rituals explained and interpreted in the Shari'a by the ulama. The ibadat generally includes rules governing ritual purity, prayer, alms, fasting, and pilgrimage.

Ihram (*iḥrām*), the state or ritual consecration required during the hajj; see *Muhrim*.

Imam (*imām*) A religious leader. In its broadest usage, the leader of the prayer (salat). In Shi'i Islam, "imam" designates the specially revered descendants of 'Ali ('Alids) who led the Shi'i community during the early centuries and whose teachings the Shi'a preserve as special sources of insight into Qur'an and Sunna.

Iman (*īmān*) The term for faith, religious conviction, in Islam.

Ja'fari (*Ja'farī*) The madhhab (school of interpretation) of the Shari'a to which the Shi'a of the Twelver sect adhere. The name is derived from the sixth imam, Ja'far al-Sadiq.

Jahiliyya (*jāhiliyya*; Djāhiliya) The Muslim designation for the cultural and religious state of affairs in Arabia prior to the rise of Islam. Jahiliyya is often translated "Time of Ignorance" or "Time of Paganism."

Jami' (*jāmi'*, Djāmi') A larger urban mosque preferred for the Friday noon prayer (*jum'a*) and sermon (*khutba*).

Jihad (*jihād*; Djihād) Striving for moral and religious perfection within the Muslim community. Generally, jihad is in response to the specific needs of the community, including bearing arms in defense of Islam. One who so strives for moral and religious perfection is a *mujahid*, a patriot or citizen of Islam. Jihad as "holy war" must be seen in this broader context; martyrdom in the context of jihad promises certain rewards in Paradise.

Junub (junub) The condition of being precluded from performing rituals (prayer, Qur'an recitation) because of a major pollution from sexual intercourse or touching carrion, corpses, blood, alcohol, and other major pollutants. The condition of Junub is removed by a major lustration or bath, known as ghusl

Ka'ba (kaaba) The cube-shaped stone building in the center of the courtyard of the Great Mosque in Mecca. In the eastern corner is set the famous black stone. The Ka'ba is the most important shrine in Islam. It serves as the focal point of the prayer (salat) and the destination of the pilgrimage (hajj).

Kafir (*kafir*) One who is "ungrateful" and unresponsive to God's blessings; hence a general term for an unbeliever.

Kalam Speech, discourse about God, His attributes, prophets, and other religious doctrines. 'Ilm al-kalam (the science of kalam) is a rough equivalent of theology.

Khawarij (*khārijiyya*, Kharijites, Khāridjites) A sect of Islam in the early Umayyad period (661–750) that seceded (*kharaja*) from 'Ali and his partisans after 'Ali failed to establish that the third caliph 'Uthman had been justly assassinated. The Khawarij, a separatist group, or series of groups in early Islam who opposed the sect called the murji'a, held that the Muslim umma should be ruled by a consensus of believers (not a single charismatic imam), and that a believers sins were grounds for expulsion from the community. Extreme Islamists today are sometimes accused of being khawarij, a heresy in Sunni Islam.

Kufr Unbelief in Islam. See *Kafir*.

Madhhab Literally, the place to which one has gone—that is, a school or interpretation of law or theology. Sunni Muslims accept four madhhabs in law (fiqh).

Madrasa A place of study, school. Madrasas are often associated with masjids, in which the religious subjects of Islam, especially law, are studied in the traditional manner. After the tenth century, madrasas were established into perpetuity by endowments known as waqfs.

Maliki (Malikite), the Sunni madhhab that traces its interpretation of Islamic law (fiqh) to Malik ibn Anas (d. 795). The Maliki madhhab is especially prominent in modern times in Africa.

Masjid (*masjid*, masdjid) Literally, the "place of prostration" for Muslim prayers. A larger central masjid in a Muslim city is known as a "jami'" because it is places of "gathering" or "assembly" for the Friday prayer, known as the *jum'a*.

Mawla (*mawla*, pl. *mawālī*) A slave or other non-Muslim captured under Islamic conquest and then freed—by virtue, usually, of becoming Muslim. Mawalis are often referred to as "clients" because in early Islam they were required to associate with Islam through a sponsoring tribe. In the early centuries there was occasional tension between Arab and Mawla Muslims.

Mihrab (*mihrāb*) A "niche" within the masjid (mosque) wall that is closest to Mecca. The mihrab serves to orient Muslim worshippers toward Mecca during the prayer (salat).

Minbar Sometimes pronounced mimbar, an ornate flight of stairs atop which is a seat from which a sermon is delivered to worshippers in a masjid, especially during the Friday midday prayer. The minbar, or "pulpit," is a podium for political and social as well as religious messages.

Muharram (*al-muḥarram*) The first month of the Muslim calendar. The first of Muharram is celebrated as New Year's for all Muslims; the tenth of Muharram (Ashura) is an especially sacred holiday for Shi'i Muslims, who observe on that and the ten preceding days rituals of mourning for Husayn.

Muhrim (*muḥrim*) A Muslim who has entered the state of consecration (Ihram, *ihram*) appropriate to entering the sacred precincts of Mecca for the purpose of pilgrimage (hajj). A Muhrim is distinguished by the special attire of simple white garments (also called Ihram).

Mu'min (*mu'min*) One who has "faith" (see iman) in the cardinal doctrines of Islamic belief. An adherent of Islam is a "Muslim" with respect to correct practice and a Mu'min with respect to correct belief.

Murji'a (Murdji'a) A sect in early Islam which held that Muslims who sin should not be expelled from the umma (as the khawarij believed), but rather that judgment as to a Muslim's faith (iman) must be postponed (*irjā'*) until God's judgment.

Mutakallim (plural, *mutakallimūn*) A member of the ulama who engages in theological disputation (kalam).

Mu'tazila (Mu'tazilites; adj. Mu'tazili) A theological school or movement in the classical period of early Islam that accepted reason as a primary criterion for establishing the validity of the content of Muslim beliefs. The Mu'tazili mutakallimun (theologians) were chiefly opposed by the mutakallimun of the Ash'ari school as well as the Traditionalists.

Pathos The social and personal collapse of a religious and social system into moral confusion and physical violence, resulting, for example, from serious conflict between normative beliefs and actual behavior or events.

Qibla (ḳibla) The direction of Mecca (more precisely, the black stone imbedded in the east corner of the Ka'ba in Mecca) toward which Muslims orient themselves for the prayer (salat).

Qur'an (*Qur'ān*, Ḳur'ān [spelled "Koran" in older sources]) The "recitation(s)" that comprise the sacred scripture of Islam. The Qur'an was revealed by Allah through His angel Gabriel to Muhammad and hence to the Arabs in Mecca and Medina. The Qur'an is regarded as a perfect Arabic revelation in both its literary and oral forms.

Salat (*ṣalāt*) Canonical prayer, the Second Pillar of Islam. The salat is performed facing the Ka'ba (in Mecca) during five periods throughout the day and evening. The times of the salat are called out from the minarets of masjids by a muezzin, "one who calls the prayer times."

Sawm (*ṣaum* or *ṣiyām*) Fasting, the Fourth Pillar of Islam. Sawm is meritorious at any time, but it is a duty during the daylight hours of the ninth month, Ramadan.

Shahada (*shahāda*) The First Pillar of Islam; the witness that "there is no god but Allah" and that "Muhammad is His Messenger."

Shafi'i (Shafi'ite) The Sunni madhhab that traces its interpretation of Islamic law (fiqh) to Muhammad al-Shafi'i (d. 820). The Shafi'i madhhab in modern Islam is found in parts of the Middle East and in Southeast Asia.

Shakir (*shākir*) A term for a Muslim in the sense of "one who is grateful" to God for His blessings. In this sense of the term, shakir is the opposite of kafir, an ingrate or unbeliever.

Shari'a (*sharī'a*) The term for sacred law which is derived from revelation (the Qur'an) and the example of the Prophet (Sunna, hadith) through the activities of the ulama.

Shaykh (Shaikh) A term for "maturity" and hence "wisdom" and "authority" in Muslim religious leaders. A shaykh is often a teacher, a Sufi master, or other respected member of the ulama.

Shaytan (Shaitān) Satan, or a satan-like unseen being or spirit that operates within the Muslim cosmology (the realms of Heaven and Earth).

Shi'i (Shi'a, Shi'ite) A designation of a minority of Muslims (about 10 percent, today living primarily in Iran, Iraq, and Lebanon) who trace their spiritual heritage to the Prophet through his cousin 'Ali. The Shi'a assert 'Ali's special knowledge of the meaning of the Shari'a, gained directly from the Prophet, and passed down through 5, 7, or 12 imams who descended from 'Ali.

Shirk A term for polytheism or "associating" other deities with Allah. Shirk was and is a particularly repugnant form of heresy in Islam. In modern Islamist (Fundamentalist) discourse, shirk is often applied to persons and practices considered to be anti-Islamic, such as Muslim leaders accused of Westernizing or secularizing Islamic society.

Sira (*sīra*) The "way" or biography of the Prophet Muhammad. The most important sira of the Prophet, by Ibn Ishaq (d. 767), is largely preserved in Ibn Hisham's (d. 834) later version, which has been translated and published in English.

Sufi (*sūfī*) A Muslim ascetic or, more recently, mystic who belongs to a spiritual brotherhood and who practices a specific life of discipline, known in Arabic as *tasawwuf*.

Sunna The customary practice of the Prophet as reported by his companions, concerning Muhammad's deeds, utterances, and unspoken approval. The Sunna is a source of authority in Islam second only to the Qur'an.

Sunni A designation of the vast majority of orthodox Muslims (about 90 percent). Sunnis acknowledge the authority of the Qur'an and the Sunna as interpreted by the ulama, but not the authority of the 'Alid Imams.

Suq (*sūq*, Sūk) the marketplace which, in Islam, has traditionally been governed by provisions in the Shari'a. Hence the suq (or *bazaar* in Persian) has religious and social as well as economic significance.

Sura (*sūra*) The name of the chapters of the Qur'an. There are 114 suras; these were revealed to Muhammad at Mecca and Medina.

Tafsir (*tafsīr*) Linguistic and historical commentary on the Qur'an.

Tahara (*tahāra*) The condition of ritual purity in Islam.

Tariqa (*tarīqa*, Tarika) A term meaning "method" or "way" which designates both a Sufi brotherhood as an institution and the special teaching and practice associated with each brotherhood.

Tawhid (*tawhīd*, tauhīd) "Making one" or "asserting the oneness" of God. The "science of tawhid" is a term for Islamic theology. Experiencing oneness or tawhid with Allah is a spiritual aspiration of Sufis.

Traditionalists Also known as hadith people, the groups in Islam that have sought to conserve traditional Islam and avoid innovations in religious belief and practice.

Traditions See *Hadith*.

Ulama ('*ulamā*') A plural form of '*alim*, "one who pursues knowledge" in the sciences of Islam. The ulama study and apply the religious sciences, such as the disciplined study of Qur'an, hadith, and Shari'a. As a class of nonordained religious functionaries, the ulama play important sociopolitical roles as a buffer between the commonality and the government.

Umma The Quranic term for a community that is part of God's plan of salvation, that is, a people to whom prophets have been sent with a scriptural message. The Islamic umma is constituted by the Qur'an and the Sunna.

Waqf (*waqf*, Wakf) A pious disposal of property, such as land and buildings, to provide an endowment income into perpetuity to be administered by the ulama for religious and charitable purposes.

World View The social construction of reality particular to a religious community, including ethical values and religious conviction. A religious world view is manifested in the social ethos of the community.

Wudu (*wuḍū'*) An act of ritual ablution (purification) to remove a minor impurity, performed prior to the prayer (salat).

Zakat (*zakāt*) "Alms" or a pious tax to provide for the poor, the Third Pillar of Islam. Calculated on the basis of certain kinds of property (including personal income), today the zakat is usually given at the end of the Hijra year on a voluntary basis to individuals in need and to charitable institutions as prescribed by the Shari'a.

Zawiya (*zāwiya*) A gathering place for Sufis, whether a room in a masjid, a saint's shrine, or an entire compound of buildings around a masjid.

Zindiq (Zindik) A term originally for the mazdakite heresy of ancient Persia. Zindiq came to designate a heretic whose teaching was regarded as a danger to the state.

BIBLIOGRAPHY

ATLASES

Bacharach, Jere L. *A Near Eastern Studies Handbook*. Revised edition. Seattle: University of Washington Press, 1983.

Useful for its maps and conversion chart of A.H. and C.E. dates.

Robinson, Francis. *Atlas of the Islamic World Since 1500*. New York: Facts on File, 1982.

An excellent collection of maps, photographs, drawings, art reproductions, and descriptions of Islam around the world since the late Middle Ages.

Roolvink, Roelof. *Historical Atlas of the Muslim Peoples*. Amsterdam: Djambatan, 1957.

GENERAL REFERENCES

Anderson, Margaret. *Arabic Materials in English Translation: A Bibliography of Works from the Pre-Islamic Period to 1977*. Boston: G. K. Hall, 1980.

A useful source for locating Islamic texts in translation, some of which are contained in larger works and not otherwise mentioned in the titles.

Encyclopaedia of Islam. Second Edition. Edited by H. A. R. Gibb et al. Leiden: E. J. Brill, 1960–.

A useful collection of articles on Islamic topics arranged according to Arabic and other Islamic terms; for example, the entry on "mosque" is found under "masdjid." The second edition is still incomplete; entries on topics from the latter part of the alphabet, for example "zakāt," are found in the first edition and *The Shorter Encyclopaedia of Islam* (see below).

Index Islamicus: 1906-1955. Compiled by J. D. Pearson and J. F. Ashton. Cambridge, England: Cambridge University Press, 1958.

Subsequent volumes compiled by J. D. Pearson and others, covering publications on Islam during 1956–1960, 1961–1965, 1966–1970, 1971–1975, 1976–1980, and then quarterly 1977–.

A catalogue of works on Islam, arranged topically, covering books, periodicals and other collective publications. An excellent resource for finding published works on virtually all topics in Islamic studies.

Kassis, Hanna E. *A Concordance of the Qur'an*. Berkeley, Calif.: University of California Press, 1983.

A comprehensive concordance of terms and verses in the Qur'an, listed by Arabic root, with a thorough English index in the back of the volume.

Muslim Peoples: A World Ethnographic Survey. Second Edition. Edited by Richard V. Weekes. Westport, Conn.: Greenwood Press, 1984.

A collection of historical and cultural descriptions of Muslim ethnographic communities, including Arabs, Persians, Berbers, Bosnians, Somalis, etc.

Sauvaget, Jean. *Introduction to the History of the Muslim East: A Bibliographical Guide*. Based on second French edition. Berkeley, Calif.: University of California Press, 1965.

A still useful, but increasingly outdated, discussion of scholarly sources for the study of Islamic history, especially in the Middle East.

Shorter Encyclopaedia of Islam. Edited by. H. A. R. Gibb and J. H. Kramers. Ithaca, N.Y.: Cornell University Press, 1953.

A convenient single-volume collection of entries on religious and historical topics, selected mainly from the first edition of *The Encyclopaedia of Islam.*

The Study of the Middle East. Edited by Leonard Binder. New York: John Wiley and Sons, 1976.

A comprehensive summary of scholarship by fields (for example, history, anthropology, political science, religious studies) by leading specialists in each field.

GENERAL HISTORICAL STUDIES

The Cambridge History of Islam. Edited by P. M. Holt, Ann Lambton, and Bernard Lewis. Cambridge, England: Cambridge University Press, 1970.

A scholarly history of Islamic civilization, including religion, politics, philosophy, art, science, literature, and warfare.

Gibb, Hamilton Alexander Rosskeen. *Studies on the Civilization of Islam.* Edited by Stanford J. Shaw and Wiiiiam R. Polk. Boston: Beacon Press, 1962.

Hitti, Philip K[uri] *History of the Arabs from the Earliest Times to the Present,* 10th ed. New York: St. Martin's Press, 1970.

An older source, still useful for historical reference.

Hourani, Albert. *A History of the Arab Peoples.* Cambridge, Mass.: Harvard University Press, 1991.

A very readable interpretation of Middle Eastern history by a leading scholar, especially good on the late premodern and modern periods.

Hodgson Marshall G. S. *The Venture of Islam: Conscience and History in a World Civilization.* 3 vols. Chicago: University of Chicago Press, 1974.

An important and widely hailed study of Islamic civilization; the author locates Islamic history more broadly and comparatively in world history.

Lapidus, Ira. *A History of Islamic Societies.* Cambridge, England: Cambridge University Press, 1988.

A comprehensive survey of world Islamic history by periods, useful for its maps and brief analyses of concepts, personalities, and movements in Islamic history.

Lewis, Bernard. *The Arabs in History.* New edition. Oxford: Oxford University Press, 1993.

A brief, well-written history of Islam in the Middle East from the beginning to the present.

Savory, R. M., ed. *Introduction to Islamic Civilization.* New York: Cambridge University Press, 1976.

A collection of articles on various aspects of Middle Eastern Islamic civilization.

TOPICAL HISTORICAL, TEXTUAL, AND SOCIAL STUDIES

Aziz, Ahmad. *Studies in Islamic Culture in the Indian Environment.* Oxford, England: Clarendon Press, 1964.

Berkey, Jonathan. *The Transmission of Knowledge in Medieval Cairo: A Social History of Islamic Education.* Princeton, N.J.: Princeton University Press, 1992.

Bowen, Donna Lee and Early, Evelyn A., eds. *Everyday Life in the Middle East.* Bloomington, Ind.: Indiana University Press, 1993.

Abu-Lughod, Lila. *Veiled Sentiments: Honor and Poetry in a Bedouin Society.* Berkeley, Calif.: University of California Press, 1986.

Beck, Lois, and Keddie, Nikki, eds. *Women in the Muslim World.* Cambridge, Mass.: Harvard University Press, 1978.

Campo, Juan Eduardo. *The Other Sides of Paradise: Explorations into the Religious Meanings of Domestic Space in Islam.* Columbia, S.C.: University of South Carolina Press, 1991.

Crone, Patricia and Cook, Michael. *Hagarism: The Making of the Islamic World.* Cambridge, England: Cambridge University Press, 1977.

Eickelman, Dale F. *The Middle East: an Anthropological Approach.* Second Edition. Englewood Cliffs, N.J.: Prentice Hall, 1989.

Eickelman, Dale F. and Piscatori, James, eds. *Muslim Travelers: Pilgrimage, Migration, and the Religious Imagination.* Berkeley, Calif.: University of California Press, 1990.

Esposito, John L. *Women in Muslim Family Law.* Syracuse, N.Y.: Syracuse University Press, 1982.

Keddie, Nikki R., ed. *Scholars, Saints, and Sufis: Muslim Religious Institutions in the Middle East Since 1500.* Berkeley, Calif.: University of California Press, 1972.

Lewis, Bernard. *The Assassins: A Radical Sect in Islam.* New York: Basic Books, 1960.

————. *The Political Language of Islam.* Chicago: University of Chicago Press, 1988.

Madelung, Wilferd. *Religious Trends in Early Islamic Iran.* Albany, N.Y.: Bibliotheca Persica, 1988.

Mernissi, Fatima. *Beyond the Veil: Male-Female Dynamics in Modern Muslim Society.* Revised Edition. Bloomington and Indianapolis: Indiana University Press, 1987.

————. *Islam and Democracy: Fear of the Modern World.* Translated by Mary Jo Lakeland. Reading Mass.: Addison-Wesley, 1992.

Mottahedeh, Roy. *The Mantle of the Prophet: Religion and Politics in Iran.* New York: Pantheon Books, 1985.

Newby, Gordon Darnell. *The Making of the Last Prophet: A Reconstruction of the Earliest Biography of Muhammad.* Columbia, S.C.: University of South Carolina Press, 1989.

Peters, Francis E. *Allah's Commonwealth: A History of Islam in the Near East, 600-1100 A.D.* New York: Simon and Schuster, 1973.

Rahman, Fazlur. *Islam and Modernity: Transformation of an Intellectual Tradition.* Chicago: University of Chicago Press, 1982.

————. *Major Themes of the Qur'an.* Second Edition. Minneapolis: Bibliotheca Islamica, 1989.

Sachedina, Abdulaziz Abdulhussein. *Islamic Messianism: The Idea of the Mahdi in Twelver Shi'i sm.* Albany, N.Y.: State University of New York Press, 1981.

Smith, Wilfred Cantwell. *Islam in Modern History*. Princeton, N.J.: Princeton University Press, 1957.

Trimingham, John Spencer. *The Influence of Islam Upon Africa*. New York: Praeger, 1960.

Voll, John Obert. *Islam: Continuity and Change in the Modern World*. Second edition. Boulder, Colo.: Westview Press, 1994.

Watt, William Montgomery. *A History of Islam in Spain*. With additional sections on literature by P. Cachia. Edinburgh: Edinburgh University Press, 1965.

Woodward, Mark R. *Islam in Java: Normative Piety and Mysticism in the Sultanate of Yogyakarta*. Tucson, Ariz.: University of Arizona Press, 1989.

ISLAM, CHRISTIANITY, AND THE WESTERN STUDY OF ISLAM

Daniel, Norman. *Islam and the West: The Making of an Image*. Revised Edition. Oxford: Oneworld Publications, 1993.

Eaton, Richard M. *Islamic History as Global History*. Washington, D.C.: American Historical Association, 1990.

Hourani, Albert. *Islam in European Thought*. Cambridge, England: Cambridge University Press, 1991.

Lewis, Bernard. *The Muslim Discovery of Europe*. New York: W. W. Norton, 1982.

Rodinson, Maxime *Europe and the Mystique of Islam*. Translated by Roger Veinus. Seattle: University of Washington Press, 1987.

Said, Edward W. *Orientalism*. New York: Pantheon, 1978.

Watt, William Montgomery. *Muslim-Christian Encounters: Perceptions and Misperceptions*. London and New York: Routledge, 1991.

SURVEYS AND STUDIES OF ISLAMIC ART

Grabar, Oleg. *The Formation of Islamic Art*. New Haven, Conn.: Yale University Press, 1973.

Kuhnel, Ernst. *Islamic Art and Architecture*. Translated by Katherine Watson. London: G. Bell & Sons, 1966.

———. *The Minor Arts of Islam*. Translated by Katherine Watson. Ithaca, N.Y.: Cornell University Press, 1970.

Nicholson, Reynold Alleyne. *A Literary History of the Arabs*. 2nd ed. Cambridge, England: Cambridge University Press, 1930.

Rice, David Talbot, ed. *Islamic Art*. London: Thames and Hudson, 1965.

ISLAMIC RELIGION

Ahmed, Kamal. *The Sacred Journey Being Piligrimage to Makkah*. New York: Duell, Sloan and Pearce, 1961.

Arberry, Arthur John. *The Koran Interpreted: A Translation*. New York: Macmillan, 1955.

———. ed. *Religion in the Middle East: The Religions in Concord and Conflict*. 2 vols. London: Cambridge University Press, 1969.

————. *Sufism: An Account of the Mystics of Islam.* London: George Allen & Unwin, 1950.

Bukhari, Muhammad ibn Ismail. *The Translation of the Meanings of Sahih al-Bukhari: Arabic-English.* 9 volumes. Translated by Muhammad Muhsin Khan. Chicago: Kazi Publications, 1976–79.

Chelkowski, Peter J., ed. *Ta'ziyeh: Ritual and Drama in Iran.* New York: New York University Press, 1979.

Cragg, Kenneth. *The Call of the Minaret.* New York: Oxford University Press, 1956.

————. *The Event of the Qur'an: Islam in Its Scripture.* London: George Allen & Unwin, 1971.

————. *The Mind of the Quaran: Chapters in Reflection.* London: George Allen & Unwin, 1973.

Gatje, Helmut. *The Qur'an and Its Exegesis: Selected Texts with Classical and Modern Muslim Interpretation.* Translated by Alford T. Welch. Berkeley, Calif.: University of California Press, 1977.

Gibb, Hamilton Alexander Rosskeen. *Mohammedanism: An Historical Survey.* 2nd ed. London: Oxford University Press, 1961.

Graham, William A. *Beyond the Written Word: Oral Aspects of Scripture in the History of Religion.* Cambridge, England: Cambridge University Press, 1987.

Lawrence, Bruce. *Defenders of God: The Fundamentalist Revolt Against the Modern Age.* San Francisco: Harper and Row, 1989.

Nasr, Sayyed Hossein. *Ideals and Realities of Islam.* Boston: Beacon Press, 1972.

Pickthall, Marmeduke William. *The Meaning of The Glorious Koran: A Bi-lingual Edition with English Translation, Introduction and Notes.* Albany, N.Y.: State University of New York Press, 1976.

Rahman, Fazlur. *Islam.* 2nd ed. Chicago: University of Chicago Press, 1979.

Schimmel, Annemarie. *Mystical Dimensions of Islam.* Chapel Hill, N.C.: University of North Carolina Press, 1975.

Trimingham, John Spencer. *The Sufi Orders in Islam.* Oxford: Clarendon Press, 1971.

Watt, William Montgomery. *Bell's Introduction to the Qur'an.* Edinburgh: Edinburgh University Press, 1970.

————. *Muhammad, Prophet and Statesman.* London: Oxford University Press, 1964.

ISLAMIC THOUGHT AND LEARNING

Fakhry, Majid. *A History of Islamic Philosophy.* Second edition. New York: Columbia University Press, 1983.

Hourani, Albert Habib. *Arabic Thought in the Liberal Age.* London and New York: Oxford University Press, 1962.

Hourani, George F. *Islamic Rationalism: The Ethics of 'Abd al-Jabbar.* Oxford: Clarendon Press, 1971.

Nasr, Sayyed Hossein. *Science and Civilization in Islam.* Cambridge, Mass.: Harvard University Press, 1968.

————. *Three Muslim Sages: Avicenna, Suhawardi, Ibn 'Arabi.* Cambridge, Mass.: Harvard University Press, 1964.

Ormsby, Eric L. *Theodicy in Islamic Thought: The Dispute over al-Ghazali's "Best of All Possible Worlds."* Princeton, N.J.: Princeton University Press, 1984

Rahman, Fazlur. *The Philosophy of Mulla Sadra.* Albany, N.Y.: State University of New York Press, 1975.

——. *Prophecy in Islam: Philosophy and Orthodoxy.* London: George Allen & Unwin, 1958.

Sharif, Mian Mumammad. *A History of Muslim Philosophy.* 2 vols. Wiesbaden, Germany: Otto Harrassowitz, 1963–1966.

Watt, William Montgomery. *The Faith and Practice of al-Ghazali.* Chicago: Kazi Publications, 1982.

——. *The Formative Period of Islamic Thought.* Edinburgh: Edinburgh University Press, 1973.

——. *Islamic Philosophy and Theology.* Edinburgh: Edinburgh University Press, 1962.

——. *Islamic Political Thought: The Basic Concepts.* Edinburgh: Edinburgh University Press, 1968.

Wolfson, Harry Austryn. *The Philosophy of the Kalam.* Cambridge, Mass.: Harvard University Press, 1976.